American Independent Cinema

American Independent Cinema

Geoff King

I.B. TAURIS

LONDON · NEW YORK

Published in 2005 by I.B. Tauris & Co Ltd
6 Salem Road, London W2 4BU
175 Fifth Avenue, New York NY 10010
www.ibtauris.com

In the United States of America and in Canada distributed by
Palgrave Macmillan, a division of St Martin's Press
175 Fifth Avenue, New York NY 10010

ISBN 1 85043 937 0 Hardback
EAN 978 1 85043 937 0 Hardback

ISBN 1 85043 938 9 Paperback
EAN 978 1 85043 938 7 Paperback

A full CIP record for this book is available from the British Library
A full CIP record for this book is available from the Library of Congress

Library of Congress catalog card: available

Typeset in Bembo by Steve Tribe, Andover
Printed and bound in Great Britain by TJ International, Padstow, Cornwall

Contents

Illustrations

Acknowledgements

Thanks to Thomas Austin for reading the manuscript before publication and to Michele Aaron for casting an eye over the section on New Queer Cinema and providing advance copies of essays from her collection, *New Queer Cinema: A Critical Reader.*

I am also grateful to Philippa Brewster at I. B. Tauris for suggesting and commissioning this project and to Brunel University for granting research leave that made its completion possible.

This book is dedicated to Alison, Jordan and Maya – and to the many independent filmmakers (and distributors) whose work continues to inspire.

Introduction

How Independent?

From the lowest-budget, most formally audacious or politically radical to the quirky, the offbeat, the cultish and the more conventional, the independent sector has thrived in American cinema in the past two decades, producing a body of work that stands out from the dominant Hollywood mainstream and that includes many of the most distinctive films to have appeared in the USA in recent years. It represents a challenge to Hollywood, although also one that has been embraced by the commercial mainstream to a substantial extent. Major formerly independent distributors such as Miramax and New Line are attached to Hollywood studios (Disney and Time-Warner, respectively), while some prominent directors from the independent sector have been signed up for Hollywood duty. The 'independence' of American independent cinema, or exactly what kind of production qualifies for the term, is constantly under question, on a variety of grounds. At the same time, the independent sector continues to thrive and to maintain an identity that is distinctive, even if not entirely separable from Hollywood.

Exactly how 'independence' is defined can vary in both form and degree. This book is organized around three main points of orientation: the position of individual films, or filmmakers, in terms of (1) their industrial location, (2) the kinds of formal/aesthetic strategies they adopt and (3) their relationship to the broader social, cultural, political or ideological landscape. Strategies vary, at each level. Some films customarily designated as 'independent' operate at a distance from the mainstream in all three respects: they are produced in an ultra-low-budget world a million miles from that of the Hollywood blockbuster; they adopt formal strategies that disrupt or abandon the smoothly flowing conventions associated with the mainstream Hollywood style; and they offer challenging perspectives on social issues, a rarity in Hollywood. Others exist in a closer, sometimes symbiotic relationship with the Hollywood behemoth, offering a distinctive touch within more conventional frameworks. In between are many shades of difference.

A degree of distance, industrially, from the Hollywood studio system often appears to be a necessary condition for substantial formal or socio-political departure from the dominant norms. Lower budgets and less marketing-driven filmmaking generally permit greater licence. But this can be relative. How, exactly, any individual title is marked as sufficiently different from the Hollywood mainstream to qualify as independent is subject to numerous variations explored in detail in this book. Some lean towards an 'artistic' form and content, merging at one end with works usually defined as 'experimental' or 'avant-garde'. Others are more avowedly 'political' or polemical in intent. The 'artistic' and the 'political' are far from separate categories, however. Formal experiment and departure from dominant conventions is, potentially, a major resource for the deconstruction of dominant ideologies. Other examples of American independent cinema are less lofty in their ambitions, taking up the inheritance of lower-budget 'exploitation' cinema, for example, or seeking to carve a niche through the creation of 'quality', stylish, cultish or offbeat films, the primary goal of which remains the provision of profit-generating entertainment.

One of the main aims of this book is to chart the contours of American independent cinema within these coordinates. Independent cinema exists in the overlapping territory between Hollywood and a number of alternatives: the experimental 'avant-garde', the more accessible 'art' or 'quality' cinema, the politically engaged, the low-

1. Not much doing really – but a milestone in the developing indie scene of the 1980s: *Stranger Than Paradise* (1984).

budget exploitation film and the more generally offbeat or eccentric. The principal focus of *American Independent Cinema* is on the particular versions of independent cinema that came to prominence from the mid 1980s with the appearance of milestone films such as *Stranger Than Paradise* (Jim Jarmusch, 1984), *sex, lies, and videotape* (Steven Soderbergh, 1989) and *Clerks* (Kevin Smith, 1994). The terms 'independent' or 'indie' – the latter often used to distinguish this particular version of independence – are used primarily in the sense in which they became established in the wider culture in this period, rather than according to a fixed or more literal definition. To understand the forces shaping this particular notion of independence, however, a number of different historical roots and predecessors have also to be considered.

   Taken literally, the 'independent' sector has a much longer and broader history than that which forms the main subject of this book. At its earliest, the term was used to describe producers operating in the shadow of the three companies – Edison, Biograph and Vitagraph – that dominated the film business in the 1890s and 1900s. Early independents faced a constant threat of legal action, control over the industry in this period being exerted partly through the ownership of patents that sought to restrict access to key aspects of film technology. From this early stage, the term 'independent' gained romantic connotation, signifying the brave efforts of rebels fighting against a powerful trust. Independent production in this era is often given the credit for a number of landmark developments, including the shift of the centre of gravity of the film business to California and the initiation of the star system, although both claims owe more to myth than reality.[1] The independents formed their own alliance in opposition to the patents company and, Janet Staiger suggests, used a number of similar strategies; the result was the division of the industry into two rival blocs.[2]

The patents company was declared to be an illegal restraint of trade and dissolved in 1915. It was soon replaced, however, by what was to become the Hollywood studio system, a vertically integrated operation in which the five major studios dominated the production, distribution and exhibition of features in the USA and much of the rest of the world. The studio system underwent substantial reorientation from the 1950s, in the face of further federal regulation and broader social change, but its dominance has remained largely in place. In the context of an industrial regime dominated by Hollywood, independent activity has tended to fall into one of two general categories: either inside or outside the orbit of the majors. Within the gravitational pull of the studios, independent production has been found at both the upper and lower ends of the business. Low-budget independent outfits such as Republic and Monogram, and many smaller entities, helped to serve the demand of the system for the production of 'B' movies, to fill the bottom half of double bills, during the 1930s.[3] At the same time, independent producers such as David Selznick and Sam Goldwyn produced expensive 'A' features, borrowing stars and leasing studio space from the majors and supplying prestige films such as *Gone with the Wind* (1939) and *Rebecca* (1940) that profited the studios by playing in their important first-run theatres. The most high-profile A-list move into independence from the studios was launched earlier, in 1919, with the founding of United Artists, a distribution company created to handle the films of Mary Pickford, Charles Chaplin, Douglas Fairbanks and D. W. Griffith.

The success of Selznick, in particular, as an independent producer working closely with the studios, pointed the way towards what was to be the future structure of Hollywood production, which became increasingly organized on a contracted-out basis from the 1950s onwards. The studio production-line system gave way to the package system, in which individual film projects were put together on a one-off basis. A great deal of Hollywood production today can be described as 'independent' in this sense, in that projects are often initiated and pursued by entities that exist formally beyond the bounds of the majors. These include production companies set up by producers, directors and stars, often working closely with one studio or another, and some larger independent companies. In most such cases the films that result belong solidly to the Hollywood mainstream. Hollywood remains the principal source of funding and distribution, even when only a relatively small proportion of production is conducted entirely in-house. Technically independent productions include Hollywood blockbusters such as *Terminator 2: Judgment Day* (1991) and *Basic Instinct* (1992), produced by the independent Carolco in an alliance with TriStar Pictures. As with the likes of Selznick, arrangements with independents such as Carolco, Castle Rock and Morgan's Creek in the 1990s gave the studios extra flexibility, to work in partnerships that reduced their risks, especially at the higher-budget end of the spectrum.[4] It is clear that formal independence of this variety in the industrial domain is, in itself, no guarantee of independent qualities of other kinds.

If some forms of independent production have worked closely in unison with Hollywood, others have operated in areas in which Hollywood has chosen not to tread, sometimes teaching valuable lessons to the dominant institution. Necessity has often driven independent operators to be the pioneers of American cinema, exploring new avenues in their search for territories not already colonized by the major studios. The early independents took cinema to parts of rural America, including the gold camps of Alaska, that were not served by the big companies.[5] Technological innovations have also come from independent sources in some cases: the development of widescreen processes and 3D in the 1950s, for example, originated outside the control of the studios. Both historically and today, independent producers have often served specialized, niche audiences of one kind or another. A good example during the classical Hollywood studio era is low-budget independent black-oriented filmmaking, which, although often white owned and financed, catered specifically for black audiences from the silent era until the Second World War.

The most significant audience for which Hollywood failed to cater in the immediate post-war decades, and which created the basis for some of the most important strains of independent production, was the youth audience. Hollywood was very slow to respond to demographic and other social changes during the 1950s and 1960s that created a large audience receptive to material targeted at teenage viewers. Into the gap stepped a number of independent producers, the best known being American Independent Pictures (AIP), supplying the teen audience with a range of low-budget horror, hot-rod, biker and beach-blanket movies. Such films tended to be in 'disreputable' genres unfavoured by Hollywood. They were sold using 'exploitation' tactics, sensational titles and posters giving the impression of more lurid thrills than were usually delivered by the low-production-value material actually presented on-screen.

If this was a version of independence that was nakedly commercial in intent, the independent scene of the later 1950s and 1960s also saw a flowering of more 'artistic' and in some cases 'avant-garde' independent filmmaking. The birth of something akin to an 'American New Wave', to match those of contemporary European cinema, was announced in the early 1960s. The more narrative- and character-led manifestations of this development – films such as John Cassavetes' *Shadows* (1960) – can be seen as direct predecessors of the indie scene of the 1980s and 1990s. Examples from the avant-garde end of the spectrum, in some cases dating back to the 1940s, include formalist experimentation by filmmakers such as Maya Deren and Stan Brakhage and the 'underground' films of Andy Warhol. The avant-garde remained largely isolated, as in almost all cases a strictly non-commercial and rigorously independent undertaking. The strands of 'exploitation', 'art' and 'underground' cinema sometimes came closer together, however, jointly forming important sources for the Hollywood 'Renaissance' of the late 1960s to the mid to late 1970s, a period in which a financially struggling Hollywood finally began to come to terms with its changed demographic and social context. The commercial success of independent youth-oriented pictures such as those of AIP was matched by that of some more edgy and disturbing independent productions in the same generic territory, especially horror. Films such as *Night of the Living Dead* (1968) and *The Texas Chain Saw Massacre* (1974) proved highly successful at the box office, pushing back the boundaries of conventional exploitation-horror material and combining this with a more negative portrait of American society that resonated with contemporary angst and unrest in the era of events such as racial uprising, the Vietnam war and Watergate.

The response of Hollywood was to embrace some of this material. A landmark move was the decision by Columbia to distribute *Easy Rider* (1969), a project originally destined to become another biker picture for AIP. The success of *Easy Rider* helped convince the studios to invest in a new generation of filmmakers seen to be more in touch with the youth audience affected by the 1960s counterculture. Hollywood learned other lessons from the independents in this period. Along with a number of foreign imports, independent features demonstrated the box-office appeal of more racy, controversial or 'adult' material, encouraging the adoption by Hollywood of the ratings system, which widened the bounds of what could be offered to audiences from 1968. Examples ranged from gory low-budget horror to the sexploitation films of Russ Meyer. Elements of independent 'exploitation' strategy were also embraced by Hollywood in its more mainstream, blockbuster productions, especially the strategy of combining wide opening release patterns with saturation advertising, in order to recoup costs quickly. A number of Hollywood's biggest-grossing films of the 1970s were, in part, bigger-budget and glossier versions of independent exploitation fare, especially *The Exorcist* (1973) and *Jaws* (1975).

Hollywood stole some of the ground of the independents during the 1970s, encouraging some independents into more extreme or 'outrageous' ground to maintain their marketable differences: the raw horror of *The Texas Chain Saw Massacre*, the harder-core sexploitation of *Deep Throat* (1972), the cult 'bad taste' trash extremes of John Waters' *Pink Flamingos* (1973). Independent operation remained the main source of development in the slasher and splatter varieties of horror, but this was another terrain onto which Hollywood was quick to move in the light of the box-office success of *Halloween* (1978) and *Friday the 13th* (1980). If the more commercial/exploitation end of independent cinema was to a large extent taken over by larger-budget Hollywood productions, the same was only partially and briefly true of the 'art' film component. The Hollywood Renaissance embraced aspects of 'art' cinema to some extent, but it proved short-lived, the product of a period of transition that soon passed in the later 1970s, with both the consolidation of a blockbuster-centred regime in Hollywood and a political turn to the right in American culture. Space for edgier, more questioning or 'difficult' filmmaking was generally reduced in Hollywood from the end of the decade. Some individuals associated with the Hollywood Renaissance continued to make less conventional films, sometimes for the studios, where past box-office achievements or status and reputation gave them sufficient clout (Martin Scorsese, for example), sometimes in the independent realm or with funding from television (as in the case of Robert Altman during the 1980s). Hollywood's loss, in terms of the general narrowing of the horizons of possibility at the heart of the studio-led machine, was to be the gain of a newly consolidating form of independent production and distribution that was beginning to take shape during the 1980s, and into which some of the inheritance of the Renaissance was carried.

The term 'independent' has had rather different connotations at different periods in the history of American cinema. In the 1930s, for example, it signified 'something less than trash'.[6] In the late 1950s and early 1960s it might have suggested both the innovations of the 'American New Wave' and the low-budget exploitation science fiction and horror made by Roger Corman for AIP. The 'New Wave' proved fragmentary and short-lived, breaking down during the 1960s into its separate art/personal/expressive feature film and more underground/experimental short components. Accessible non-Hollywood features were still produced, but, as Geoff Andrew suggests, 'they were so infrequent, and usually achieved such a low audience profile, that there was little sense of continuity, let alone of any kind of "movement".'[7] From the mid 1980s, however, the more arty/quirky, sometimes politically inflected, brand of independent cinema began to gain a higher profile and a more sustained and institutionalized base in the broadly off-Hollywood arena. Explanations for this development will be suggested in greater detail in Chapter 1, which focuses on the industrial dimension of recent and contemporary American independent cinema, but the generally inhospitable climate of the Hollywood mainstream during the 1980s and into the 1990s was certainly a factor.

The industrial realm is, clearly, an important part of any definition of independent cinema. In Greg Merritt's account, *Celluloid Mavericks: A History of American Independent Film*, it is the single, defining characteristic. An independent film, for Merritt, is 'any motion picture financed and produced completely autonomous of *all* studios, regardless of size'.[8] Films made by smaller studios or given a guarantee of distribution by one of the majors before production are classified as 'semi-indie'. In neither case, in Merritt's account, is style or content a consideration. Any other basis of definition is 'too slippery', including 'the widely held belief that independence is determined not by financing but by "spirit", by professing an alternative vision'.[9] My argument, however, is that independent cinema is not best defined in such narrow and literal terms. Industrial factors are important, but do not provide the only grounds for definition of the particular varieties of filmmaking to which the label independent has most prominently been attached in recent decades. Other definitions may be somewhat slippery, but the feature-length, narrative-based independent cinema examined in this book is not a single, unified entity. 'Independence' is a relative rather than an absolute quality and can be defined as such at the industrial and other levels. It is this dynamic quality, drawing on a range of traditions, that makes it such a rich, variable and fascinating part of the cinematic landscape.

American Independent Cinema starts with consideration of the industrial context because it is in this dimension that many of the conditions of existence of independent cinema are set. The gradual establishment of an industrial infrastructure, particularly in distribution, was a key factor in the emergence of the type of indie scene that came to fruition in the 1980s and 1990s. In general – but with some exceptions – the term 'independent' as used in this book requires an industrial location that is either clearly independent or somewhere in the grey area often known as 'Indiewood', which includes studio-owned/affiliated 'specialist' or 'independent' labels. But it would be an impoverished definition of independent cinema that ignored the qualities of the films themselves. If indie films are often described by the use of somewhat vague terms such as 'quirky' and 'offbeat', one of the aims of this book is to examine some of the particular devices that create such qualities, to seek a grasp on the slippery notion of 'alternative vision' at the levels of both form (principally in Chapters 2 to 4) and content (principally in Chapter 5). Where departures from mainstream convention are found at the formal level, they tend to be in two main directions: either in making greater claims to verisimilitude/ realism, or in the use of more complex, stylized, expressive, showy or self-conscious forms. In content, many independent films offer visions of society not usually found in the mainstream, although the bounds of difference are often limited. The characteristic location of that which is designated by the terms 'indie' or 'independent', in the dominant senses in which they are used here, is a space that exists between the more familiar-conventional mainstream and the more radical departures of the avant-garde or the underground.

Unlike many accounts of American independent cinema, this book does not take the individual filmmaker as a major point of organization (there are no chapters devoted specifically to figures such as Jim Jarmusch, John Sayles, Hal Hartley, Todd Haynes or Quentin Tarantino). The indie sector is, clearly, a place where more scope generally exists than in Hollywood for the pursuit of auteurist individual freedom of expression; for filmmakers to express their own particular visions of the world through choices of form and content.[10] What this book seeks to identify, however, is the existence of a number of different (overlapping) modes of independent practice, institutionalized or partially institutionalized forms that include but also go beyond the particular concerns of the many individuals whose work has contributed to the vibrancy of independent alternatives to the Hollywood mainstream.

1

Industry

While it's true that, in the best of all possible worlds,
independent films are genuinely alternative, genuinely original
visions, there's no such thing as an absolutely independent film.
There's still an economy at work: The movie has to go into the
marketplace, and people have to want to see it.

Christine Vachon[1]

At the industrial level, the American independent sector stretches
from extremes of low- or (according to legend) almost no-budget
filmmaking to the margins of Hollywood; from grainy images shot
in 16mm or digital video to glossy products that look more like
those of the commercial mainstream; from small one-off, home-based
production to the world of suits, offices and consolidated business
enterprises. Here, as much as elsewhere, the term 'independent'
encompasses a wide range of activities in the broad territory located
between Hollywood and the outer reaches of 'non-industrial'
experimental or avant-garde cinema.

Part of the romance of independent cinema is the notion of
producing films at extremely low cost, outside or on the edges of

the mainstream, free from dependence on the corporate oligarchy comprised by the major studio system. Successive generations of filmmakers, as well as critics and enthusiasts, have been inspired by tales of feature-length movies being made on tiny budgets, shot in spare time, financed on credit cards or through funds scrambled together from other unlikely sources. One of the most often cited examples is *El Mariachi* (1992), shot single-handed by Robert Rodriguez and edited on borrowed equipment for the absurdly low sum of $7,000. Others include Robert Townsend's use of a string of newly acquired credit cards to pay for the completion of *Hollywood Shuffle* (1987) and the stupendous return on investment achieved by *The Blair Witch Project* (1999), which grossed an extraordinary $140 million in the USA on an initial budget estimated at between $22,000 and $60,000. In one of the more unlikely sounding endeavours, Michael Almereyda shot his second feature, *Another Girl Another Planet* (1992), on a plastic toy Fisher-Price PXL 2000 camera costing just $45, recording images onto audio cassette. Over a period of four decades, the potential for access to the otherwise seemingly expensive, closed and exclusive arena of feature filmmaking has been demonstrated by the appearance of films ranging historically from John Cassavetes' *Shadows* at the start of the 1960s to the latest explorations of ultra-low-budget digital video (DV) production in the 2000s. Previous claims to the status of all-time-low budget were put in the shade by the production of James Portolese and Rene Besson's DV feature *Boxes* (2000), which was sold to the Independent Film Channel after being made for the princely sum of $285.12 (half of that spent on haircuts for the principal characters!).

Microbudget production was the norm for first-time independent filmmakers by the mid 1990s, but this was not always the case. Ultra-low-budget films such as John Sayles' *Return of the Secaucus Seven* (1980; $60,000) and Spike Lee's *She's Gotta Have It* (1986; $80,000 to initial prints) were occasional exceptions during the 1980s, when low-budget generally meant $500,000 to $1 million, figures for which finance was usually available in the independent sector at the time.[2] Two factors were responsible for change in the early 1990s: a financial squeeze and the success of three microbudget features that appeared in the same year, 1992 (*Laws of Gravity*, directed by Nick Gomez, budgeted at $38,000; Gregg Araki's *The Living End*, $22,700; and *El Mariachi*). A series of articles by Peter Broderick in *Filmmaker* magazine served as a catalyst for the shift of emphasis, giving a detailed breakdown of each of the three budgets and underlining the strategies that permitted feature production at so little expense.[3] The key to the new model was scripting on the basis of a prior assessment of resources that were already available at no cost, classic examples including a bus and a dog used by Robert Rodriguez in *El Mariachi* and the convenience store at which Kevin Smith worked that served as the principal location for *Clerks*. Other ingredients of the microbudget recipe include the use of small and committed casts and crews prepared to work without salary, other than deferred payments to be secured in the event of future profits, a very low shooting ratio and the use of borrowed equipment.

Production on these lines can be remarkably inexpensive, especially when compared with the tens of millions routinely spent by Hollywood. Lowness of budget has been played up as a publicity and marketing device on numerous occasions. Production at this end of the spectrum can have the appearance of something closer to a non-industrial, home-movie enterprise. Substantial sums of money are still involved in most cases, however, especially for those without the benefit of wealthy and generous relatives or other sources of personal income. (If Townsend put $40,000 on credit cards for *Hollywood Shuffle*, for example, less trumpeted was the fact that he was able to supply an initial $60,000 from his earnings as an actor.) A great deal of effort can be expended, sometimes over a period of years, on the frustrating business of putting together from various sources the funds for even a modestly priced independent feature, a process that can become as creative as making the film itself. The ultra-low-budget model was designed in part to cut through such delays, reducing significantly but not entirely the extent to which filmmakers were dependent on outside sources of finance.

The variety of independent cinema examined in this book remains best characterized as an 'industrial' activity, even if it sometimes overlaps with the extreme low-budget, no-budget or artistic-grant-funded territory of home-made, experimental or avant-garde cinema. This is even more the case when it comes to the realms of distribution, marketing and exhibition. The business of actually getting indie movies *seen* by audiences entails very much higher costs than the headline budget figures associated with examples such as *El Mariachi, Clerks, The Blair Witch Project* or the latest DV marvel. Getting a film in the can, in a sufficient state to secure a deal with a distributor, is one thing. Having it at the stage where it is ready to be shown commercially, in the cinema or on videotape or DVD, can be quite another. The completion of a version of *El Mariachi* for $7,000 was an extraordinary achievement, but that was not for a film print on 16mm, let alone the favoured release format of 35mm. For $7,000, Robert Rodriguez had a master tape on three-quarter-inch video, the medium onto which he transferred to edit the film.[4] It was originally intended to be sold to the ultra-cheap Mexican direct-to-video market. Obtaining a 16mm print alone would have cost more than $20,000, nearly three times the headline figure. At around $27,000 taken to 16mm, *El Mariachi* would be in the same budget league as the cheaper of the late-1980s and 1990s indies: examples such as *Slacker* (1991; $23,000), *Laws of Gravity, Clerks* ($27,000) and *The Blair Witch Project*.

These are still very small numbers for the production of a feature, but they remain incomplete. Budgets such as these can be multiplied several-fold to include a number of requirements that have to be met before a film can go into distribution. It will have to be blown up to 35mm unless it is to be shown only in the limited market with facilities for projection in 16mm or digital video. A sound remix, to replace what may be a crude original, is another often-obligatory requirement. These and insurance costs were estimated to add at least another $60,000 in 1995 by John Pierson, a producers' representative who helped many of the earlier indie 'classics' to find distributors. Other average costs – including music rights, deferments and laboratory costs such the 'music and effects' mix, in which the sound and dialogue tracks are separated out to permit redubbing for international distribution – take the total up to $100,000.[5] Figures of a similar scale are suggested by the independent producer Christine Vachon, whose credits include *Poison* (1991), *Swoon* (1992), *Go Fish* (1994) and *Happiness* (1998).[6] A higher estimate is reached by James Schamus, co-founder of the production company Good Machine, who suggests a cost of $300–500,000 for an international release of a 'no-budget' film.[7] These costs may be incurred by the distributor

2. Ultra-low-budget, but much more spent on completion and promotion: *The Blair Witch Project* (1999).

and deducted from future revenues. Alternatively, the deal with a distributor might require the producers to supply a print taken to some or all of these stages of completion, in which case a higher advance might be expected to be paid. It is important to note that these are only *pre*-release costs. They do not include the potentially huge costs of distribution and marketing, including the expenses of attending festivals, making multiple prints for exhibitors and, especially, advertising. In the case of *Clerks*, Pierson suggests, completion costs totalled $200,000 with another $1.7 million spent by the distributor Miramax on print, radio and television advertising during the six-month theatrical run. Completion costs for *The Blair Witch Project* were some $300,000 for transfer to 35mm and sound editing. The first stage of promotion was very cheap, making innovative use of the internet. The distributor, Artisan Entertainment, initially intended to spend $4.5 million on prints and advertising. Once the film started to become a media phenomenon, however, $20 million was committed, the equivalent of the originally anticipated domestic gross.[8] A growing tendency of the early 2000s was for advances paid to filmmakers to shrink or disappear in all but the most favourable cases, often replaced by a commitment to invest a particular sum in marketing and a guarantee to open a film in an agreed number of markets. Such commitments may prove short-lived, however, in the event of a disappointing initial opening.

The story of American independent cinema in recent decades is partly one of innovative and enterprising filmmaking, whether on relatively lower or higher budgets. But it is also the story of the development of industrial and institutional frameworks that have provided the infrastructure for a sustained base of production. This chapter begins by outlining the historical background of these developments, including the broader social and economic context in which independent cinema underwent an upsurge from the mid 1980s. It also includes closer analysis of the distribution and marketing strategies that have typified the indie scene. In recent years distinctions between the top end of the independent sector and Hollywood have blurred to a significant extent, a phenomenon examined in the latter part of this chapter, which also considers the space still available today for more innovative and low-cost indie filmmaking.

Creating an Infrastructure

If the roots of the independent cinema that took off from the 1980s can in some respects be traced back to the late 1950s and early 1960s, a major difference between the two periods lies in the extent to which any sustained infrastructure was created. A few small-scale institutions were created in an attempt to consolidate the avant-garde sector during the 1950s, including the Creative Film Foundation established by Maya Deren in 1955, which granted funds to experimental filmmakers.[9] The exhibition of avant-garde films was a fragile business, relying on museums, galleries, temporary spaces and specialized 'little cinemas' in major cities. A distribution outlet was created by the exhibitor Cinema 16 in New York in 1950, handling experimental films and the more accessible international art cinema of directors such as Ingmar Bergman and Michelangelo Antonioni. This was followed by the non-profit-based Filmmaker's Cooperative, founded in 1962 by Jonas Mekas, who became the most vocal proponent of the American avant-garde.

The avant-garde remained an extremely marginal activity in commercial terms, but the market for international art cinema thrived in metropolitan centres such as New York and San Francisco, benefiting from a number of factors including a decreased level of production by the Hollywood majors.[10] The number of art cinemas in America had increased from twelve in 1945 to some 550 by 1960.[11] The main attractions for audiences in the 1950s and 1960s were imports but also a small number of noted American independent films, including Shirley Clarke's portrait of inner-city life, *The Cool World* (1963), and *One Potato, Two Potato* (Larry Peerce, 1964), a study of interracial marriage. A key player was Don Rugoff, whose Cinema V controlled a number of art-house theatres in New York. Cinema V branched out into distribution in 1963, an important move in the development of a nascent infrastructure. Cinema V, as Justin Wyatt suggests, has often been seen as a model for larger independent distributors such as Miramax and New Line in the 1990s, particularly in its use of niche-marketing strategies designed to respond to the particular qualities of each individual film. A similar move from exhibition into distribution was made by the smaller New Yorker Films and Bauer International.[12] The former was founded in 1965 by Dan Talbot, owner of the New Yorker Theatre; seeking access to a number of international films, including Bertolucci's *Before the Revolution* (1964) and Godard's *Les Carabiniers* (1963), Talbot was obliged to import them himself.

Distribution is a critical component of the film business, the vital link required if films are to find their way into cinemas and to receive the necessary marketing and promotion to secure an audience. For exhibitors such as Cinema 16 and Cinema V, and others that followed, a move into distribution was a way to secure access to films that might not otherwise be available to be screened. The process by which distributors obtain the rights to individual films usually takes either of two forms. In some cases the distributor may also be the producer, paying the entire cost of the production or investing a proportion of the cost in a joint production deal. A distributor may be involved from the start or may come on board at some stage during the production or post-production process. Many films are acquired after completion, however, as what are termed 'negative pickups'. Involvement in production gives the distributor more control and potential access to greater profit, but at the cost of exposure to more risk. Most of the initial breakthrough, low-budget independent films of the 1980s and 1990s were completed without the aid of investment from distributors, although advance sales from sources such as video, cable television and the overseas theatrical market came to provide an important source of stability. These would probably qualify for the restricted definition of independence offered by Greg Merritt: films financed and produced independently of any entities involved in distribution and sold to a distributor (a domestic theatrical distributor, at least) only after completion. This definition is rather static, however, failing to allow for changing strategies adopted in what remained for the most part the same branch of the industry. As the independent sector grew during the 1990s, distributors came increasingly to invest in production as a way to guarantee access to a supply of suitable films and to gain an early start in the process of marketing and promotion, a move that continued into the 2000s without in itself changing the nature or status of the films produced.

Even after being forced out of the exhibition business by legal action against their oligopoly powers, the Hollywood studios retained control over the main networks of distribution, in both America and much of the global market. Where independent films have been taken up by studio distributors, the results have often been unsatisfactory, the Hollywood approach not usually being best suited to the particular demands of marketing more offbeat material. One of the numerous ways John Cassavetes marked his status as a hero to later independents was his move into the distribution of his own films with the creation of Faces Films to release *A Woman Under the Influence* in 1974, a development inspired by dissatisfaction at the handling of two previous films he made for the studios. The establishment of its own distribution network on a larger scale was a central requirement if American independent cinema was to have a sustained impact.

One of the key independent players of the 1980s, 1990s and 2000s also had roots in the 1960s, a period in which New York exhibitors and distributors flourished on the basis of the baby-boom college audience, 'which ravenously consumed specialized movies in both theatres and on campus'.[13] New Line Cinema, founded by Robert Shaye in 1967, started life as a non-theatrical distributor serving the campus market with films such as *Reefer Madness* (1936) and Jean-Luc Godard's Rolling Stones documentary *Sympathy for the Devil* (1970).[14] New Line moved into theatrical distribution in 1973, its slate mixing European art films with low-budget exploitation titles such as *The Texas Chain Saw Massacre* and *Pink Flamingos*. A limited move into production followed in 1978 as the independent marketplace strengthened and increased funding became available. The college audience was also the starting point, as bookers of rock concerts and concert films, for the careers of Harvey and Bob Weinstein, whose Miramax was to become the other major indie distributor from the 1990s.

The beginnings of the festival circuit that forms another part of the institutional and higher-profile basis of independent cinema can also be traced back to the late 1950s and early 1960s. The San Francisco International Festival started in 1957, followed by the New York Film Festival in 1962. As with the art cinemas of the period, their principal fare was foreign rather than American independent. Further developments followed in the 1970s, including the establishment of the Telluride festival in Colorado in 1973, Toronto and Seattle in 1975 and Montreal in 1977. The US Film Festival was born as a modest event in Salt Lake City, Utah, in 1978, moving to the more attractive location of the nearby Park City skiing resort in 1981. It was built initially around a retrospective accompanied by panel discussions by high-profile filmmakers and critics, but from the first year its most widely attended component was a competition for what were then known as 'small regional films'.[15] In 1984, the festival, burdened by debt, was taken over by Robert Redford's Sundance Institute, formed in 1981 to support independent filmmakers. The model for the institute was the Eugene O'Neill Theater in Connecticut, a retreat at which new plays were performed, revised and reworked with the aid of established practitioners.[16] The involvement of Sundance gave the event security and increased the profile of both the festival and the entire independent scene. It established itself as the premier landmark in the annual calendar of American independent cinema (its name changed to the Sundance/United States Film Festival in 1990, thereafter becoming just the Sundance Film Festival). Strong connections were established between the Sundance Institute and major Hollywood players, a number of whom found places on its board during the 1980s. By the mid 1990s, Sundance was a key marketplace (although there has never been a formal market section), crowded with agents and executives from the studio and independent distribution sectors. Competition to gain entry became fierce, many independent film production and post-production schedules being organized around the entry deadline for the January event.

The late 1970s and start of the 1980s was a period in which the infrastructure began to consolidate. A number of new, small-scale distributors came onto the scene, including Samuel Goldwyn, Castle Hill, Island/Alive, Cinecom and First Run Features.[17] In 1979, the broadcaster PBS started funding independent films as part of its 'American Playhouse' series in return for initial television screening rights, providing a key source of finance and a guaranteed outlet to viewers.[18] The same year saw the creation of the Independent Feature Project (IFP), a non-profit body that developed out of an American Independent sidebar at that year's New York Film Festival. Initially based in New York City, but with branches later established in Los Angeles, Chicago, Miami and Minneapolis, the membership-based IFP was designed to act as a forum for the development of independent features. Its principal showcase, the annual Independent Feature Film Market (later renamed the Independent Feature Project Market), joined the Sundance festival as one of the major events of the indie season. The IFP Market differs from Sundance in its greater emphasis on the work of new and emerging filmmakers, a strategy underlined by a decision in 2002 to restrict screenings of fiction features to rough cuts and works-in-progress in search of completion finance. Parallel to the market runs a conference that provides filmmakers with the opportunity to benefit from the experience of leading figures in the independent sector. Bodies such as the Sundance Institute and the IFP created a support network for practising or would-be independent filmmakers, the activities of Sundance including film workshops at which projects could be developed collaboratively with the help of experienced industry figures.

Another important development around the turn of the decade was the first move of the big studios into the art/indie film arena. The way was led by United Artists, a struggling studio that merged with MGM, another great name from the classical studio era that had become a shadow of its former self.

United Artists Classics was created in 1980 as a speciality division to handle art-house films, mostly foreign, but it became one of the major players in the American independent sector in the early 1980s. Twentieth Century Fox and Universal followed, creating their own classics divisions. All three proved short-lived, although studio involvement in the independent sector was to increase, in various forms, in the 1990s. A significant role in the emerging infrastructure of the second half of the 1980s was also played by John Pierson, as a pioneering producers' representative, mediating between new or emerging filmmakers and distributors and in some cases providing development funds such as the $10,000 invested in *She's Gotta Have It* and $53,000 contributed towards the completion of *Go Fish*. Pierson subsequently took up office under the wing of Miramax before creating a new forum with his *Split Screen* show on the Independent Film Channel, which has commissioned numerous short segments from established and up-and-coming filmmakers.

American independent features remained quite thin on the ground in the early years of the 1980s, but much had been done to provide the institutional base from which the sector would grow during the next two decades, a critical mass that was lacking when the would-be American 'New Wave' broke early in the 1960s. Early successes, if generally modest, included *My Dinner with Andre* (1981), *Chan is Missing* (1982), *Smithereens* (1982), *Eating Raoul* (1982), *El Norte* (1983) and *Liquid Sky* (1983). Milestone films that followed, and further established the profile and impact of the indie sector, included *Stranger Than Paradise*, *She's Gotta Have It*, *sex, lies, and videotape*, *Slacker*, *Reservoir Dogs* (1992) and *Clerks*; along with increasing numbers of others, many of which disappeared without much trace.

The Wider Industrial and Social Context

The creation of an infrastructure comprised of independent distributors, festivals and institutions such as Sundance and the IFP played an important part in enabling the independent sector to flourish from the mid 1980s. Other factors also contributed to the creation of a climate in which independent cinema was able to grow. Two of these were mentioned in the Introduction: the generally conservative state of Hollywood from the late 1970s, which forced both filmmakers and audiences to look outside the mainstream institutions for more challenging or unconventional fare, and the 1980s boom in home video. The latter was the largest of three components that created a general increase in demand for films that could not be met by the Hollywood studios, the others being a significant growth in the number of theatrical screens and the expansion of cable television.[19]

The growth of home video during the 1980s was astronomical. Penetration of video recorders into US households increased from three per cent in 1980 to nearly 75 per cent in 1989, creating an enormous demand for product. Total revenue from pre-recorded cassette rentals and sales grew from $76 million to an estimated $7 billion in the same period. Video companies seeking product to keep up with the demand became a major component of independent film financing. Video operations such as Vestron, RCA/Columbia and Nelson established deals with independent distributors who provided the theatrical release on the back of which success on home video usually depended. Cable television also underwent rapid growth, as did the numbers of cable services and cinema screens (the latter increasing from 17,500 to 23,000 in the 1980s, the outcome largely of the development of multiplex cinemas with larger numbers of smaller screens). Increased overseas film sales, particularly to Europe and Japan, added another new source of potential income for independents.

The major studios were unable to match these new demands because of their commitment to a strategy in which resources tended to be concentrated primarily on a limited number of expensive films with the potential to earn blockbuster profits. Independent filmmakers and distributors were provided with 'a unique opportunity'.[20] The total number of features released in the USA from 1980 to 1988 increased by half, from 342 to 513. Historically, as David Rosen suggests, independents have always supplied a substantial share of releases, but the proportion increased significantly during the 1980s. In 1980, the Hollywood majors and mini-major studios accounted for 40 per cent, a share that fell to 26 per cent in 1987 (135 major releases,

380 independent) and recovered slightly to 31 per cent in 1988 (161 major, 352 independent).[21]

Another important factor, in the broader economic context, was the increase in the availability of capital created by the debt-based 'Reagan revolution' in the American economy from 1982 to 1988. Investment capital was made available for film production and distribution while consumer expenditure also increased.[22] The independent sector was particularly likely to gain from this situation, despite the relatively low sums involved, because, as Rosen puts it, investment in low-budget independent films 'is more akin to high-risk "play money", from investors with money they can afford to gamble rather than to put into safer hands'.[23] A range of financial mechanisms, including loans, grants, limited partnerships and public offerings, were available to filmmakers.

> Beyond one-shot investments in individual films, increased capital
> availability to small distributors, homevideo companies, cable
> networks, and even venture-capital groups (e.g. FilmDallas) provided
> an important new revenue stream in the form of presale, acquisition,
> and negative pickup arrangements.[24]

An audience was also available for independent cinema during the 1980s, the demographic product of the maturing 'baby boom' generation of the 1960s. This is usually characterized as a generally more 'discriminating' audience than that attracted by the products of mainstream Hollywood. Such viewers, often older than the main audience targeted by Hollywood and more than averagely likely to be urban and college educated, have continued to constitute a core target group for independent films, although, as will be seen below, production, marketing and distribution strategies often involve attempts to extend the appeal of individual films to a variety of other distinctive social groups.

A number of setbacks were faced by the independent sector in the late 1980s, although the level of production continued to increase into the 1990s. Overall demand for films began to slacken. The growth in the numbers of theatrical screens slowed at the end of the 1980s, a period in which the Reagan administration's policies of industrial deregulation allowed the major studios to move back into the exhibition sector. The result was often a reduction of space for independent films in multiplex cinemas. The blockbuster-based approach of the studios favoured a strategy in which big-budget films were held over for longer runs, moving onto the smaller screens that might have provided suitable accommodation for independents. The video boom that had seen unlikely sums of money advanced on the basis of anticipated sales or rentals also came to an end. The video market began to flatten and shifted to a pattern that tended to mimic that of Hollywood theatrical performance: a market dominated by big video chains rather than smaller neighbourhood stores and by large sales of relatively few hit titles. As Rosen puts it: 'Depth-of-copy (increased copies of hits) replaces breadth-of-copy (number of titles carried) as retailer purchasing criteria.'[25] The problem was exacerbated by a shift towards the sell-through market – direct sales to consumers – which increased more rapidly than rentals. The sell-through market is even more hit-driven, further limiting the value of video to the independent sector.[26] One exception to the tendency for independents to lose out in home viewing was the advent of DVD in the late 1990s, the audio-visual quality of which, and the potential to include extra features, made it a format of choice for more film-literate viewers, more than averagely likely to be drawn to less mainstream fare.[27]

The stock market crash of 1987 brought an abrupt end to the easy availability of capital, making money harder to raise and usually on stricter terms. Other sources of funds also dried up, the Reagan era seeing a significant reduction of federal support for features from agencies such as the National Endowment for the Humanities, without which a number of indie films of the late 1970s and early 1980s such as *Heartland* (1979) and *The Ballad of Gregorio Cortez* (1982) might never have been made.[28] At the same time, the cost of independent features was rising, partly as a result of the increasingly competitive nature of the business. This and some of the other difficulties faced by the sector at the end of the 1980s were products of its success in the preceding years. Quantity took over from quality of production, according to Pierson. That it was possible not just to make but to find a market for low-budget indie films had been demonstrated: 'Suddenly, there was no excuse not to make a feature film and the desire to make a film, *any film*, replaced the need to express a vision.'[29] The high profile attained by independent films in the 1990s was such that the dream of becoming a filmmaker came to occupy the place in the culture for some Americans that had previously been held by the aspiration to become a writer, a desire 'fueled by examples of success – young people with little or no experience, training, or family advantage who managed to break through'.[30] For Rosen, the development of the independent market also brought with it a change in the character and motivation of those who achieved the ambition. More appeared to be academically trained professionals, from the dominant film graduate schools in New York and Los Angeles, motivated less by an alternative vision than by the prospect of using the independent sector as a route to work in the established studios.[31] Many independent films failed, whether through lack of quality or because too many were being produced, as did a number of the small distribution companies that had come onto the scene earlier in the decade.

Some small distributors made the risky but tempting move into the financing or production of features, effectively becoming micro-studios. Early examples included the co-financing by Cinecom of John Sayles' *Matewan* (1987) and a multi-picture deal between Circle Releasing and Joel and Ethan Cohen.[32] As Rosen suggests, the micro-studios thought they could pick winners, but were put at risk when they invested in a number of films that turned out to be commercial failures. Success brought its own problems for some companies that overextended themselves on the basis of isolated box-office bonanzas. The labour-intensive nature of distribution can mean that a single big success requires expansion in personnel to perform tasks such as shipping prints and collecting revenues from theatres.

With such expansion, suggests the indie business veteran Ira Deutchman, then president of Fine Line Features, a division of New Line, 'comes a self-fulfilling pressure to release future pictures as if they will break out as well, and this is the catch-22 that has put many of New Line's competitors out of business'.[33] A notable example was Vestron, which profited heavily on the enormous (by independent standards) $63 million domestic gross of its first in-house production, *Dirty Dancing* (1987), but was forced out of business in 1989 after increasing production with what proved to be a series of box-office failures. Other victims of the shakeout included Island/ Alive, FilmDallas, Skouras, Atlantic Releasing and the De Laurentis Entertainment Group.

During the 1990s, independent distribution became concentrated in the arms of fewer and larger companies, most notably New Line and Miramax, although a considerable number of small and in some cases very small outfits continued to hold their own into the new millennium. The business, like that of the major studios, came to revolve to a greater extent around the search for significantly larger-grossing independent box-office hits, films that crossed over into a more mainstream audience, a process that culminated in the $108 million gross of *Pulp Fiction* in 1994. The preceding year witnessed a big move into the independent sector by the Hollywood studios with the takeover of New Line and Miramax by Time-Warner and Disney, respectively. The implications of that development will be considered below. First, however, a closer look is needed at some of the distinctive marketing and distribution strategies that have characterized the indie scene.

Marketing and Distribution Strategies

Since the mid 1970s, Hollywood has moved increasingly towards a marketing and distribution strategy based on very wide releases of films accompanied by heavy television advertising. It was common by the end of the 1990s for films to open simultaneously in the United States on 3,000 screens. At the top end of the market, on which the fate of the industry depends to a disproportionate extent, the aim is to reach a very large audience rapidly, across a range of particular target groups. The general message is that films that do not succeed at the box office relatively quickly are likely to be pulled from distribution to make way for others. The needs of smaller, offbeat independent films are very different, as are those of some of the more unconventional films handled by the majors. The basis of much of the success of independent distributors has been their ability to give specialized attention to the particular requirements of individual titles that need careful nurturing if they are to achieve their full audience potential.

The traditional approach is to open indie or 'art' films gradually, a 'platform release' strategy. An effort is often made to create advance awareness through pre-release showings at festivals, extra attention being gained by films that win prizes, especially at high-profile events such as Sundance and Cannes. The release of Todd Solondz's *Welcome to the Dollhouse* (1996), for example, was preceded by a series of festival appearances carefully orchestrated by the distributor to create a profile for an otherwise potentially hard-to-market and somewhat downbeat, although blackly comic, account of the travails of a 'nerdy' schoolgirl.[34] For films without distribution arrangements, key festivals are among the best places to gain the attention of acquisitions executives. Festival screenings are also a source of reviews from critics in both the mainstream and trade press. Reviews play a particularly important role in the independent sector, far greater than in the commercial mainstream, as the art-house audience is one that tends to both read and be influenced by critical opinion. Positive reviews are also relatively cost free, unlike the very expensive mass television advertising used by the majors (although gaining press attention in the highly competitive environment of leading festivals such as Sundance is far from easy and can require the pricey services of a publicist). Prominent critics can become significant allies in the marketing and promotions process. Many reviewers like to 'discover' and champion unknown films, a process that can provide positive comments for use in trailers, posters and other forms of advertising; good reviews can also be one of the best ways of attracting a distributor in the first place.[35]

Exploitation-cinema-style gimmicks are also used in some cases in an attempt to create viewer awareness and anticipation, the most celebrated example in recent independent history being the campaign mounted by the makers of *The Blair Witch Project*, Daniel Myrick and Eduardo Sanchez.[36] An eleven-minute teaser trailer about the Blair Witch myth, and the supposed 'disappearance' of the three central characters, was shot in advance of the film, initially as a device designed to attract potential investors. The segment was sold to Pierson's *Split Screen* for $10,000, a substantial chunk of the budget that, along with savings and credit card debts, enabled shooting of the feature to commence. It was shown with no indication of whether the story was real or not. A second segment was shown on *Split Screen* some months after shooting was completed, provoking an enormous response on message boards on Pierson's website. It was at this stage that the filmmakers decided to create the website that became almost as famous as the film itself, generating enormous publicity at low cost and demonstrating to both Hollywood and other independents the value of the internet as a marketing tool.

Initial release for independent films is usually limited to a small number of theatres in one or two of the most important urban markets, usually New York and/or Los Angeles. An opening of this kind is another crucial source of reviews and further building of profile and the word-of-mouth recommendation or 'buzz' that remains the most important factor in the success of all commercial films, whether those of the independent sector or the Hollywood mainstream. New York openings are especially favoured, providing access to key critics from nationally circulated publications such as the *New York Times* and *Time* magazine. Release is then widened, gradually. In some cases, the second tier is a larger number of theatres in the initial market/s. In others, it involves an expansion to other major urban centres, the extent and pace of which is likely to depend on the health of box-office returns in the earlier stages. In the case of *Welcome to the Dollhouse*, the initial opening was in New York and Los Angeles. After three weeks of good performance, the film moved out to more screens in the New York and Los Angeles areas. It expanded further to 85 screens around the country, eventually reaching a total of 700 and achieving a healthy gross of $6 million. *The Blair Witch Project* was kept in exclusive runs in selected markets for two weeks, where it sold out and its reputation grew, before being opened onto 1,100 screens.

The timing of the opening is another important factor. Distributors will often try to avoid opening directly against other films that are too close in style or subject matter, so as not to dilute the potential audience, a strategy also adopted by the major studio–distributors. The opening of *Welcome to the Dollhouse* was deliberately timed to coincide with that of the heavily promoted Hollywood blockbuster *Mission: Impossible* on the Memorial Day weekend of 1996. The assumption was that few other films would risk opening against so prominent a studio feature but that a sizeable audience would remain for which *Mission: Impossible* would not be the first choice of viewing.[37] The film was also placed purposely in theatres that would not be large enough to accommodate the expected audience, a tactic used in the release of a number of independent films, including *The Blair Witch Project*, to create lines outside and a sense that the film was in demand and difficult to see, contributing to the positive 'buzz'.

The platform release strategy was designed to allow independent films to build an audience from relatively smaller beginnings than is generally permitted in the commercial mainstream. Smaller indie movies have often depended entirely on reviews and word-of-mouth recommendation. Where advertising is affordable, the tradition has been for it to be modest and print-based rather than on television, the expense of the latter usually requiring larger simultaneous release patterns if it is to be viable. The core market lies in the regular art-house audience but one of the key tasks of the independent distributor is to reach out to other audience groups, either distinct social subgroups or a wider and more mainstream audience. Getting the balance right is far from an easy process.

A good example of the tensions that can exist between different potential release patterns is offered by the handling of *The Ballad of Gregorio Cortez*, one of a number of case studies included by Rosen in a collection produced in association with the Sundance Institute and the IFP.[38] The film, an account of linguistic/cultural misunderstanding that leads to a Mexican American farmer in turn-of-the-century Texas becoming the subject of a manhunt, was financed principally by public funds from the National Endowment for the Humanities and the Corporation for Public Broadcasting. It was developed as a product with a strong social/political message. A deal for theatrical release was made with Embassy Pictures, a small studio (subsequently taken over by Columbia). The filmmakers, including star Edward James Olmos, were committed to a distribution and marketing strategy based on a 'grassroots' outreach campaign. The aim was to generate awareness of the existence of the film among particular social groups, in this case the Hispanic American community.

The deal struck with Embassy included an agreement to hire Olmos and a team of six as a marketing unit separate from the studio's own department, to conduct the grassroots campaign. The film was shown by Olmos at Hispanic community centres, schools and juvenile detention centres, with discussions about the importance of promoting cross-cultural understanding. Relevant local and national organizations were contacted, including the American Historical Association and the National Council of Teachers of English. A number of exploitation-cinema-style gimmicks were used to create awareness for the film, including the distribution of 3,000 tickets for one promotional screening at a 300-seat theatre in San Francisco, at which a range of suitably Hispanic street entertainment was provided for those who turned up but were unable to be accommodated inside. The group was given a relatively free hand to develop these aspects of the campaign, although Embassy retained decision-making power on issues such as the national release and marketing strategy. In the event, two competing release plans were developed simultaneously, 'reflecting the inherent conflict between Embassy's traditional studio launch strategy and that of the *Cortez* group'.[39] The studio favoured a more rapid spread into the major national markets, a strategy that conflicted with the slower pace required if the grassroots campaign was to be able to keep up:

> The success in San Francisco led Embassy to move the film to
> Berkeley and then into a nineteen-city regional "breakout" over
> a single weekend. This scale of exposure was too much for the
> *Cortez* group to handle, and subsequent box-office performance was
> inconsistent.[40]

Tensions often exist between distributors and filmmakers, each of which has a shared interest in the success of a film but might have different priorities or a different sense of how that success is best achieved. Keenen Ivory Wayans, co-writer and star of *Hollywood Shuffle*, complained about the strategy adopted by the Samuel Goldwyn Company, which he argued was focused too much on the art-house audience with which the distributor was familiar rather than seeking out what he considered to be a potentially large but untapped black audience.[41] The key question for the distributor is where to seek to 'position' a film in the marketplace: what kind of advance image and expectations to create, a decision that plays a central role in determining the kind of audience most likely to be attracted. First impressions tend to stick and can largely determine the chances for success or failure in one market or another. The aim of the publicity campaign accompanying the release and pre-release of *Welcome to the*

Dollhouse was to create the impression that it was 'a very cool, hip, entertaining thing to go see' rather than a serious art feature.[42] To this end, the distributor worked with two public relations companies to place interviews with the director and the star, Heather Matarazzo, in youth-oriented magazines and on MTV.

In the case of *Welcome to the Dollhouse*, the strategy was to seek a crossover from art-house to a wider youth audience, something rarely achieved on any scale. Films such as *Dollhouse* or Wes Anderson's critic-ally lauded high-school movie, *Rushmore* (1998), can easily become caught between two stools. Ideally, they appeal to both the specialized and a more general audience. But trying to have it both ways can be risky. There is a danger of appearing too 'arty' and 'adult' for teenagers and too youth-oriented for older art-house viewers. *The Blair Witch Project* is a rare example of a low-budget independent that achieved enormous crossover into the mass teen audience, but that was for a product clearly located in a genre of youth-oriented appeal.

If art-house territory is the one generally known and served best by specialist independent distributors, it can in some cases lose out to efforts to move into other markets, as was the case with *Wild Style* (1982), a portrayal of the exploits of a New York graffiti artist who is embraced by the 'legitimate' art world.[43] The distributor, First Run Features, invested considerable effort in a grassroots marketing strategy designed to reached an inner-city youth market. Unable to afford the television advertising usually seen as the most effective way to reach this audience, First Run concentrated on more innovative and labour-intensive strategies to generate word-of-mouth within the youth constituency. The campaign in New York included the use of runners wearing *Wild Style* T-shirts to distribute 36,000 advertising fliers to schools. Breakdance parties and performances by rappers featured in the film were staged at a number of popular music clubs. More than 1,500 posters were displayed, especially in inner-city neighbourhoods, while sound trucks toured distributing fliers, badges and other materials on the opening night. Advertisements and ticket giveaways were also used on appropriate radio stations in New York and some other markets. The film opened successfully in New York, but to the disappointment of writer-director-producer Charles Ahearn it did not make it into an established art house: 'Because of its appeal to the youth market, where it did so well, it never "crossed back" to the art-house audience.'[44]

A balancing act is often involved in the handling of films with specific constituencies, as opposed to the more general art-film audience. Playing up the specifics might be detrimental to the art-house appeal, while exclusive concentration on the latter can leave potentially significant markets untapped. The success of the bigger independent distributors, especially Miramax and New Line, has been based on their ability to achieve a crossover into larger audiences, beyond those of both the art-house and specific social groups defined through categories such as class, ethnicity or gender. Miramax grew into the biggest name in the indie scene through the use of a strategy often associated with the exploitation market, handling a number of films that lent themselves to controversial media coverage.[45] This approach also characterized the earlier operations of Rugoff's Cinema V, which went out of business as one of the victims of the shakeout of the late 1980s. Controversy was used by Rugoff to promote European titles such as Dušan Makavejev's *WR: Mysteries of the Organism* (1971) and the Swedish film *I Am Curious (Yellow)* (1967).[46] Miramax courted controversy by repeatedly challenging the ratings system after X or NC17 ratings were given to *Scandal* (1989), *The Cook, The Thief, His Wife and Her Lover* (1989), *Tie Me Up! Tie Me Down!* (1990) and *You So Crazy* (1994).[47]

The strategy of Miramax was to highlight the sexual aspect of many of its releases, both American and overseas in origin. The publicity campaign for the British feature *The Crying Game* (1992) focused on sexual enigma (the fact that one of the central characters turns out to be a man rather than a woman) rather than the IRA-related political dimension of the film. The result was a US gross of $62.5 million, extraordinary at the time in the indie sector. As reported in *Variety*: 'Miramax sold the film as an action-thriller with a big "secret". If it had been realistically pegged as a relationship film with gay connotations, it might never have broken beyond the major cities.'[48] The film is credited with having saved the company after a series of costly flops from 1991 to 1993.[49] Miramax's biggest hit, *Pulp Fiction*, which grossed even more than *The Crying Game*, entering into the $100-million-plus bracket that was once the benchmark of success for a studio blockbuster, also benefited from a campaign designed to achieve crossover from the art-house to a much wider audience. The strategy was encapsulated in the trailer, as Justin Wyatt suggests, which moves from a title stating that the film won the prestigious Palm d'Or at the Cannes Film Festival to the appearance of gunshots through the screen and a fast-paced sequence that establishes the film as being filled with action, comedy and sex.[50]

New Line has profited through a mixture of both arty/alternative and much more mainstream genre-based independent features.[51] The distributor enjoyed huge revenues through two franchises that owe more to the world of exploitation than to the art-house or 'quality' art-house/crossover fare with which Miramax is usually associated. The first was launched by the success of A Nightmare on Elm Street (1985), a low-budget teen horror film that generated a series of even more profitable sequels. A key to the stability of New Line at the time was the fact that revenue from the franchise 'was funnelled back into the company rather than into hasty and sizeable production and distribution expansion',[52] the latter being the case with some of the distributors that went to the wall at the end of the 1980s. The Nightmare films were followed by an even more profitable franchise, Teenage Mutant Ninja Turtles, the first instalment of which grossed $135 million in 1990. The film single-handedly took New Line into profit.[53]

The two franchises enabled New Line to invest in the creation of its own home video division, giving greater access to video revenue and more control over the coordination of theatrical and video releases. They also funded the creation of Fine Line Features, a separate distribution arm to handle the more specialized market; Fine Line would make 'character, story and film-maker driven' films while its parent focused on 'genre and high concept movies'.[54] The mainstream branch went on to enjoy a string of further Hollywood blockbuster-style successes, including the Jim Carrey vehicles The Mask and Dumb and Dumber (both 1994). Future hits continued the trend for New Line to operate more like a major studio operation, especially in its commitment to the establishment of high-grossing mainstream franchise properties, examples including Austin Powers: The Spy Who Shagged Me (1999; gross $205 million) and the extremely lucrative Lord of the Rings trilogy. New Line has continued to invest in less mainstream/commercial material, including the multi-strand narrative *Magnolia* (1999), but such films appear very much as a sideline. Crossover successes for Fine Line included returns of $21 million for Robert Altman's *The Player* (1992) and $36 million for *Shine* (1996).[55] Most of its products and films picked up from elsewhere for distribution have performed more modestly, although Fine Line has remained a fixture on the independent scene and New Line's principal source of more arty/indie credibility.

Miramax and New Line led the way in the expansion of independent distribution from the mid 1990s, a growth that had mixed results. In some areas, the business became more like that of the studios. Even in its more distinctively 'indie' guise, the sector has followed Hollywood in becoming a more hit-driven phenomenon, in which promoters and distributors are constantly on the lookout for the 'next big thing', which has come to involve some box-office performances (and budgets) indistinguishable from those of the Hollywood majors. The result has become a sharply delineated 'boom or bust' economy in which a small number of films receive headline-making advances at Sundance and/or large investments in marketing while large numbers fail to find distribution of any kind. Sales of films completed without the involvement of distributors were increasingly squeezed from the mid 1990s into the 2000s by the prevailing tendency for distributors to invest in production themselves, leaving less capacity to make outside acquisitions. The number of films able to occupy the middle ground of more stable and moderate success has been reduced. This is a process that dates back to the unexpected scale of commercial success enjoyed by *sex, lies, and videotape*, a break-though film for Miramax and for the Sundance festival, at the end of the previous decade. Initially envisaged as a much lower-budget production, in the region of $60,000, *sex, lies, and videotape* was made for $1.2 million on the basis of advances for video rights from RCA/Columbia and Virgin. It was a hit at Sundance and won the Palme d'Or at Cannes before going on to gross $25 million in the USA and a global total of $100 million. The effect was to give a boost to the independent sector in general but also to raise the bar of expectations for future box-office performance.

The change was not only one of box-office expectations, but also in the speed and strategy through which revenue would be accrued.

3. A box-office breakthrough for Miramax, Sundance and the independent sector in general: *sex, lies, and videotape* (1989).

In the early 1990s, as James Schamus explains, 'a distributor might have hit the $2 million mark by cycling twenty or so prints of a film on a continuous, long-term roll-out that would, over the course of as many as sixty weeks, see the film play in as many as 300 markets.' By 1997, 'even a small film might open on six to twenty prints within its first two weeks, breaking to ten or twenty cities within a month.'[56] A more concentrated release strategy of this kind requires more intensive spending on advertising, including the use of expensive television spots. Films are under pressure to earn rapidly or lose their place in theatres. The number of independent films on offer increased rapidly from the late 1980s, creating a more crowded marketplace in which advertising and more general media hype was increasingly important. Escalating costs meant a film could not be released with less than $2 million spent on promotion and advertising alone by the turn of the century, according to Geoff Gilmore, director of the Sundance festival.[57] Pressures such as these have an impact on the kinds of films most likely to get funded or picked up for distribution, increasing the threshold for profitability and generally favouring those capable of making a quick impression over those dependent on slow-burning recognition.

ᵉ exhibition end of the business was exacerbated
ıany 'art' theatres by larger cinema chains that
̣g to the Hollywood model of each week eliminating
 ̣ı the lowest gross, instead of nurturing it over a longer
 ̣ ̣ Independent features face the problem of being pushed off
 ̣reens even if they are still earning healthy returns, by new products
handled by larger distributors that have more power over exhibitors.
Independent distributors also receive a smaller share of box office takings
than the big studios, some 38–40 per cent compared with 50–60 per
cent or more for the studios. The number of art-house screens available
to American independents or imports was on the increase in the early
2000s, especially in major indie markets such as New York, but not at
a rate that could begin to keep up with the level of production.

'From an independent film-lover's standpoint, times could hardly
be better,' wrote a correspondent for *The Hollywood Reporter* in January
1997, looking back on the previous year.[59] Never before had so many
high-profile and critically acclaimed independent movies been on
offer, with subject matter as broad as ever. From the point of view of
the industry, however, the situation was less rosy. It was 'reeling' from
a serious case of overproduction. Excessive numbers of indie features
were competing for the same limited market, usually thought to be
about five per cent of the total film-going public. Estimates vary, but
the production figure by the end of the 1990s was put in the region
of 1,300 to 1,500 features a year, far from all of which would find a
distributor. As Amir Malin, then co-managing director of October
Films, put it: 'With the amount of quality films in the marketplace,
there's no question that we are all cannibalising each other's potential
gross.'[60] Competition was not just between rival distributors but
also internal. Miramax, for example, released the performance-based
friendship drama *Walking and Talking* (1996) within days of two of
its biggest films of the year, adaptations of Jane Austen's *Emma* and
Irving Walsh's *Trainspotting*. The result, according to Ted Hope of
Good Machine, producer of *Walking and Talking*, was that the film
got 'squeezed', Miramax inevitably concentrating its investment in
marketing and release costs into the two bigger films.[61]

Overproduction was encouraged by the windfall returns on
investment earned by some films, much-cited examples including

Sling Blade (1996), produced for some $1.8 million, sold to Miramax for $10 million and grossing $26 million in the USA.

> Stories such as these put stars in the eyes of Hollywood mogul wannabes – Park Avenue bankers, young Wall Streeters and Texas real estate investors – who believe they can make a killing with just a small upfront investment.[62]

A strong stock market provided the means for such investment. Banks were also lending more to independent producers in the latter part of the 1990s, following the squeeze on credit of the late 1980s and early 1990s.[63] A significant development was the renewed willingness of banks to arrange 'gap' financing, to bridge the difference between budgets and revenue guaranteed by pre-sales but not paid until after delivery of the film.[64] Exactly how independent films are financed – and how easily – tends to change in line with both the general economic climate and factors more specific to the film and television industries. The early 2000s saw a renewed financial squeeze, including the disappearance of gap finance, the result largely of a turndown in foreign pre-sales (especially from Europe) on which independents have often relied for more than half of their budgets and which in many cases formed the basis on which banks loans were made available.[65] A major loss was money that had been available through taxation regulations in Germany, which dried up as a result of changes to the rules and a slowdown in the German economy.[66] Financial arrangements tended to become more complicated than ever, although there was little sign of a reduction in the level of production.

Hardest hit by problems of overproduction are the smaller independents, which have less clout with exhibitors and often struggle to get their films onto the screens they want or to keep them there long enough to achieve their potential; or even to get paid their agreed share of box-office receipts. The difficulty exists throughout the life cycle of independent features, including festivals and post-theatrical television sales. The festival circuit expanded during the 1990s but became heavily oversupplied. Applications for the Sundance festival mushroomed from some 200 films at the start of the decade to 840 fictional features in 1999, plus another 360 documentaries and more than 400 overseas entries; a far cry from the early years, in which the organizers had to scratch around to find enough films to show.[67] By 2004, the feature total reached a record 2,426 applications. Overspill from Sundance led to the creation of the nearby Slamdance festival in 1995 and assorted other alternatives such as Slumdance, Lapdance and No Dance. To fail to get into Sundance or one of the other major festivals is a blow for many independents, significantly reducing their chances of gaining distribution, although films can sometimes get picked up as a result of screenings at smaller festivals. Some complain that Sundance has become dominated by films filled with stars, star-directors or star-producers that are already assured of a place in the market, rather than primarily being an opportunity for the discovery of new and innovative work, although the precise mix tends to shift somewhat from year to year (2004, for example, saw a diverse range, including top dramatic prize for the ultra-low-budget *Primer*). The market for international television sales, a key source of advance funding for many independents, has also become more star-driven and far less hospitable than it was in the 1980s and early 1990s.

A crowded or over-crowded marketplace is a sign of health, in some respects, but it is likely to restrict the opportunity for smaller, more unconventional and less commercial features to find an audience. A question often asked by industry insiders and commentators is: would a *Poison* or a *Slacker* make it to first base today, to gaining festival and critical prominence, a distributor and a visible release? Not that all of the earlier generation 'indie classics' were given an easy time. *Slacker* was shown as a work in progress at the Independent Feature Film Market in 1989 and gained a £35,000 advance sale to German television. It was turned down by Sundance (and later by Telluride and Toronto), however, and opened theatrically by the director himself at the on-campus Dobie Theatre in his home town of Austin, Texas, playing to a very local constituency before eventually being picked up by Orion Classics and gaining the high profile that resulted from the film and its title being played up in the media as an embodiment of the 'Generation X' lifestyle. An example of a more recent film of non-conventional narrative structure that struggled to find a distributor is Christopher Nolan's *Memento* (2001). The only offer was from Paramount Classics, but was rejected for being too low. *Memento* eventually found its market, however, after former exhibitor

Bob Berney offered to distribute it if funded by the production company, Newmarket Capital Group. It went on to gross nearly $24 million as the independent hit of the year.[68]

The following year, Berney played a central part in the substantially larger box-office triumph of another feature that was turned down by almost all the indie distributors, the more conventional comedy *My Big Fat Greek Wedding* (2002). It was eventually picked up by the newly created IFC Films, headed by Berney, in a deal in which the financiers paid for prints and advertising, and went on to take an extraordinary $241 million in the USA alone, overtaking *The Blair Witch Project* as the most successful indie feature in history (the total including overseas box-office and video/DVD is put at some $600 million). IFC saw only a small proportion of the windfall, the distributor in this case having received a flat fee of $300,000 for its limited commitment, a figure that was increased to more than $1 million, still a tiny share of the revenue, after an agreement by the producers to make bonus payments.[69] The success of the $5 million feature was based, significantly, on a return to more traditional indie marketing and distribution strategy, starting with a small-scale release tied to a grassroots campaign focused on urban Greek American communities. *My Big Fat Greek Wedding* remained in cinemas from April until the end of the summer blockbuster season in the autumn, expanding only gradually to a larger-scale release. The distributor resisted pressure to expand more rapidly, keeping the film in a relatively small number of screens, thus ensuring that it played to full houses, a particularly effective strategy to build positive word-of-mouth for a crowd-pleasing comedy.[70] The scale of the film's success prompted much debate in indie circles about the extent to which it might (or might not) encourage a broader return to such a classically indie-style approach.

Even when all distributors pass, grassroots strategy remains an option at the smaller end of the indie sector, especially for films that can establish connections with distinctive niche audiences such as those based on ethnically defined constituencies. Gene Cajayon used such an approach to self-distribute his $1.2 million Filipino American coming-of-age feature *The Debut* (2000) after it failed to make major festivals or to secure a distributor.[71] Cajayon was able to secure a $104,000 loan from private investors to pay the costs of a release in markets containing more than 20,000 Filipino American residents, into each of which a small team moved in advance to promote the film to the core audience of Filipino and Asian American teenagers, young adults and families. To reach such viewers, multiplex and major chain theatres, rather than art-houses, were targeted. Because of his lack of any clout in distribution, Cajayon was initially required to rent screens on a weekly basis. The film went on to achieve modest success, grossing a total of $1.7 million at the US box office. The smaller-festival circuit also offers an arena in which films that fail to achieve distribution can eke out a reasonably extended lifetime on screen.

To play in the higher-stakes end of the business, the principal independent distributors had to become bigger institutions with more staff and larger headquarters. Heavier overheads brought changes in the nature of the game, away from its small-scale beginnings rooted in modest profits on low-budget films, driving further the tendency towards expansion and escalation. Breakout crossover hits have become a requirement rather than a bonus for the larger independents. On the one hand, the independent sector has become bigger and stronger, in its industrial and institutional base. Other developments in the second half of the 1990s included the creation of its own cable television channels: the Independent Film Channel, launched in 1994 (by Rainbow Media Holdings, a subsidiary of Cablevision, a substantial telecommunications and entertainment corporation), which subsequently diversified into both production (IFC Films) and distribution (IFC Productions); and the Sundance Channel, a joint venture between Robert Redford, Showtime Networks and Universal Studios. (Sundance also moved into limited theatrical distribution in 2003, launching an initiative in which groups of films taken from the festival circuit were promised a guaranteed two-week run with generous marketing on Loews Theater screens in at least 10 markets across the country.)[72] On the other hand, some fear that its essentially – or relatively – independent, low-budget and unconventional character has been undermined by such developments. None more so than the reappearance on the scene of the big Hollywood players.

Re-enter the Majors

The unprecedented scale of box-office success and high profile achieved by some independent films in the late 1980s and into the 1990s did not escape notice by the major Hollywood studio-distributors. They soon became significant contributors to the ability of the big independents – if they can retain that label – to operate on such a large-scale basis. Major studio-distributors joined the ranks of those bidding for independent features, contributing to the driving up of prices, both for the films they targeted and the reduced number of attractive prospects left to the indie distributors. In 1993, as mentioned above, Miramax and New Line were sold into the arms of the majors. The Weinsteins sold Miramax to the Walt Disney Company for $60–80 million, plus the assumption of significant debts. New Line was sold for $500–600 million to Ted Turner, a subsequent merger making it part of the giant Time-Warner conglomerate. Other moves into the territory of the independents included the establishment of Sony Pictures Classics (SPC) in 1992, a division of Sony Pictures, owners of the major studio Columbia; Fox Searchlight, created by Twentieth Century Fox in 1994; and Paramount Classics, an offshoot of Paramount Pictures, in 1998. Universal Studios went through a convoluted series of relationships with a number of independent labels during the late 1990s and early 2000s, eventually taking over Good Machine and combining it with its own affiliates under the Focus Features label in 2002. The move under a studio umbrella by Good Machine, one of the higher-profile independents of the early 2000s, was described by *Variety* as a shift 'that signals just how dependent so-called independent film has become'.[73] The benefit for Good Machine, in exchange for some of its autonomy, was access to finance and to Universal's domestic distribution network. United Artists returned to the independent scene in 2000, transformed into the speciality arm of MGM/UA. The complete set of studio-owned 'independent' arms was completed in 2003 with the long-anticipated creation by Warner Bros. Entertainment of Warner Independent Pictures, with plans to produce or acquire between five and ten films a year, and the launch of Dreamworks SKG's speciality unit, Go Fish.

Ownership by major studios gave former independents such as

Miramax and New Line access to greatly increased financial and institutional resources. It was the resulting influx of capital that enabled New Line to increase its level of production and to play effectively in the world of Hollywood-scale blockbusters. Miramax, given unlimited rights to borrow from its parent, increased its rate of acquisitions sharply. Suddenly flush after surviving from hand-to-mouth for several years, the company was able to outbid its competitors and dominate the market, largely on the strength of video and TV deals within the Disney empire.[74] It could also draw upon Disney's power in the market to orchestrate the wide release of *Pulp Fiction* and subsequent breakout features.[75] Disney and Turner granted a significant measure of autonomy to Miramax and New Line. The aim was to benefit from the expertise they had demonstrated in the specialized/independent sector, rather than to subsume them to the strategies of the parent companies. A lesson was learnt from the experience of the earlier 'classics' divisions of the majors, the films of which had been handled without any special care or attention by the mainstream domestic distribution offices.[76] Both Miramax and New Line were given control of distribution and marketing strategies for their films. The Weinsteins were retained by Disney to run Miramax, initially on a five-year contract. Shaye remained in place at New Line, as did Schamus as co-president of Universal's Focus. Disney agreed to finance the development, production and marketing of Miramax features, giving the subsidiary complete autonomy for any acquisition or production up to $12 million.[77]

Corporate ownership has caused some frictions, as well as more general criticism from those for whom heavy studio involvement is anathema to any idea of a distinctive independent cinema. The Miramax policy of using controversy as a marketing tool caused difficulties in the case of the handling of two films in 1995: the British import *Priest*, which centres on the experiences of a gay priest, and Larry Clark's *Kids*, a frank portrayal of the sexual and other activities of New York teens. A number of prominent stockholders sold shares in Disney in protest at the company's involvement in *Priest*, which was initially slated to open – in a typically provocative Miramax move – on Good Friday. *Kids* became a touchstone in national and international debate about the fate of inner-city youth. Miramax had, eventually, to form a new company, Shining Excalibur Pictures, to release the film after it was given an NC17 rating, a category Miramax was contractually forbidden to handle. Pressure on Disney from Catholic organizations, which organized boycotts of *Priest*, led Miramax to offload Kevin Smith's 1999 comedy *Dogma*, featuring Ben Affleck and Matt Damon as fallen angels. The film, financed by Miramax, was personally bought back from the company by Bob and Harvey Weinstein for a reported $14 million, at the request of Disney head Michael Eisner (domestic distribution rights were subsequently sold to Lion's Gate Entertainment).[78] The willingness of Miramax to continue to court or risk controversy in the face of criticism from the Catholic League for Religious and Civil Rights appeared undiminished, however, when it signed up to distribute *The Magdalene Sisters*, winner of the Golden Lion award at the 2002 Venice Film Festival, the story of three Irish women abused in a home run by nuns. Objections from Disney also prevented Miramax from distributing Michael Moore's provocative Palme d'Or-winning documentary *Fahrenheit 911* (2004), an examination of post-September 11th foreign policy and links between the family of president George W. Bush and prominent figures in Saudi Arabia. Like *Dogma*, the film was bought back by the Weinsteins (for an estimated $6 million, the sum invested in the picture by Miramax), who formed a new company, Fellowship Adventure Group, to distribute the film jointly with Lions Gate and IFC Films. *Fahrenheit 911* was opened just three weeks after the deal was signed, to take advantage of the publicity created by the row, in which Disney was accused of fearing that handling the film through Miramax would threaten tax breaks it received in Florida, and the film's success at Cannes. Ted Turner was reported, in similarly controversial territory, to have delayed the release of *Crash* (1996) because of his personal distaste for David Cronenberg's adaptation of J.G. Ballard's novel about the sexual fetishization of car crashes.[79] October Films, at the time a division of Universal, abandoned plans to distribute Todd Solendz's *Happiness* in June 1998 as a result of objections reportedly raised by the studio's then-parent, Seagram, about aspects of the film, including the fact that one of the central characters is a paedophile. An uncut and unrated version was released directly by the producer, Good Machine, although Universal helped, quietly and in the background, to secure the necessary bank loan.[80]

Ownership by the majors undoubtedly helped to reinforce the position of Miramax and New Line and to blur the distinction between some of their operations and those of the Hollywood mainstream. Its impact on the rest of the independent scene was less favourable. The creation of 'major independents' has tended to polarize the market. Prices for many independent features were forced up by the strength and aggressive marketing approach of Miramax in particular, leaving smaller distributors struggling to find suitable films at affordable prices. Miramax and New Line retained some commitment to the more traditional notion of independent production and distribution, the latter in the form of the relatively modest operations of Fine Line. Miramax has faced regular criticism from smaller independents for 'selling out' and abandoning its origins or for distorting the marketplace.

A substantial chunk of the commercial success of Miramax in the past decade has come through its genre-film label, Dimension Films, created in 1992 and headed by Bob Weinstein, the lower-profile of the Weinstein brothers. The strength of Dimension was built on horror titles such as the *Scream* series (1996, 1997, 2000), *Scary Movie/Scary Movie 2* (2000/2001), *Halloween H20* (1998) and Alejandro Amenábar's rather more subtle *The Others* (2001). The creation of Dimension, inspired by the success of New Line with genre/exploitation franchises such as *Nightmare on Elm Street*, enabled the Disney subsidiary to profit from very mainstream-seeming genre features while maintaining the 'quality' market associations of the Miramax brand, critical and box-offices successes in that bracket including the Oscar-winning *Good Will Hunting* (1997) and *Shakespeare in Love* (1998). Miramax has continued to demonstrate its ability to achieve unlikely-seeming breakout successes, including the $58 million gross of the Italian concentration camp tragi-comedy, *Life Is Beautiful* (1997). The company maintains that it is committed to a range of products at all levels, including more traditionally indie-seeming material such as the Oscar-nominated family drama *In the Bedroom* (2001), although, as Biskind suggests, the decision to throw weight behind such productions is largely opportunistic, often contingent on the disappointing performance of other contenders for box office and/or Oscar success. Miramax has also demonstrated an increased commitment to larger-scale productions, seeking studio or other equity partners in 2003 to follow the $100 million Martin Scorsese historical epic *Gangs of New York* (2002) with two or three such high-budget studio-style 'tentpole' pictures a year.[81] The same year also saw a shift to higher-budget co-funding partnerships with the majors by Dimension, launched with Terry Gilliam's $75 million *The Brothers Grimm* (2004), a co-production with MGM.[82]

Miramax was a leading force in the shift of emphasis towards increased involvement in production rather than acquisitions, a move that, according to Peter Biskind, amounted to abandoning its original recipe for success: the acquisition of large numbers of films, a few of which would be identified as the most potentially profitable on opening, and thus be singled out for heavy investment in areas such as marketing and campaigns for Oscar nominations. A production-led enterprise meant involvement with fewer films, in each of which the company had a larger investment. The result, Biskind suggests, was an increasingly conservative strategy, in which star names were sought as box-office insurance and riskier projects were likely to be avoided or to have any rough edges smoothed down.[83] A more mainstream audience became not so much a potential bonus, for occasional breakthrough hits, as the principal target market to which Miramax products became tailored. Dimension, meanwhile, became an increasingly important contributor to the company's profits, its share rising from 25 per cent in 1992 to nearly 75 per cent in 2000.[84]

For the Hollywood studios, involvement in the independent sector generally represents a good investment. Whether through the acquisition of previously independent operations or the creation of their own semi-autonomous divisions, the majors increased their ability to share in the very high levels of profit enjoyed by specialized/indie-type features that break out into the mass audience (not to mention the benefits of more mainstream properties supplied by New Line and Miramax/Dimension). The new generation of classics divisions generally fared reasonably well, handling modest numbers of imports and home-grown independent films. Their aim has been to focus carefully on limited numbers of projects, generally resisting the trend in other parts of the indie/Indiewood sector towards a more hit-driven market.

The closer involvement of the majors was almost inevitable once the independent scene began to become a cultural phenomenon, gaining widespread media treatment, from the end of the 1980s. It would be surprising if no move had been made into independent territory at an institutional level to match the tendency of the studios to cash in on the success of individual films that demonstrate the existence of viable niche audiences or catch particular social currents. As Chuck Kleinhans puts it: 'The success of independent gay features shows that you can sell a *Philadelphia* (1993).'[85] Julie Dash's *Daughters of the Dust* (1991), an evocative portrait of a community of American women descended from West African slaves, proved the viable existence of an audience defined as that comprised of women who read novels by writers such as the African American author Toni Morrison; the studio response, from Twentieth Century Fox, was *Waiting to Exhale* (1995). While independents can gain an initial edge through the discovery of such markets, Kleinhans suggests:

> once those markets are identified, independents must compete with the mainstream industry's attempt to exploit the same market. Thus, the Gen X hit *Slacker* (1991) opens up the space for the star-powered *Reality Bites* [1994].[86]

A toe in the independent waters also has other potential benefits for the studios. Association with 'quality', arty, edgy or 'cool'/alternative features is good for the image; that of individual executives with pretensions to something more than noisy blockbuster productions, and that of branches of large corporations often subject to criticism for their business practices and much of their not-so-creative output. Connections with the independent arena can help studio executives to stay in touch with upcoming social/cultural trends and fashions, particularly those oriented around aspects of youth cultures with which they might otherwise have little contact. Involvement in or around the indie scene has also proved useful to the studios as a way of gaining access to new talent. Production deals might be offered to promising filmmakers in the hope of bringing them on to perform in the mainstream arena. For both independent distributors and those closer to the orbit of the majors, modest expenditure in supporting low-budget first features is often seen as a worthwhile investment against the potential returns of a future relationship.

In some cases the majors have produced mainstream efforts to tap into markets opened up by the independents, or have recruited independent filmmakers to produce more conventionally studio-oriented material. In others, they have themselves produced features that have something in common with indie films, if tending towards the glossy end of the scale, squeezing further the space available for the independent sector. A number of examples appeared at the end of the 1990s, the most prominent being the $15 million budgeted midlife-crisis drama *American Beauty* (1999), produced and distributed by DreamWorks, which grossed $130 million on an indie-style platform release of extended duration. 'Just as indie distributors have begun to settle into the normalcy of an overcrowded marketplace,' Thom Geier wrote in *The Hollywood Reporter* in January 2000, 'they have found themselves faced with encroachment by the majors into their territory.'[87] This is another way the lines between the independents and Hollywood can become blurred. It can be attributed to both the commercial success of some independent films and their ability to garner critical acclaim and – perhaps especially – the Oscar nominations and awards so highly coveted by the studios. A large number of Oscars went to films from the independent or semi-independent sector during the 1990s, a source of the highest-profile coverage available in the industry and a key part of the marketing strategy of the independent features that have benefited. Apart from their almost guaranteed effect of adding a substantial bonus to box-office takings, Oscar nominations or awards are a valuable currency in the efforts of independent operators to raise finance and attract higher-level talent to future products. A best screenplay award and five other nominations for *The Crying Game*, for example, was played up by Miramax to draw *Pulp Fiction* to the company from initial development at a rival studio (the latter went on to achieve very similar Oscar recognition).[88]

Whether indie-style films from the Hollywood majors or the top end of production/distribution by larger formally or partially independent companies merit inclusion under the label 'independent' remains open to debate. Some studio films are undoubtedly closer in spirit to the independent tradition than some features produced or distributed within the independent or semi-autonomous sector (compare, say, *American Beauty* with New Line's *Lord of the Rings* trilogy). A gap exists between glossier productions – whether from independents, autonomous or semi-autonomous studio divisions or the studios themselves – and the lower-budget end of the independent market, even if the distinction is far from absolute. It is the difference, generally, between productions budgeted in millions as opposed to tens or more usually hundreds of thousands of dollars. There is also a significant and substantial middle ground, neither as exploitation/ mainstream-based as some of the bigger-earning independent or quasi-independent films nor as raw as the cheapest low-budget entries. The same goes for distribution and/or production companies. A number of middle-ranking outfits have managed to sustain a place in the market beneath the 'major independents', as have a variety of smaller, niche-based entities.

From Mid-Level Independents to the New Cutting Edge

Of companies entirely independent of the Hollywood studios, the two largest names were merged in December 2003 with the takeover of Artisan Entertainment by Lion's Gate Entertainment. The move, in which Lion's Gate bought Artisan for $160 million, plus the assumption of some $50–60 million of Artisan's debt, consolidated two mini-major studio operations, each of which involved film production and distribution as well as television production. The principal appeal of Artisan for Lion's Gate was its video back-catalogue of some 7,000 features established through the purchase of titles from companies including Republic Pictures, Carolco and Hallmark. Substantial libraries of this kind offer an important source of stability, producing reliable revenues that smooth out many of the financial ups and downs of the film business. Artisan's biggest claim to fame was its handling of *The Blair Witch Project*, from which it gained a reputation for innovative approaches to marketing. Its ability to achieve unlikely-seeming success in the youth market was also demonstrated by the $3.2 million gross of Darren Aronofsky's obscure, black-and-white $60,000-budget *Pi* (1998). Artisan released Aronofsky's second feature, *Requiem for a Dream* (2000), un-rated to prevent cuts it said would have compromised the director's vision, a move designed to increase the company's appeal to filmmakers on the basis of its respect for artistic integrity.

Artisan is a good example of a company that was run as a rationalized and efficient consolidated business operation but that managed to combine this with an openness to films of a genuinely independent-seeming cast. The aim of such outfits is partly to beat the studios at their own game, often making and/or distributing highly marketable films at lower cost and handling them with an extra degree of imagination. Both larger and middle-ranking independents are often accused of abandoning the original independent spirit. But a key part of their strategy is the creation of an identifiable market difference from the major studios. Artisan based much of its success on being identified as a home for quirky, indie-style directors such as Aronofsky, Steven Soderbergh (*The Limey*, 1999), Robert Altman (*Dr. T and the Women*, 2000) and figures from the international art cinema such as Wim Wenders (*The Buena Vista Social Club*, 1999).

Somewhere beneath the studio-owned Miramax/Dimension and New Line/Fine Line, Artisan and Lion's Gate, both separately and combined, are still high in the independent food chain. If there has been a general move towards consolidation in the independent sector, as manifested by the Lion's Gate/Artisan merger – along with much of American capitalism in general – plenty of smaller operations continue to exist, if not always to thrive, in the lower-budget or more import-oriented sphere. Micro-indie distributors – usually not large enough to invest in production – come and go on a regular basis. The independent sector is an unpredictable business. Exactly which films will succeed or fail cannot be guaranteed. The same goes to a large extent for Hollywood, but the strength of the major studios is that they operate at a sufficiently large scale, and under the auspices of larger media conglomerates, to be able to absorb substantial financial disappointments. Hence the appeal for independent outfits of finding shelter under a studio wing. By themselves, they tend to be vulnerable to the vagaries of the market. Some have stuck around for a long time, however, including New Yorker Films, still in business in the early 2000s, having expanded into the video release market in 1990. New Yorker was acquired by the independent operator Madstone Films in 2002, along with its library of 500 titles, subsequently taking over Madstone's traditional distribution and marketing responsibilities.[89]

Small- to medium-sized independents that go to the wall tend to do so as a result of over-expansion, often on the basis of isolated success that tempts them into higher-cost/higher-risk levels of production and marketing. A spectacular breakout success for one producer or distributor, such as that enjoyed by Artisan with *The Blair Witch Project*, can create unrealistic pressure on others to come up with mega-hits of their own. The occasional hit can be a lifeline for struggling independents, however, as was *My Big Fat Greek Wedding* after a number of disappointments for IFC Films, even if it only received a small piece of the cake.

The secret appears to be not to allow one-off success to lead to a wholesale change in strategy. Micro-distributors that survive tend to rely on carefully choosing from the films passed over by their larger rivals and keeping costs low, especially in marketing, at a scale appropriate to realistic expectations of box-office return. The number of small independent production or distribution companies was on the increase in the early 2000s, despite the level of competition, increased marketing costs and prominent failures such as the demise in 2001 of The Shooting Gallery, a production cooperative that gained attention for a novel deal in which it put together touring packages of non-mainstream films shown in Loews Cineplex multiplexes in 15 cities.[90] Some producers have pooled resources by creating joint marketing/distribution arms, such as Independent Distribution Partners, which releases films from Samuel Goldwyn, Fireworks Pictures and Stratosphere Entertainment.[91] Other companies have established additional sources of revenue such as the creation of in-house video/DVD divisions (First Look), while one trend in the early 2000s was for micro-distributors to open their own theatres (Madstone Films, Magnolia Pictures).[92] The subsequent purchase of Magnolia by Mark Cuban and Todd Wagner's 2929 Entertainment in 2003 created a more ambitious form of indie vertical integration, following 2929's takeover of the largest independent cinema chain, Landmark Theatres, and its creation of a digital production outfit, HDNet Films. (Cuban and Wagner also own the high-definition cable network, HDNet, giving control over another in-house outlet.)[93]

One of the secrets of longevity is knowing and sticking to a specific niche. For New Yorker and a number of other small outfits, this is US distribution of international/foreign-language art films. Where the distribution end of the business is concerned, non-American films remain a significant sector of the indie scene, if usually with modest box-office performance, although this is another part of the market that has followed the pattern of success tending to concentrate on a small number of breakout hits. Other smaller distributors specialize in particular sectors of the market for American independents. Strand Releasing, for example, handles foreign-language films and a range of American independents but made its name in the gay and lesbian market with low-budget films such as Gregg Araki's AIDS-era road-movie, *The Living End*.

Small, offbeat, unconventional and sometimes radical independent films do still exist and gain distribution, despite all the pressures created by the higher-spending, screen-dominating end of the spectrum. The nature of the low-budget scene is such that it is never likely to disappear, even if it goes through relative periods of rise and fall. Filmmakers will continue to have films to make that cannot be nurtured in the mainstream and the persistence to see them through, even if they do not always reach much of an audience. An oft-repeated mantra at events such as the annual IFP Market is the extent to which low-budget production is driven by the compulsive *need* of the filmmaker to produce, regardless of the obstacles faced. At the production end, especially, independent filmmaking can be an intensely personal activity, less subject to the vagaries of the commercial marketplace. Conditions of relative financial difficulty might even be a spur to higher quality, increasing the extent to which the pictures that survive into production are those in which higher levels of creative passion are invested, an argument made by Sundance director Geoff Gilmore in relation to the 2002 line-up.[94] If the low-budget sector has been squeezed to some extent in recent years it has also been given a boost by the advent of ultra-cheap digital video equipment, a development seen as offering to take parts of the indie scene back to its roots, although one that has also been embraced by the bigger players.

Digital video is an extremely inexpensive medium, compared with film. Cameras capable of decent image quality, shooting in low or available light, can be bought for as little as $1,000 at the bottom end, while editing can be done on software available for higher-end home computers. DV permits independent filmmakers to own the means of production and post-production themselves, rather than being restricted to what they can borrow or rent (expensively) for limited periods of time. One of the biggest expenses for very low-budget filmmakers – film and processing – simply disappears, initially at least. DV cameras are also very small, light and portable, lending themselves to 'guerrilla-style' filmmaking with minimal crews and little impact on the locations used. Low-profile shooting has a number of advantages for those on shoestring budgets, including the ability to avoid the cost of permits often required for shooting on location and to escape the attentions of local union representatives checking up on the extent to which they are conforming with cast or crew hiring requirements that can significantly increase budget requirements, even with reduced-rates deals for smaller-budget films.[95] DV has been embraced enthusiastically in the New York indie scene, a key point of inspiration being the work of the Danish Dogme 95 movement, especially Thomas Vinterberg's hand-held *Festen/ Celebration* (1998). The potential of the format was demonstrated at the International Documentary Film Festival in New York in spring 1998, which included two films shot with Sony Mini-DV cameras, including Bennett Miller's *The Cruise*, a portrait of a New York City tour guide, which 'became a case-study for would-be digital filmmakers'.[96]

The following year saw the creation of Independent Digital Entertainment (InDigEnt), a collective formed by a group including the independent filmmaker Gary Winick, the producers' representative John Sloss and Caroline Kaplan from the production arm of the Independent Film Channel. InDigEnt was funded by the latter to produce ten low-budget digital features for a total of $1 million, with cast and crew taking reduced fees in return for a share in any profits (a further slate of four films was announced in 2002). The first, Winick's *Sam the Man* (2000), was shot on location in New York with a cast of established professionals, without permits, for close to the intended budget of $60,000.[97] InDigEnt went on to triumph at Sundance in 2002, Rebecca Miller's *Personal Velocity* winning the grand jury prize for dramatic features while *Tadpole*, made for $150,000, won a directing award for Winick and was picked up by Miramax for an eye-catching $5 million.

A number of star names were attracted to InDigEnt's initial slate, including Sigourney Weaver in *Tadpole* and Ethan Hawke and Uma Thurman in *Tape* (2002), a one-location drama directed by Richard Linklater. The scaled-down mechanics of shooting in DV lends itself to performance-led material likely to appeal to actors seeking a more intimate and flexible arena in which to work. Commercially, star-led DV movies are an attractive prospect, at minimal cost compared with studio films and virtually guaranteed distribution because of the names attached. Distribution rights to InDigEnt's first package were bought, unseen, by Lion's Gate. In its use of stars in some films, InDigEnt is not operating at the lowest end of the DV budget scale. The same is true of other technical standards. Reliance on natural lighting and small crews is combined with investment in higher-end sound recording, editing and digital effects to permit a blow-up to 35mm for theatrical release and broadcast.[98]

Digital filmmaking without stars or the augmentation necessary for transfer to 35mm can be exceptionally inexpensive, permitting almost anyone with the necessary ideas and commitment of time to make an independent feature. Distributors warn against being misled by the low initial costs, given the investment of at least some $50,000 to $70,000 required to make the transfer to 35mm required for conventional theatrical exhibition. The final budget might not be much lower than that of productions in 16mm and there is no guarantee that distributors will be prepared to pick up the bill. The key difference, though, is that DV makes it possible to get a feature completed to a stage at which it can be screened for distributors and, increasingly, at festivals, creating the opportunity to test its potential at a significantly lower level of expenditure. It also enables a great deal more material to be shot than would be affordable on film and, where the filmmaker owns camera and editing software, permits more extended and integrated periods of shooting and editing. The proportion of films shot on DV screened at Sundance was about 25 per cent in 2002, rising to 30 per cent the following year; in dramatic shorts, the number of submissions rose more rapidly, a 62 per cent increase from 2,100 to 3,345, an indication of the widening of access created by the increased availability of inexpensive digital cameras and home computer editing software.[99]

Digital formats are also compatible with the cheapest and most accessible new mode of distribution: the internet. A number of websites are available to showcase independent or 'underground' films (for example, the IFILM site, www.ifilm.net, and AtomFilms, atomfilms.com). Initially restricted largely to shorts, the internet has in recent years become a viable means of distributing features, as a result of the development and wider uptake of broadband connections. As with all new indie frontiers, internet distribution has been exploited both by those at the more experimental margins and those seeking to move closer to the mainstream. For the former it offers an outlet for which little if any involvement is necessary with industrial/commercial structures. Putting an experimental-type film on your own website might not be the way to gain an enormous audience, given the crowded nature of the internet and the number of competing attractions. But it is likely to gain more exposure than is available through more traditional underground networks.

Self-distribution of films on the internet is likely to increase, following the model established in music, in which garage bands have distributed directly over the web using the MP3 format. It is not restricted to movies shot in DV. Feature-length examples on film include *alt.sex* (2001), shot in Boston for $32,000, which was posted for free viewing (www.altsexmovie.com) by writer-director Eric Bickernicks, in the hope of gaining attention after failing to get into Sundance or Slamdance. The first film credited with being shown in full online before theatrical release is *Party Girl* (1995), although at the time it would have been seen by few viewers and in low-resolution form.[100] Sundance itself launched an online component in 2001, a showcase for shorts running alongside the main festival. Online distribution as a commercial entity in itself in still in its early years, but a number of outlets are available. One of the largest, CinemaNow (www.cinemanow.com), is majority-owned by Lion's Gate (other principal investors being the big players Microsoft and Blockbuster Video), giving it a clear investment in the indie as well as the mainstream sector. CinemaNow and IFILM sell themselves to independent filmmakers as conduits to both general film-going audiences and to industry insiders who might pick up their films for theatrical distribution.

New ways to distribute and exhibit DV films at low cost in locations ranging from small, specialized theatres to coffeehouses are also being explored. Ira Deutchman, head of Emerging Pictures and Emerging Cinemas, announced plans to open 200 theatres with digital projection systems in venues including museums and performing arts centres by 2005, using satellite delivery systems to supply films in easily downloadable files.[101] The extent to which this is likely to become a significant alternative channel remains the subject of much debate among distributors and exhibitors. Digital exhibition is becoming a reality more generally, as a way of cutting distribution costs for both Hollywood and the independent sector. Larry Fessenden's offbeat horror film *Wendigo* became the first feature to be shown using Microsoft Windows Media technology during its release in 2002. The following year, Landmark Theaters announced plans to equip its entire circuit of more than 50 cinemas for digital projection and to work directly with filmmakers lacking distribution for low-budget DV features (a commitment to digital maintained after the subsequent purchase of Landmark by Wagner and Cuban). The involvement of Microsoft in the venture, and the use of its lower-end technology, was expected to reduce the usually high cost of conversion.[102] Another non-mainstream option is release of DV movies directly onto DVD, copies of which can be made at relatively low cost and sold via the internet. The Film Movement, a new initiative launched in 2002 by Larry Meistrich, founder of The Shooting Gallery, offered a DVD subscription service, acquiring the rights to films that would receive a limited theatrical release in major cities such as New York and Los Angeles at the same time as they were distributed to subscribers. The aim was to overcome the problem of presenting films theatrically to viewers outside a few key markets, a situation in which the size of the potential audience is rarely commensurate with the costs of the promotion needed to make them aware of its existence.[103]

Digital video combined with online distribution, digital projection or DVD release has the potential to open up and decentralize aspects of the independent scene. It is also likely to increase the problem of overproduction, however, not to mention the prospect of the appearance of a rash of inexpert material, the effect of which is to reaffirm the importance of filters such as major festivals, markets, producer's representatives and other mediating figures.

As an industry, American independent cinema has come a long way since the burst of activity that characterized the second half of the 1980s. A substantial infrastructure is in place, comprising distributors both large and small, affiliated to the Hollywood studios or more 'truly' independent; a body of expertise in distribution and marketing, not to mention the filmmakers themselves, whether their ambitions are to break into Hollywood or to remain at the more artistic/ alternative end of the independent spectrum; a thriving festival circuit and dedicated cable channels; its own equivalent of the Oscars, the Independent Spirit Awards, conferred by the IFP's Los Angeles branch and including a category for films made for under $500,000; a number of forums in which independent filmmakers are able to communicate and get together, including the IFP and publications such as *Filmmaker* and the online *indieWIRE* (www.indiewire.com); all this and a place in the wider film and cultural landscape.

Parts of the indie scene have become so institutionalized as to put into question the suitability of the 'independent' label, in terms of both industrial structure and the kinds of films produced. The independent sector has become much more of a business than was the case in the 1980s or early 1990s, to which people might be attracted to gain fame and fortune rather than to pursue an artistic or political vision. The success of independent cinema has turned the notion of independence into an exploitable marketing angle, a claim made for many films that have been confected deliberately in an attempt to gain 'indie' cachet in the marketplace; a more cynical and calculating approach than what many would see as the true 'spirit' of indie cinema, in which the business of 'positioning' and selling would be a secondary process, a perhaps necessary evil that comes only after a film has been made on its own terms. Some independent films have been produced without much concern about their commercial fate, especially at the lower end of the budget scale, but it is easy to over-romanticize an earlier and supposedly 'purer' notion of independence.

A vibrant, smaller scale version of independence continues not just to exist, if often struggling financially, but to be linked organically to the larger body; the latter drawing on the former wherever opportunities are identified, the former relying on the gaps in the market left by the latter. The relationship between the commercial mainstream and various different degrees of independence is dialectical and dynamic rather than fixed, in industrial as in other respects. That an audience continues to exist for independent films that depart from the norms associated with Hollywood remains beyond doubt, even if the competitive nature of the market makes it hard to reach for many individual productions. So, what exactly is offered by independent films? One major respect in which they often depart from, or complicate, the Hollywood model is in the realm of narrative, the subject of the next chapter.

2

Narrative

I can't stand plots, because I don't feel life has plots. There is no beginning, middle, or end, and it upsets me when things are tied up so perfectly.

Harmony Korine[1]

Feature-length American independent cinema is, primarily, a narrative-based form, one that involves the telling of a story of some kind. Stories can be told in different ways, however, and can figure more or less largely in the overall mix. A particular version of narrative structure has become dominant in the mainstream, especially in Hollywood and its imitators: a form known generally, if often somewhat loosely, as 'classical' Hollywood narrative. One of the key identifying features of many American independent films is the extent to which they depart from the familiar conventions of the classical Hollywood variety. Some independent features are marked by their lack of strong, forward-moving narrative drive, opting instead for more relaxed or decentred structures akin to those associated with some forms of international 'art' cinema. Others are more complex than the typical Hollywood narrative, which usually revolves around a small number of major strands. Independent films of recent decades include several varieties of intersecting, multi-strand narrative and at least one example in which the narrative is told backwards.

A total abandonment of narrative is sought in some avant-garde or experimental films. These have, in some cases, influenced more accessible independent features, but it is rarely if ever the case that narrative is entirely absent in the more commercial/industrial independent sector that is the main focus of this book. It is usually a substantial presence, in one form or another. Certain aspects of 'classical' narrative structure remain central to many independent features, even when others are undermined, minimalized or complicated. In narrative terms, as in many others, indie cinema tends to occupy a place closer to Hollywood than to the outer experimental margins, although a range of alternative approaches has been explored, including some quite significant departures. This chapter starts with a sketch of the principal characteristics associated with the classical Hollywood style of narrative, the 'norm' against which other forms are often measured. It then considers a number of alternative strategies employed by independent filmmakers, examining the extent to which they challenge the Hollywood norm at a formal level and the consequences this might have for the viewing experience.

Classical Hollywood Narrative

Classical Hollywood narrative is defined according to a set of interlinking characteristics, some of which are derived from other narrative sources. At the most basic level, classical narrative entails an overarching structure found in many narrative forms: a clearly marked beginning, middle and end. An initial state of equilibrium is disrupted and, after various complications, eventually restored or reinstated in a different form. Classical narrative moves through these stages in a linear, forward-directed manner. A clear process of cause and effect is identified, tying individual scenes into a coherent and readily comprehensible sequence. Each scene is divided into distinct phases, as suggested by David Bordwell, the most influential theorist of the classical Hollywood narrative style. An initial stage of exposition is followed by action towards the goals of characters: 'In the course of this, the classical scene continues or closes off cause–effect developments left dangling in prior scenes while also opening up new causal lines for future development.'[2] Classical narrative usually contains a high level of redundancy, material that is repeated or reiterated to ensure that no crucial information in the cause–effect chain is missed. The end usually offers a form of closure, in which the main narrative issues are resolved, even if in some cases this is best defined as a 'closure effect' or 'pseudoclosure', in examples in which closure might be asserted rhetorically more than it is demonstrated literally in all details.[3]

The classical narrative structure usually revolves around two major plot lines. The 'main' plot is the defining situation that gives a narrative its particular character and establishes qualities such as the film's generic identity. It often involves a quest or a mission of some kind, as Bordwell suggests: the scenario to be investigated in a detective story, for example, or the professional or other ambition of a central character. The second plot line is usually a (heterosexual) romance, although in some cases this can be of importance equal to or greater than that of the other component. The two strands are usually closely interlinked, resolution of the latter often forming an important dimension of the way closure is asserted emotionally in the former. A key aspect of the classical style is the role played by a small number of central characters, especially the romantically linked couple or couple-to-be. Character-centred causality is, as Bordwell puts it, 'the armature of the classical story', the driving force of the narrative.[4] Characters are goal-oriented, narrative emerging largely from their desires. The characters are defined by clearly identified, unambiguous and consistent traits, the model for Bordwell being that of the short story: 'an average between the fixed character types of the melodrama and the dense complexity of the realist novel.'[5]

Classical narrative can also be identified according to the particular strategies through which story information is delivered to the viewer: the *process* of narration. A useful distinction can be made between the underlying story and the way it is actually represented on-screen, a distinction that dates back to Aristotle but was most fully elaborated by Russian Formalist literary critics writing in the 1920s.[6] From the limited amount of narrative material selected for presentation on-screen, termed *syuzhet* by the Formalists, the viewer is encouraged to construct a sense of the broader story, or *fabula*. Events depicted in a typical 100-minute film might, for example, tell a story that unfolds over a period of days, months, years or centuries. One of the main acts of narrative comprehension is the ongoing construction of fabula from syuzhet, which might be more or less easily achieved. The syuzhet material presented on-screen might be designed to create maximum access to the underlying story. This is usually the case to a large extent in the classical model, although not entirely; some degree of blocking or delaying of access is normally employed for dramatic effect, to create elements of mystery, tension or suspense, for example. The classical variety tends to be *omniscient*, displaying a wide range of knowledge about the narrative situation. It tends to be highly *communicative*, giving rather than withholding relevant information. It also tends to be *unselfconscious*, not laying bare the process of narrative address to the audience.[7] Each of these is subject to qualification in specific circumstances. Narrative omniscience or communicativeness may be reduced according to the conventions of particular genres such as the detective or mystery film, for example, while a higher degree of narrative self-consciousness might be found in certain privileged moments, especially at the opening or close of the story. These are generally exceptions that prove the rule. The style of a classical Hollywood film – the way it is performed, shot and edited – is generally subordinate to the priority of establishing narrative clarity, in Bordwell's account. Narrative is defined as the dominant organizing principle, creating 'a marked hierarchy of systems in the classical film'.[8]

The extent to which narrative dominates classical Hollywood films remains open to question. Bordwell tends to play down the importance of qualities such as spectacle or the presence of stars with images and performance styles that transcend those of any particular narrative situation. Films of the classical Hollywood era, the heyday of the old-style studio system from the 1920s to the 1950s, often depart to varying extents from the ideal model described above, exhibiting qualities such as episodic or sometimes less than very coherent narrative structure.[9] It is a useful model, however, if considered as an ideal type rather than one that is manifested fully in any or all examples; an analysis of tendencies rather than absolutes, with which particular examples from either Hollywood or alternatives such as the American independent sector can be contrasted or compared. Most if not all of its characteristics remain broadly applicable to contemporary mainstream features and have not, generally, been undermined to any great extent even in the most spectacular of recent Hollywood blockbusters, as I have argued at length elsewhere.[10]

The effect created by departures from the type of narrative usually found in Hollywood is dependent to a large extent on the degree to which the broad outlines of the classical narrative style have been internalized by viewers. Dominant or familiar narrative structures operate as templates or schemata, against which the ongoing events of the individual work are tested. Departures from the canonic or classical form can undermine such expectations, even if the difference between what might be found in Hollywood or the independent sector is often only one of degree. In general, independent features are more likely to employ devices designed to deny, block, delay or complicate the anticipated development of narrative, to reduce clarity or resolution and in some cases to increase narrative self-consciousness.

The Moments Between: Decentred, Downplayed or Fragmented Narrative

Two skinny boys, an adolescent and one who appears pre-teen, cruise the fictional small-town streets of Xenia, Ohio, armed with B-B guns, in search of cats to kill and sell into the local restaurant trade to fund their glue-sniffing habit. Three sisters, two teens and one younger, hang out together in various largely aimless activities, their own black cat initially surviving a close encounter with the preceding characters. The two groups form what might loosely be described as two main polarities in writer-director Harmony Korine's first feature *Gummo* (1997). Only loosely, though. *Gummo* is one of a number of independent features that largely abandons any conventional sense of linear plotting. Developing or sustained narrative drive is replaced by a more fragmentary portrait of an assortment of dead-end lives in a community of the disaffected and/or disadvantaged. A rationale for this approach is provided in the form of a framing device: home-video-style footage and voice-over commentary refers to a tornado

4. A narrative red herring? 'Bunny Boy' (Jacob Sewell) in the opening of *Gummo* (1997).

that struck the town a few years previously, contributing, it seems, to the desolation of the place and its inhabitants, a device used by Korine to justify the presentation of a selection of individual scenes rather than the development of a strong narrative line.

For the unsuspecting viewer of *Gummo*, a number of narrative expectations are undermined. After the initial tornado-era video footage, the film opens, over the credits, with images of a young boy dressed in shorts and pink rabbit ears, playing on a footbridge, pissing and dribbling onto the cars driving below. He might be expected to be the main – maybe even the title – character, but he is not. Bunny Boy (Jacob Sewell) turns up on several more occasions during the film, but as a marginal figure (among marginals), whose presence and behaviour are as unexplained as his attire. The next few scenes introduce the two boys, Tummler (Nick Sutton) and the younger Solomon (Jacob Reynolds), and the three girls, Darby (Darby Dougherty), Dot (Chloe Sevigny) and Helen (Clarissa Glucksman). Some kind of coming-of-age narrative might be anticipated, even if an offbeat one. Or we might expect some form of romantic or sexual union to occur, or to be attempted, between some or all of what appear to be the male and female principals. No such expectations are fulfilled, however. They tend to be either ignored (in most cases) or deliberately subverted. The only resemblance to a conventional youth-dating-movie moment, for example, occurs in a very early scene in which Tummler is 'making out' with a girl in a wrecked car in a junkyard, only to inform her, deflatingly, that she has a lump in her 'titty' (she is seen again, much later, informing her family that she has to have both breasts removed).

The presence and activities of the two main groups of characters knits *Gummo* together, to some extent, but into a fabric that is far from narrative led. The focus of the film slides in and out, tracing some connections between the main protagonists and a range of other figures, represented directly or alluded to, sometimes in brief voice-over commentaries and grainy video footage. The major dynamic is as much centrifugal as centripetal. Korine has just established what appears to be the narrative centrality of the two boys, and has introduced the girls, and connected the two groups via their cat, when we shift, seemingly arbitrarily, to a sequence featuring two skinhead brothers said to have murdered their parents. Next we are given video footage of a young girl, accompanied by a voice-over in which she (presumably) talks about having been sexually abused by her father. The film continues in this vein, in some cases bringing its gallery of minor characters (including some non-actors with disabilities) into contact with those who take relatively central stage, but quite often not doing so, and in no sense offering an impression of overall narrative progression or forward momentum. There is an absence in many instances of any classical-style continuation or closing of incidents or character-material left dangling in prior scenes. A viewer coming to *Gummo* armed with the classical schemata might spend some time trying to identify an overarching narrative thread or a central enigma, in keeping with canonic expectations, only to find that the central enigma lies partly in the lack of any such ruling plot device.

Korine's next feature, *Julien Donkey-Boy* (1999), is more closely focused than *Gummo*, but exhibits many similar qualities. The organizing principle is a single family, that of the schizophrenic title character, Julien (Ewen Bremner), rather than a community, although the family group is equally damaged: Julien himself, his pregnant sister,

Pearl (Chloe Sevigny), a would-be-wrestler brother, Chris (Evan Neumann) and the raving authoritarian father played by the German director Werner Herzog. *Julien Donkey-Boy* begins with what proves to be a narrative red herring. Blurry opening video images of a skater – a motif repeated throughout the film – give way to a sequence that culminates in Julien drowning (we are led to assume) a young boy. This is a powerful moment, an arbitrary and disconnected act (the boy is pushed under the water because he declines to give Julien a turtle he has found in a pond). In a conventional dramatic narrative, we would expect consequences, or at least an arc of suspense (will he be found out, what will happen?), especially in the case of so dramatic an event positioned in the privileged opening moments during which major plot premises are often established. In this case, though, there is nothing. The incident remains isolated, just one moment in a film filled with digressions, like *Gummo*, in which the emphasis much of the time is on the scene playing rather than its place in any more than a loose accumulation of scenes. There is a degree of narrative progression in some respects, including something like a climax, in which Pearl falls while ice-skating, the unborn baby dies and Julien takes the foetus from the hospital, carries it home by bus and lies with it under his bedclothes, as if himself returned to the womb. But many scenes are digressions, or would be if there were a more solid central narrative core from which to digress: sequences, for example, in which the father, variously, rambles, expounds and berates, sometimes alone, sometimes aiming his complaints at members of his family, especially Chris.

Gummo and *Julien Donkey-Boy* received very mixed critical notices, including many attacks for both the nature of the material presented (the alleged 'exploitation' of disabled non-actors and the 'anti-social' behaviour of the central characters, especially in *Gummo*) and the absence of conventional narrative development. There is a considerable logic to the departure from linear narrative, however. In *Julien Donkey-Boy*, the fragmented structure might easily be understood as part of the figuration of the disintegrating mental state of the title character, even if the material is not presented as a manifestation of his subjectivity as such. More generally, in both films, the lack of classical plotting seems entirely appropriate to the subject matter: a portrayal of lives that are essentially directionless, lived without the contrivances of conventional-mainstream narrative arc. This is one of the major justifications available to filmmakers who depart in this way from dominant or classical narrative form: a claim to the status of something more closely approximating the reality of the lives of most people and especially, perhaps, those on the socio-economic margins. There is, very clearly, a politics to this. To impose the usually affirmative Hollywood arc onto such material – to portray characters as heroically lifting themselves out of their difficulties, triumphing through adversity, and so on – is to impose a typically American-capitalist ideological framework, rooted in the notion that America is a society in which even those from the lowest reaches can achieve the dream of prosperity. Without being overtly critical-political in emphasis, the implicit message of *Gummo* and *Julien Donkey-Boy* puts the lie to such illusions.

What is involved here, to use another analytical tool from Russian Formalist criticism, is a different form of 'motivation', a different rationale or justification for material presented on-screen. Motivation according to the expectations or requirements of narrative is known as 'compositional' motivation. Certain events occur, and might be anticipated, precisely because they are what is expected according to the schemata of canonic/classical narration. An obvious example would be the Hollywood happy ending, which might often make little sense other than in terms of familiar compositional motivation, or the eruption of some threatening or destabilizing event in the midst of the equilibrium portrayed in the earlier stages of any kind of action-adventure film. One alternative to compositional motivation that plays a large part in some independent films is motivation according to verisimilitude, or realism. Material 'makes sense' because of its claims of proximity to the way things are in the outside world, rather than the extent to which it accords with the dominant conventions of fictional narrative. The two are often viewed as diametrically opposed: the extent to which material is motivated by verisimilitude is often understood as precisely the extent to which it departs from canonic forms of narrative, and vice versa.

Films such as *Gummo* and *Julien Donkey-Boy* are certainly not unshaped reflections of reality, in their narrative or any other dimensions; that is not a claim Korine or many other independent filmmakers would make. *Gummo* and *Julien Donkey-Boy* offer a mixture of the seemingly 'real/authentic' and the 'poetic/impressionist' (issues to which we return in the next chapter), their basis of organization owing as much to montage or collage as to narrative or story. They remain constructs, even if constructed according to principles different from those associated with the commercial mainstream. It can be argued that they are relatively closer to, or more adequate evocations of, a particular kind of reality, however, in that the degree to which an artificially heightened narrative frame has been imposed is greatly reduced. 'Real life' is a complex phenomenon, and not something experienced entirely in the raw, as it were, purely, immediately and without the imposition of meaning-generating frameworks. There is a widespread human-cultural tendency to read narratives and other metaphorical or mythic frameworks into our lives, to shape perceptions of experience, both at the time of experience and in retrospect. The fact remains, though, that the lives of very few individuals accord with the kinds of plottings and character developments found in the classical Hollywood narrative model. The events of life tend not to have clear-cut beginnings, middles and ends, as Korine suggests, beyond the minimal biological framework of birth, life and death. Life tends, on the whole, to be rambling and without a great deal of tightly structured development. It just 'goes on', most of the time, rather than being subject to a regime of interlocked and forward-moving dynamics or moments of major crisis. Dramatic developments prompting equally dramatic responses are not the norm. One of the major appeals of classical Hollywood narrative as a form of fantasy-entertainment is precisely its distance in this and other respects from the texture of life as it is generally lived.

Hollywood-style narrative might be characterized as a heightened portrayal of aspects of very particular lives, in very particular circumstances – with most of the dull bits left out. Leaving the dull bits in, or building films around successions of 'dull' bits, has been one persistent tendency in the independent sector. This is found at its most extreme in some works of the experimental avant-garde or underground. The films of Andy Warhol are among the most obvious examples of a cinema built around either a complete absence of narrative development or its reduction to vestigial status. Something close to a zero-degree of non-narrative minimalism is reached in examples such as *Empire* (1962–1963), Warhol's eight-hour stationary shot of the Empire State Building, or *Sleep* (1963), a five-hour recording of the poet John Giorno sleeping. A move towards something closer to character-based drama is found in a later work such as *Flesh* (1969), a Warhol 'presentation' conceived and shot by his collaborator Paul Morrissey. *Flesh* runs to a conventional feature-narrative length (86 minutes) and is structured around the experiences of a single central character, the hustler Joe (Joe Dallesandro), and his interactions with characters including his wife, clients and acquaintances. There is something approximating an overarching narrative situation. At the start, during exchanges between Joe and his wife (Geraldine Smith), the latter says she needs $200 to pay for an abortion for a girl friend. This resembles a conventional-enough narrative frame, even if not one of the most original or exciting examples: a quest to raise a sum of money to fulfil character need. The central part of the film can be read as a response to this requirement, as Joe hustles on the street. Towards the end, we are introduced to the wife's friend, Patti (Patti D'arbanville), which establishes a degree of closure, although Joe claims at the end not to have made any money and says he will get some the next day. The bulk of the film is not driven by linear narrative, however, 'driven' not being a term that springs to mind at all in relation to the structure of any Warhol and/or Morrissey films. The bulk of *Flesh* is comprised of lengthy individual sequences marked by desultory talk and a sense of very little happening from moment to moment.

Many of Warhol's films can be understood as close to documentary portraits of the world occupied by a recurring group of performers, mostly playing themselves or performed versions of the self. Banality is, in many cases, close to an aesthetic principle. A central interest of the 1960s underground, Juan Suárez suggests, was the capturing of 'ordinary, everyday occurrences that seemed too small for Hollywood pictures'.[11] For Stan Brakhage, the aim was to halt 'the overwhelming influence of drama in film' in favour of a concentration on 'the glories of an undramatic present, which is literally the tabletop'.[12] The impulse to downplay narrative drama, or melodrama, in favour of an emphasis on something closer to the 'undramatic present', has also figured strongly in parts of the more commercial/industrial independent sector, although not taken to the degree of abstraction found in Brakhage or the minimalism of Warhol. This has often entailed a reduction of the emphasis on narrative in favour of greater attention to the smaller details of the lives of characters or the milieux in which they are found. This is an approach that also follows a strong tradition in international art cinema, influential examples including the products of Italian Neorealism in the 1940s and early 1950s, the work of directors such as Satyajit Ray in India and Yasujiro Ozu in Japan, and, taken closer to its limits, the extended minimalism of Chantal Akerman's 225-minute study of the minutiae of routine domestic oppression in *Jeanne Dielman, 23 Quai du commerce, 1080 Bruxelles* (1975).

The classical Hollywood narrative model is one in which characterizations, events and other details are to a large extent subordinated to, or composed of, their place in the narrative design. In its ideal form – however rarely that might fully be realized – every component would be locked securely into place, performing a narrative function (which might include establishing a particular mood required by the plot as well as more obvious story-development-related material). Nothing, or at least nothing of substance, is meant to be arbitrary or unmotivated. In independent features – or other alternatives to the Hollywood model – qualities such as arbitrariness or less focused narrative might be considered to be virtues, characteristics of a form in which the impression is given that individuals exist or things happen in their own right rather than in a context in which they are expected to 'lead' explicitly somewhere or become cogs in a linear-narrative-led machine.

Classical narrative usually establishes a clear hierarchy between moments that are presented as more or less important. The rhythms of narrative structure move between heightened, key moments of development ('plot points' as they are termed in screenwriting manuals) and action, and the balance provided by quieter or more discursive periods. It is the heightened moments or major plot points that are discarded or downplayed in some independent features, leaving a more even, de-dramatized or rougher structure of events. Points of dramatic crisis might arise more abruptly and not be subjected to the kind of reconciliation or closure typical of the Hollywood model. A good example is John Cassavetes' *Shadows*, a film that stands as a bridge between the alternative American cinemas of the 1950s and 1960s and the later independent movement. The main narrative crisis lies in the racial tension that emerges when one character, Tony (Anthony Ray), discovers that the woman with whom he has just had sex, Lelia (Lelia Goldoni), is black, although she does not appear to be (and is played by a white performer), a realization that comes when he is confronted with her more obviously black brother, Hugh (Hugh Hurd). Tony reacts with an unspoken horror, provoking an angry response from Hugh and discomfort all round. The film is not structured specifically around or to build up to and develop this theme, however. As David James puts it, the approach is an 'indirect sidling up to moments of thematic tension and dramatic release that produces an angular, fragmented narrative'.[13] Tony tries later to see Lelia, unsuccessfully, and offers an apology, via her other brother Ben (Ben Carruthers), but this is only an oblique development or reconciliation of the incident. The impression created is that racist reactions are part of the texture of life, subject to its vagaries, rather than the stuff of heightened or carefully plotted and patterned melodrama. (Hollywood narrative typically offers a reconciliatory structure, the implication of which is that thematic issues such as racial tension can be reconciled along with the relationships between the principal characters.) Tony, Lelia and Hugh are three of the main protagonists, but among a group of several others, none of which is the exclusively central focus of the film. *Shadows* climaxes with a brawl in which Ben, Tom (Tom Allen) and Dennis (Dennis Sallis) clash with three others with whom they compete for the attentions of two young women in a café. They lose, get beaten and drink afterwards in a bar, but the film ends in dissipation rather than any sense of progression or the learning of any lessons: Tom heads for home, Dennis goes into a shop to buy cigarettes and Ben, rather than waiting, drifts off alone across the street.

A similar sense of narrative drift, even around significant points of departure, is found in Jim Jarmusch's *Stranger than Paradise*, one of the breakthrough films of the independent scene of the mid 1980s. (A more fragmented narrative structure, based on the various encounters of its wandering central character, is found in Jarmusch's debut feature, *Permanent Vacation* [1980].) One of the distinguishing qualities of *Stranger than Paradise* is the sense that nothing much ever seems to happen, as the principals Willie (John Lurie), his visiting Hungarian cousin Eva (Eszter Balint) and friend Eddie (Richard Edson) hang out, largely aimlessly, in locations ranging from Willie's New York apartment to a Florida beach. A typical example is a single-shot sequence in the apartment in which Willie and Eddie sit drinking beer from cans and say nothing, a shot held for nearly a full minute. Much of what occurs in the film is not so much understated as unstated. A year after Eva moves on to stay with her aunt in Cleveland, a decision by Willie and Eddie to visit is made obliquely: in one scene, Willie talks about borrowing a car and getting away from the city; in the next they are driving and he is asking whether Eddie thinks the car will make it to Cleveland. A decision to move on to Florida, with Eva, instead of returning home, is made in a similarly arbitrary manner, for which no preparation is made. Despite all the miles covered, in a series of uneventful car-interior scenes, the dominant sense is of an absence of change. 'You come to someplace new and everything looks the same,' as Eddie observes in a snowbound scene in Cleveland, the truth of his words for the viewer demonstrated in a later scene in Florida in which an overexposed background of sand and sea creates a similarly whitened-out effect.

A major turning point towards the end of *Stranger Than Paradise* is another product of the arbitrary, this time taken to an absurd degree of chance that seems to mock classical narrative convention. Eva buys a wide-brimmed hat. Walking near the beach, she is stopped by a man who gives her a package that turns out to be a large sum of money; shortly after her comes the woman for whom she has been mistaken, dressed almost identically, in wide-brimmed hat and long dark coat. The final, decisive move in the plot is another that occurs obliquely, off-screen. Eva appears to have bought a ticket back to Europe, the only flight available being, as chance would have it, back to Budapest. Willie, in pursuit, buys a ticket to get onto the plane in order to remove her. We see the plane take off. Eddie watches, resignedly, assuming that Willie has abandoned him to leave with Eva. But then we see Eva's return to their motel room, the result of a decision to stay to which we are not allowed any access. Another prominent elision is found in Jarmusch's next feature, *Down by Law* (1986): the three principals escape from prison, but exactly how is glossed over and undepicted. One of the appeals of this style of filmmaking is the emphasis it places on aspects of life that are usually edited out in the interests of speed and economy of narrative movement. In *Night on Earth* (1991), for example, Jarmusch constructs an entire feature through a series of taxi rides, events that are not usually seen as significant. As Jarmusch puts it:

> [I]n a film when someone takes a taxi, you see them get in, then there's a cut, then you see them get out. So in a way the content of this film is made up of things that would usually be taken out. It's similar to what I like about *Stranger than Paradise* or *Down by Law*: the moments between what we think of as significant.[14]

Narrative obliqueness is part of a broader aesthetic of the minimalist and deadpan that became the Jarmusch trademark, but it is a quality, influenced by various works of international art cinema, that has appealed to other independent filmmakers as a way of marking a difference from the Hollywood style. What a mainstream feature would show, usually with great flourish and spectacle, is often left implicit or shown only at varying degrees of remove. In *Living on Tokyo Time* (1987), the shallow nature of the marriage-of-convenience that allows Kyoto (Minako Ohashi) to remain in America is figured through its off-hand occurrence off-screen, conveyed to the viewer only through a letter she writes home to a friend. The low-key tone of the film matches Kyoto's stilted relationship with the taciturn Ken (Ken Nakagawa). A similarly off-hand approach is used towards murder in *Henry: Portrait of a Serial Killer* (1990), signifying the casual, everyday nature of Henry's acts of violence. In one instance we see Henry (Michael Rooker), who has been prowling for a victim, pick up a hitchhiker carrying a guitar case. All we know directly of what happens next (although we can assume plenty) is that, a couple of scenes later, he is giving a guitar to the ex-con acquaintance with whom he is staying, Otis (Tom Towles). Much of the focus is reoriented, away from the usual concerns of the serial-killer narrative format, towards an emphasis on the more banal and everyday, and the everyday potential for violence in more 'normal' figures such as Otis (a reflection of the fact that murder is usually a function of lives much more ordinary than the lurid fantasies of Hollywood serial-killer movies). A sequence in which Henry kills Otis, during a bloody struggle that follows the latter's rape of his sister, Beckie (Tracy Arnold), is depicted directly, but *Henry* reverts to its oblique mode, to powerful effect, in the denouement. Beckie and Henry appear to have established a personal connection, rooted partly in the fact that each was the victim of parental abuse. Beckie helps Henry to kill Otis, intervening when Otis is about to stab Henry with a long-handled comb. The pair dispose of the body then head off together, he answering, less assuredly but in kind, her declaration of love. We see them putting up for the night at a motel. Next morning, Henry shaves. He leaves early, alone. Dissolve to a lonely spot on the road where he pulls over. He lugs a large suitcase from the back of the car. Sombre music. As he drives off, the camera moves in slowly, closer to the case (the clear implication being that it contains her remains), an image that is held before a fade to black and the end titles.

The main focus of the films of Cassavetes is on the delineation of character rather than plot. If the classical Hollywood narrative style tends to be relatively lean and linear, with the emphasis on forward momentum, that of Cassavetes and many of his successors is broader and thicker in texture, particularly in the rendition of character and performance. Characters tend to be more complex or ambiguous, defined less in terms of clearly established goals or morality than is usually the case in Hollywood. An absence of unambiguous moral tone is one of the strengths of Korine's *Gummo*, as well as being one of the prime sources of criticism from some sources. How, exactly, are we meant to take characters such as Tummler and Solomon? For some critics, habits such as killing neighbourhood cats, sniffing glue and turning off the life-support system of the grandmother of one of their contemporaries, make them suitable only for condemnation and, with them, the filmmaker himself. The film takes no clear line. By giving them a relatively central place, it might be assumed to be celebrating as well as documenting their activities, but no very strong lead is provided. A sequence such as the break-in that culminates in what amounts to the murder of the grandmother sounds shocking, but the act itself is conducted in what might be seen as a spirit of kindness and release as much as coldness or malice. Tummler and Solomon might well be judged as victims of their own squalid circumstances.

The point, though, is that the film leaves such questions open. The characters just 'are', essentially; they do what they do and viewers are left to come to their own conclusions. This is not a quality usually associated with the Hollywood mainstream, the productions of which tend to display clear-cut, often Manichean, oppositions between those established as good or evil.

The films of Cassavetes devote large amounts of running time to the more overt exploration and laying bare of character, through extended acts of foregrounded 'performance', as might be expected of the work of an actor-turned-director. Centre stage in a film such as *A Woman Under the Influence* (1974) is taken by the performance of Gena Rowlands in the title role. Narrative here emerges from character and character relationships, rather than vice versa. Events seem to develop more organically, out of the situations in which characters are found, rather than being imposed artificially from less plausible-seeming outside intrusions. The focus generally is on relatively 'ordinary' characters in 'ordinary' situations, rooted in their life-worlds, rather than 'ordinary characters in extraordinary circumstances' – a Hollywood model given explicit voice in a reference to the protagonists of Spielberg's *Close Encounters of the Third Kind* (1977) – or extra-ordinary characters in the kinds of situations that might be normal in their worlds (police officers, secret agents, space travellers, and so on).

Another option is to give a low-key, 'ordinary' quality to the lives of characters who occupy worlds that are usually depicted in Hollywood in a heightened or salacious manner, the classic example of which is Lizzie Borden's *Working Girls* (1986), a portrait of women working in a New York brothel. *Working Girls* uses a 'day-in-the-life' structure, an ideal framework within which to provide a 'slice of life' that has some shape without the imposition of any grand narrative design. The whole point of the film is to emphasise the mundane quality of the life, as one among other ways in which women are exploited. The diurnal frame offers a beginning-middle-and-end structure – starting with the central character Molly (Louise Smith) waking in the morning, having breakfast and cycling to work, as if to any other job – but one that is largely in the background. Most of the film revolves around the alternating rhythms of wryly observed sessions with clients and the routines and relationships among the girls and between them and their posturing employer, Lucy (Ellen McElduff). A more conventional narrative movement is developed towards the end, however, in keeping with both canonic norms and what is presumably a feminist-political commitment to represent the possibility of change. Molly becomes upset after being asked to stay late and seeing one abusive customer too many. She keeps a business card from an avuncular client who offers to pay enough to see her 'on the outside' for her to give up the job and, as she leaves at the end of the day, she tells Lucy she will not be coming back. This marks the imposition of a stronger narrative shape on the material, satisfying, even in a low-key manner, something closer to classical expectations of character growth and development of situation.

Narrative structure is not abandoned in any of these examples, although its forms and sources may be variable. The films of Cassavetes and Korine are constructed through a balance between pre-established structure and improvised performance. With the exception of parts of *Shadows*, Cassavetes' films are scripted narratives rather than works of improvisation, although with suggestions from performers often integrated into the script during periods of rehearsal. *Gummo* was scripted in advance but in an episodic manner, with the emphasis on individual scenes that were only subsequently worked into a sequence.[15] In the case of *Julien Donkey-Boy*, improvisation played a larger role, the script outlining the general thrust of what might happen in scenes but without much in the way of pre-determined dialogue.[16] Downplayed or low-key narrative can also be combined with more conventional frameworks, as suggested by Jarmusch in the case of *Stranger than Paradise* and *Down by Law*, each of which conforms to an overarching structure of three acts followed by a coda.[17]

If some independent films depart substantially from the Hollywood norm, with fragmented, oblique or minimal narrative development, others do so in more subtle or nuanced fashion. This is one of many respects in which the distinction between independent and mainstream is often relative rather than absolute, embracing gradations of difference. An 'indie' impression might be created through a relative resistance to familiar narrative cliché or a relaxation rather than a halting of linear narrative dynamics. When Greg Harrison sought industry funding for his rave subculture feature *Groove* (2000), for example, he came under pressure to add conventional plot elements to the account of one night's experiences at an unlicensed rave. 'They wanted to add a gun [to the story] or have someone die of a drug overdose, but that wasn't the film I wanted to make.'[18] To make the film his own way, without the imposition of such devices, Harrison had to make it independently on a low budget. *Groove* is far from being an obscure or 'arty' film, in its approach to narrative or in any other dimensions. It has very accessible and commercial dimensions, especially to an audience attracted by the music and general youth-culture ambience. It is a clear illustration, however, of how formal qualities such as narrative can be shaped quite directly by industrial imperatives: in this case how a particular approach to narrative, even if not a radical one, necessitated recourse to an independent mode of production.

Paul Thomas Anderson's *Hard Eight* (originally *Sydney*, 1997) is one of many examples that might be cited of independent features that have plenty of narrative material, including some strong hooks, but that do not quite conform to dominant conventions. *Hard Eight* opens with a strong narrative enigma, setting up firm expectations: a seemingly chance meeting between broke, down-on-his-luck John (John C. Reilly) and well-heeled Sydney (Philip Baker Hall). Sydney treats John to coffee and cigarettes in a roadside diner. John, it emerges, is on his way out of Las Vegas after failing in an effort to win $6,000 to pay for the funeral of his mother. Sydney has a proposition. He will give John $50, take him back to Vegas and teach him something. John is suspicious, amusingly wary of a sexual motivation, but goes along. The opening scenes thus set up a number of questions, primarily: who is Sydney, what is he up to, what is he to teach John and what will come of the relationship? The tone is wry and a touch offbeat. In Vegas, Sydney introduces John to a simple scam that enables him to secure free board in a casino-hotel, but nothing more. He says he has a friend in Los Angeles who might be able to help. That night, Sydney is going down to the casino to gamble and agrees to let John accompany him to watch. Fade to black, followed by the title 'Two years later, Reno NV'.

We now take up a story in which John is established in some capacity within Sydney's orbit, as a gambler of some kind, it seems, although very much the protégé. We have, in effect, leapt over what might have been expected to be the next stage of the narrative, without any explanation or anything more than a partial answer to the enigma posed in the opening sequence. The film moves along in a low-key, measured manner, dialogue and character-centred, tracing the relationships between Sydney, John and a waitress, Clementine (Gwyneth Paltrow), none of which appear to be strongly plot-directed. A crisis eventually occurs when John telephones Sydney in the middle of the night seeking his help to escape from a kidnapping/ransom dilemma (John holding hostage a man who reneges after agreeing to pay for sex with Clementine, abruptly revealed now to be John's wife). This is the stuff of 'real' plot-point narrative development and complication, except that it is somewhat absurd. It is the product not of goal-driven, dynamic characters but of rather bumbling, slow and semi-hopeless figures. Sydney eventually sorts out the difficulty and the couple leave. It is only after this, more than three-quarters of the way into the film, that the solution to the initial enigma is provided. Jimmy (Samuel L. Jackson), a somewhat shady acquaintance of John's, blackmails Sydney, demanding $10,000 not to tell John what he knows: that Sydney, who has become a surrogate parent-figure, killed John's real father some years previously in Atlantic City. Everything falls into place, although by this stage the character/relationship-based quality of the film is such that narrative enigma is less likely to be in the foreground. The answer is provided, but at a point at which it no longer seems pressing and where the character of Sydney has been established in other relationships (especially with Clementine) as precisely the kind of 'decent' figure who might have helped John on his way without any guilty ulterior motive. *Hard Eight* conforms to the classical or canonic format in many respects, including its focus on a small group of characters and its tracing of a mixture of milieu-specific (the world of gambling and related spheres) and personal relationship-based narrative threads. Central narrative enigma remains important, and is subject to strategies of retardation and partial answer that might be found in Hollywood, but there is also a degree of sustained delay and displacement that would not usually be expected in the mainstream.

The denial or delay of moments when narrative crisis is expected to culminate in explosions of more conventionally 'movie-type' action can create powerful effects, as in Nick Gomez's first feature, *Laws of Gravity*. A chronicle of the lives of a group of small-time New York crooks that owes more than a little to Scorsese's *Mean Streets* (1973), *Laws of Gravity* sets up a series of simmering resentments and confrontations between its characters. That some or all of these are likely to break out into full-scale conflict seems inevitable, especially given the presence of a haul of guns that the central characters Jimmy (Peter Greene) and Jon (Adam Trese) are trying to sell on behalf of the hot-headed Frankie (Paul Schulze). Frankie hits a stranger during an argument in a bar; tension exists between Jimmy and the imposing Sal (Saul Stein), to whom he owes money; Sal accuses Frankie of informing on a relative to the police and the two square off and have to be kept apart on more than one occasion; the boyish and irresponsible Jon has a stormy relationship with his girlfriend Celia (Arabella Field), with a potential customer for the guns who takes Celia for a ride in his car, and with Jimmy, who tries to act as his mentor and keep him in line. On numerous occasions, brooding tension threatens to be released in acts of serious violence. Anticipated crisis is constantly deferred until the last moments, however, when a series of events culminates in an angry stand-off between Jon and Frankie. Shots ring out and Jon is left dead on the ground, although the climax is treated obliquely, the shooting occurring off-screen. A conventional/mainstream Hollywood feature in the same broadly generic territory would be likely to offer a frequent provision of action set-pieces rather than such a withholding of violent release. It would also be expected to offer more goal-oriented characters and more in the way of contrived overriding plot devices; narrative tension remains a function of character, the gun-sale plot playing a relatively minor role. The commitment of *Laws of Gravity* is to a more 'authentic' and gritty portrayal of the rhythms of petty criminal life, although it is far from being fragmentary or unshaped. The structure is low key and slow burning, but it builds carefully to create its own particular effect. It does eventually offer the anticipated climax, which could have been denied altogether, an effect that would have marked a further departure from the mainstream.

Many more independent features could be cited in which, without greatly radical formal innovation, narrative is downplayed or displaced, slower-paced or de-melodramatized. Such strategies reduce the potential for lapses into sentimentality in examples such as *Sling Blade*, starring and directed by Billy Bob Thornton, which traces the relationship between a young boy and the mentally impaired Karl, released into the community twenty years after killing his mother and her lover, and Allison Anders' portrait of two sisters coming of age with their hard-pressed mother in a trailer park in *Gas, Food, Lodging* (1992). In their major relationship scenarios, films such as these are conventional enough, but they are structured to resist the kind of heightened melodramatic dynamics that would be expected in more mainstream, Hollywood equivalents. In the case of *Sling Blade*, this is largely a matter of leisurely pacing, atmospherics and Thornton's tightly controlled performance, in a narrative situation that in itself is very much the stuff of fictional contrivance. Scenes are allowed to play out in a generally static, laconic fashion, in keeping with Karl's own mode of delivery. In *Gas, Food, Lodging*, it is a question of focusing on something closer to the rhythms and textures of ordinary life. Each is organized around key, life-changing experiences for the central characters. These are not handled as obliquely as in some of the examples cited above, but neither are they given the full Hollywood treatment.

A similar effect is found in *The Good Girl* (2002), which sets up broadly conventional dynamics within a drolly humdrum background, but pointedly refuses to fulfil them, giving the film more serious and substantial resonance than might otherwise be the case. *Friends* star Jennifer Aniston, in a striking career move, plays Justine, a fairly drab and dull character, working in a supermarket. Into her life comes a romantically alienated would-be artistic figure with a *Catcher in the Rye* complex, who calls himself Holden (Jake Gyllenhaal) and promises to be a source of awakening. But he turns out to be a loose cannon, disturbed and unstable rather than the quirky rebel of easier convention. Towards the end, Justine is faced with the choice between staying in her job and a lifeless relationship with a dim husband (a relationship unlikely to be revived by the prospect of a baby, Holden's) or escaping. A tempting shot is given of the open road – desert, sky, big empty spaces, the stuff of American mythologies of frontier/freedom – but she stays, trapped, in a life/plot without convenient resolution. Elsewhere, conventional narrative dynamics can be thwarted, displaced or short-circuited by more quirky developments, as in examples such as Wes Anderson's first feature, the would-be crime-caper movie *Bottle Rocket* (1996), and Greg Mottola's *The Daytrippers* (1996), a not-so-very-epic 'quest' narrative involving a carload of family members seeking to confront an apparently errant husband and featuring what one claims to be 'the world's shortest car chase'.

In these and other examples, narrative drive, enigma and climax often take second place to the establishment of character and dialogue of a quirky or offbeat character, including some of the indie 'classics' of the 1980s and 1990s. Kevin Smith's *Clerks* is another example that uses the diurnal format, in this case a reluctant day-in-the-life of 22-year-old Dante (Brian O'Halloran), called in to work at a convenience store on what should be his day off. Expectations of some narrative movement within this format are established in the early parts of the film. Dante only agrees to go in on the basis of a guarantee that the boss will relieve him by 12 p.m., setting up the question of how far this promise will be kept and anticipation, judging by the tone of the piece, that it will not. The most sustained plot thread concerns Dante's love life: his relationship with his current girlfriend Veronica (Marilyn Ghigliotti) and with the long-term ex, Caitlin (Lisa Spoonauer), whose engagement has been announced in the local paper. The combination of matters to do with the central character's responsibilities in the store and the romantic dimension is, in itself, close enough to the Hollywood model, as is the focus on a small group of core characters, a feature of very many independent productions. The main thrust of the film, however, is the loose accumulation of assorted comic scenes featuring a range of oddball characters and customers in and around the store (business such as a customer with a Pringles tube stuck on his arm and a lengthy debate about the relative merits of two different episodes of the *Star Wars* series).

There is a 'major dramatic event' in *Clerks* (involving a traumatic encounter between Caitlin and a dead man's erection) but, as in *Hard Eight*, it is too wilfully absurd, and deferred, to serve anything like the usual central and defining narrative purpose of such developments. A series of chapter-type titles creates an impression of structure, although one that is at least partly tongue-in-cheek and includes entries such as 'Vagary' and 'Whimsy' that apply to much of the format of the film itself. There is development in the narrative dimension, however, conforming to some more conventional dynamics. Dante seems at the end to be in the process of sorting out misunderstandings about his relationships with Veronica and Caitlin and is reconciled after a spat with ultra-slacking neighbouring video-store clerk Randal (Jeff Anderson). Closure is effected literally, through the closure of the shop at the end of the day. This creates something of the kind of rhetorical closure frequently employed in Hollywood. It is heartfelt in some respects and not entirely ironic, although titles such as 'Catharsis' and 'Denouement' give it a self-conscious twist of a distinctly indie character.

The patterning of events in *Clerks* is motivated through verisimilitude, up to a point, the disparate structure of much of the material having its basis in the random selection of customers visiting the store. It is also a stylized pattern, however, designed to establish a particular aesthetic, an eccentric impression courted by many indie features. The form of motivation in effect in this dimension is 'stylistic' or 'artistic', a variety seen by Bordwell as less common in canonic or mainstream narrative. Material that is motivated stylistically is understood as existing to create an effect in its own right, drawing attention to the form of the work or the skills of the creator, rather than being subordinated to any other rationale. In Hollywood, this might include the protracted song-and-dance numbers of a musical, large-scale displays of special effects in the contemporary science fiction blockbuster, bravura camerawork or foregrounded examples of actor performance. Numerous examples of artistic motivation can be found in the independent sector, including other films characterized by downplayed or digressive narrative styles.

If the oblique style of Jarmusch can be seen as motivated in part by verisimilitude, as a tribute to the low-key and unspoken nature of much of what goes on in real life, it is also a heavily stylized minimalism that draws attention to itself as a formal–artistic device. Digression as a mark of stylization is also found in the films of Quentin Tarantino, especially in the character/dialogue-based riffs around various issues of popular culture found in *Reservoir Dogs* and *Pulp Fiction*. In one sense, again, this could be seen as making a claim to a degree of verisimilitude. Hit-men such as Vincent (John Travolta) and Jules (Samuel L. Jackson) in *Pulp Fiction* might be just as likely to engage in trivial discourse about items such as the merits of various types of burger, before and during their work, as anyone engaged in more humdrum activities. Inserting such material, incongruously, into this context gives the very fictional world of such characters some grounding. But it is also a stylistically motivated flourish, a marker of the distinctive presence of the director (and, as such, a valuable tool in his establishment of a marketable identity). The same can be said of the offbeat and often stylized dialogue and characters found in the work of other notables in the indie scene, including figures such as Joel and Ethan Cohen and Hal Hartley. Relatively low-key, fragmented or disjointed narrative need not be the product of commitment to notions of quotidian authenticity, as is the case in a film such as *Working Girls*. It can also be a licence for enjoyably unfocused romps such as the Cohen brothers' *The Big Lebowski* (1998), the kidnap/ransom plot at the centre of which is largely an excuse for an assortment of eccentric digressions. The fragmentary narrative style and imagery of Korine is another example of an approach that combines elements of motivation by claims to both verisimilitude and the poetic-artistic.

In the independent sector, in general, a relative shift might be expected from compositional motivation towards those based in verisimilitude and/or artistic stylization. The latter often involves a degree of self-consciousness of the kind embodied by the chapter-title headings in *Clerks*, a departure from the unselfconscious norm of the classical Hollywood style. Another example of this tendency is *Totally Fucked Up* (1996), Gregg Araki's gay-teen-angst homage to Jean-Luc Godard, described in its opening titles as 'another homo movie by gregg araki… in 15 random celluloid fragments' (a play on the '15 precise acts' subtitle of Godard's *Masculin-Féminin* [1966]). Another title, about a third of the way into the film, reads 'start narrative here', from which point its fragmentary depiction of 'lifestyles of the bored and disenfranchised' does begin to undergo relatively more conventional narrative development with the establishment of one central (but doomed) relationship and the undermining of another. Drawing attention to narrative structure in so explicit a manner is very much against the Hollywood norm. It can be playful, flattering niche audiences for independent films by letting them feel superior to those apparently 'taken in' by the devices used in more conventional features. It also has a more radical potential: demonstrating the constructed nature of narrative fictions can be a step on the way to demonstrating the constructed/fictional nature of the ideologies they embody. Some independent features are strongly committed to notions of unvarnished authenticity, as in the case of Cassavetes, who criticized some of his own camerawork in *Shadows* for being too showy and arbitrary, not sufficiently grounded in the expression of character. One of the pleasures offered by many films, however, is a revelling in form and technique, or more subtle allusion to the devices employed, including aspects of narrative structure. Departures from dominant conventions are, generally, more visible than the conventions themselves, which often gain invisibility-through-familiarity. Playing around with narrative can be a source of both pleasure and frustration, sometimes combined, depending on the orientation of both individual films and viewers.

Tangled Webs: Multi-Strand Narrative

If some independent features play down narrative, reducing or undoing its classically smooth and driving qualities, others increase its presence through the use of strategies to link or combine a multiplicity of different narrative threads. A number of approaches can be identified. In some cases a complex web of narrative strands is woven, more or less easy to untangle. Different narrative elements can be closely tied together, or their relations left implicit or uncertain. The same action might be viewed from different perspectives or re-enacted in different circumstances. More work is often required from the viewer in such cases than would usually be expected in Hollywood, a process that also tends to increase consciousness of the process of narration itself. A film that offers a point of transition between examples included in this and the previous section is Richard Linklater's *Slacker*, another of the landmark indie films of the early 1990s. *Slacker*, in its portrayal of an assortment of eccentric characters in the director's home town of Austin, Texas, certainly belongs to the school of decentred and downplayed narrative, but it also offers an example of a novel approach to the linking of its numerous components. The narrative line, as far as it can be described as such, is passed along from one character to the next. In one typical sequence, near the start, an arrested youth is taken from his doorstep to a police car. Two others comment as they pass by, one carrying a guitar case. Cut to the latter busking. A girl puts in a coin, and we follow the girl. She goes into a coffee shop, where we pick up a group of youths talking at a table. The camera follows one as he goes outside, and is joined by another as he walks down the street. So it goes on.

Slacker is comprised entirely of micro-narrative fragments. The structure is different from that of *Gummo*, in which certain elements can be described as *threads*, in that their character-groupings and activities are revisited on numerous occasions, even if others remain entirely fragmentary. *Slacker* has a principle of unity much like that of *Gummo*, however: the evocation of a particular kind of community, in this case mostly college and post-college young people talking and hanging out around the vicinity of the Austin campus. There are similarities in the obsessions shared by some of the characters, especially in the realm of assorted rambling conspiracy theories. The structure is one of repeated short ends, linked clearly enough one to another through the passing-on of the line (compared with the abrupt leaps of *Gummo*), but in a pattern that displays no sign of progression (it does not prove to be a 'round' format, in which a return is made to characters introduced at the start). There is a logic to this, as in the case of *Gummo* and *Julien Donkey-Boy*, that might be described as a 'thematic' source of motivation. The structure of *Slacker* is appropriate to the evocation of a landscape in which many characters are tied up in worlds of their own quirks, concerns, obsessions and theories, largely disconnected from others (there is much talk, but often 'at' rather than 'to' the addressee). Self-conscious allusion to the narrative format is also made, as in *Clerks*, including the ramblings of the character played by the director himself, about splitting and parallel realities. A quotation is read aloud from James Joyce's *Ulysses*, a reference to one individual imagining himself the first but always being the last term of a preceding series (in this case, the lovers of Molly Bloom), and the comment towards the end that 'the underlying order is chaos'.

A low-key approach is also found in Wayne Wang's multi-stranded *Smoke* (1995), a collaboration with the novelist Paul Auster that traces a group of characters linked principally through the cigar store run by Auggie (Harvey Keitel). The cigar store acts as a central location, in which an assortment of figures hang out during the film, often telling stories themselves, although it is not a fulcrum around which the narrative components of the film are very tightly organized. The effect of interwoven multi-strand narrative structure of this kind is to defer the process of narrative progression in each thread and, in some cases, to create a proliferation of material that can reduce narrative clarity. Developments in one strand tend to be put on hold and left dangling for longer than is usual in the classical format, except at moments in which one or more strands cross or are tied together. A certain degree of shifting from one narrative strand to another is familiar in the dominant Hollywood-style model, but some independent features go further in the multiplication of threads that can be more or less neatly brought together to form a unified fabric. The effect created can be one of confusion for the viewer, the result of a lower degree of narrative communicativeness, especially during the earlier stages, in which connections between an array of sub-narratives might not yet have been established or become apparent. Three good examples, each of which offers a slightly different emphasis, are *Short Cuts* (1993), directed by Robert Altman, *Happiness*, directed by Todd Solondz, and Paul Thomas Anderson's *Magnolia*. Each offers a balance between centrifugal and centripetal tendencies; between a diversity of narrative components, on the one hand, and a number of linking devices and thematic continuities, on the other.

The least integrated of the three in terms of explicit narrative connections is *Short Cuts*, reflecting, perhaps, its source in material from a number of separate short stories by Raymond Carver. Its multi-strand style is also a long-standing Altman trademark, his best-known earlier example of the format being *Nashville* (1975). *Short Cuts* offers a mosaic portrait of life in the Los Angeles area, featuring at least 20 principal characters. The narrative style is restless, moving swiftly from one component to another. Characters and relationships are no sooner established, briefly, in the opening moves, than we switch to others. Any sense of sustained narrative focus is constantly undermined in the early part of the film, in which, on first viewing, it can be difficult to keep a sense of which characters are which and what, exactly, is the nature of some of the relationships sketched on-screen. This can create a sense of discomfort that goes against the Hollywood norm; it is not always immediately apparent who is who and what is what in the very opening stages of Hollywood films, but clarification is usually provided sooner rather than later. Two main devices are used in the opening and closing scenes of *Short Cuts* to create a sense of unity, at least at the level of the geographical (and, by implication, social) community. The fast-moving credit and immediately post-credit sequences, a point at which fragmentation of narrative focus and potential disorientation for the viewer are at their highest, are tied together through the presence of a flight of helicopters spraying the area with chemicals to protect against an outbreak of medfly. The closing stages are linked through the eruption of an earthquake, a succession of scenes depicting its impact across a variety of narrative components. These are marked as somewhat arbitrary devices, however, in a feature that does not seek to offer any single focal point or intersection for the multitude of narrative threads but that captures, as Jonathan Romney puts it, 'the cellular essence of LA, as city in which separate zones, separate homes, are linked by highways'.[19]

Some narrative threads in *Short Cuts* intersect, with one or other components, but in only a partial and limited overlap between the separate elements of what remains closer to the structure of a patchwork quilt. Links in the diegetic world (the fictional universe on-screen) are in some cases supplemented through formal devices imposed by the filmmaker. One example follows an incident in which a young boy, Casey Finnigan (Lane Cassidy), is hit by a car driven by a character from another narrative thread, Doreen Piggot (Lily Tomlin): a random (literal) collision of two narrative elements. Back home the boy's mother, Ann Finnigan (Andie MacDowell), allows him to fall asleep, and into a coma. She telephones her husband, Howard (Bruce Davison), a television news commentator, at work. Howard tells her to take the boy to the emergency room, an ambulance visible and audible on a monitor behind him. An overlap of sound places the call of the siren over the scene at home, where Ann attempts to wake Casey and give him a glass of milk. She puts the glass down at the bedside. The camera moves in on the milk as she sits Casey up, increasingly desperate. Cut away to the image of a glass of milk on a television screen. It is knocked over, a voice-over intoning that 'accidents happen every day', and we realise that we are now at the Piggot home, where Doreen comments – ironically, for the viewer – on what a close call the incident had been for the boy. This is a very slick sequence, characteristic of many in the film, and very different from the resolutely un-slick style of the films of Harmony Korine and the other examples cited in the first part of this chapter. Considerable effort is made in *Short Cuts*, *Happiness* and *Magnolia* to *orchestrate* the different narrative components, a narrative style that shares with Hollywood a commitment to the production of a smooth and glossy finish, even if at a level of narrative density or complexity untypical of the mainstream.

Stronger diegetic connections between narrative elements are offered in *Happiness* and *Magnolia*. *Happiness* is organized around the lives of three sisters, their parents, and others who come into their orbit, although this is not apparent from the start. The film begins in the story of one sister, the inaptly named Joy Jordan (Jane Adams), breaking up at the end of what appears to be the latest in a series of failed relationships. It then switches to that of Bill Maplewood (Dylan Baker) and it is only several scenes later that we find out that he is married to Joy's sister, Trish (Cynthia Stevenson). In between, we are introduced to the third sister, Helen (Lara Flynn Boyle), although the relationship is not made clear at this stage. As is the case with *Short Cuts* and *Magnolia*, the viewer has to work harder than is the norm in Hollywood to trace the nature of the relationships that exist between characters established in separate narrative threads. The mutual implications and resonances of events in different parts of the narrative weave gradually become increasingly clear as films such as *Happiness* and *Magnolia* progress. The diegetic structuring principle of *Magnolia* takes longer to establish than that of *Happiness*, although some connections are made from the start.

The ubiquity of television, drawn upon on occasion in *Short Cuts*, is used as a major linking device in *Magnolia*. The opening image of the narrative-proper is one of the main characters, the male sexual-assertiveness guru Frank T.J. Mackey (Tom Cruise), appearing on-screen in an advertisement for his latest book. The ad is showing in an empty living room, then in the background at a bar, where another of the principals, later identified as Claudia (Melora Walters), is picked up by a stranger. Back at her apartment, as they make love, a TV show is profiling Jimmy Gator (Philip Baker Hall), the presenter of a long-running children's quiz show. That Claudia is Gator's daughter will only be established much later (unless the very sharp-eyed viewer recognizes her in a photograph during the early sequences); and, later still, the fact that her hatred of him, manifested when he visits her the following morning, is the result of apparent sexual abuse when she was a girl. We then see Gator and a woman we might assume (rightly) to be his wife, at an unidentified location (probably a hospital; we learn later that he has been diagnosed with inoperable cancer). Cut to them arriving home – and entering the room in which the television was initially playing – where the Gator profile is focusing on current child-prodigy performer, Stanley (Jeremy Blackman). Cut to Stanley at home, rushing to get to school. Shift to archive footage of his predecessor, Donnie Smith from 1968, playing on the Gator household television, and on to the hapless 'Quiz Kid' Donnie Smith today (William H. Macey). Television screens continue to play an important role in the creation of smooth continuity between segments throughout much of the film, particularly during the broadcast of an episode of Gator's show, 'What Do Kids Know?', which forms one of the central narrative episodes. The opening movement of *Magnolia* is completed with the introduction of the viewer to the other principals: the household of an elderly dying man, later identified as Earl Partridge (Jason Robards) – who turns out to be the father of Frank Mackey – including his nurse Phil (Philip Seymour Hoffman) and his much younger wife, Linda (Julianne Moore); and a relationship-hungry cop, Jim (John C. Reilly), who will form an alliance with Claudia.

This is a breathtakingly fast and fluid example of initial multi-strand-narrative exposition, the effect increased through the use of highly mobile camerawork and emphasis-creating zooms, introducing all the major characters in a sustained sequence of about six minutes. 'What Do Kids Know?' proves to be a link between all of these components, although it is nearly two hours into the film before the closing credits reveal the show to be 'A Big Earl Partridge Production', thus including the Partridge contingent in its orbit. The fluid style of *Magnolia* has something in common with *Short Cuts*, as does its use of environmental factors as another form of organization and linkage.

Chapter headings in *Magnolia* are supplied by titles giving weather conditions ('Partly Cloudy. 82% Chance of Rain', 'Light Showers. 99% Humidity. Winds SE 12 MPH', 'Rain Clearing. Breezy Overnight') that reflect something of the rising and falling dramatic arc that flows across the various narrative components. Heavy rainfall in the central portion of the film is both a temporal continuity device, establishing a clear sense of simultaneity, and expressive of the emotional outpourings it contains. *Magnolia* climaxes, very much like *Short Cuts*, with a freak of nature, in this case a deluge of frogs, the moment of impact of which is traced across the various narrative strands.

Restless camera movement, including rapid whip-pans both across and between scenes in the more heightened instances, impose a formal design across the different narrative strands of *Magnolia*, but the strongest unifying device in this dimension is provided by music, including a number of songs by Aimee Mann. The introduction sequence described above owes much of its impression of unity to its accompaniment by the song 'One', with the strong thematic resonance of its refrain 'One is the loneliest number'. A line of building tension and expectation is sustained in large parts of the film through the use of a simple, insistent and repeating strings theme, a device that enables the film to keep all of the major narrative components rapidly intercut in a state of close-to-crisis for remarkably sustained periods. The use of music is at its most overt in a sequence in which, in turn, Claudia, Jim, Gator, Donnie, Phil and Earl, Linda, Frank and Stanley sing along, in lip-synch, to Mann's 'Wise Up', a highly unconventional and non-naturalistic usage. This, and some of the other, more 'showy' devices, here and in *Short Cuts*, can be said to be motivated artistically, as much as in compositional terms, as demonstrations of the virtuoso use of cinematic technique to keep so many narrative balls in the air. There is a compositional logic to the 'Wise Up' sequence, in the sense that it marks a particular point of emotional development in each strand, but the device exceeds purely compositional bounds.

The structure of multi-strand narratives such as *Smoke*, *Short Cuts*, *Happiness* and *Magnolia* can also be understood in terms of claims to the status of verisimilitude, like the more downplayed narratives considered earlier. They depict a wider canvas of life than is usually found in the more conventional or classical Hollywood format, coming at least relatively closer to the dense complexity of real life. At the same time, this might easily be read in more 'artistic' terms. If classical Hollywood narrative has some features in common with the short story, especially in the delineation of character, these films are more 'novelistic' in scope, displaying complex structure and a wider array of characters. The move from one format to the other is most explicitly traceable in *Short Cuts*, the individual segments of which are based on short stories and could in some cases, separated out, have provided the scale of material suitable for a more conventional feature. The thematic resonances of these films also have more in common with their literary/novelistic equivalents than with the stuff of dominant Hollywood narrative.

Loneliness and alienation, and attempts to forge connections, are pervading themes of *Short Cuts*, *Happiness* and *Magnolia*, material that is entirely appropriate to their principles of narrative design. Characters are separated from one another in their lives, in many instances, as are the narrative components they inhabit. Where narrative strands are brought together, relationships can be established in some cases – the fragile but promising relationship of Claudia and Jim in *Magnolia*, for example – if not in others. *Magnolia* has a narrative and emotional impetus that moves, generally but far from absolutely, towards degrees of reconciliation between those previously alienated, a respect in which it is relatively closer to what might be expected in a Hollywood feature. The same cannot really be said of *Happiness*, even if most members of the central extended family are together for dinner at the end. Relationships remain brittle all round and Bill Maplewood is absent, facing prosecution for serial acts of child sexual abuse. Many potential connections prove abortive. Typical of the style of *Happiness* is the almost entire failure of some characters to appreciate either the fragile nature of their own existence (Trish's smug assessment of the virtues of her life, in a scene that immediately follows one in which we see her husband masturbating with the aid of a kids' magazine) or the hurtful impact of their comments on others (Trish, again, trilling away to Joy that she never thought she would amount to much, insensitively mistaking for the truth Joy's claim to be happy and, in the process, hammering nails into the coffin). Connections, where they occur in these films, are the product of chance as much as goal-directed design on the part of characters, an issue highlighted in a prologue sequence in *Magnolia* that documents three purportedly real cases of unlikely coincidence.

A more radical example, in which different narrative strands have no internal connections, is Todd Haynes' first feature, *Poison*, which won the Grand Jury Prize at Sundance in 1991. A key marker in the establishment of what became known as New Queer Cinema, *Poison* comprises three intercut stories, the titles of which ('Hero', 'Horror' and 'Homo') are only provided in the closing credits. Each occupies a very different stylistic and generic territory, although a number of resonances carry across from one to another. 'Hero', shot in pseudo-documentary style, investigates a bizarre incident in which a young boy shoots his father and disappears, jumping out of the window and flying away, according to his mother. 'Horror' is a pastiche of 1950s B-movie horror, in which a scientist becomes victim to a leprous disease after accidentally consuming his own newly discovered formula for the essence of the sex drive. 'Homo', inspired by the writing of Jean Genet, is a tale of homosexual longing and memory divided into two elements: the drab, grey-toned realism of a 1940s prison and the gauzy lushness of remembered teenage experiences in a reformatory. A number of transitions between these elements contain links that encourage the viewer to seek deeper thematic continuities. A key quotation from Genet that ends the introduction to the prison narrative finishes on the word 'horror', followed by a cut to the start of the horror strand (even if its nature is not fully apparent at that moment). John Broom (Scott Renderer), the central character of 'Homo', talks in voice-over about making up stories about fellow inmate Jack Bolton (James Lyons) that always come to a violent end; cut to the horror narrative, that can also be expected to come to a violent end. The mother of Ritchie Beacon, the boy who disappears in 'Hero', tells how he was picked on and hurt at school; cut to Bolton displaying his scars to Broom. Some thematic connections can be made without too much difficulty, although it is left up to the viewer to do the work. It is hard not to read 'Horror' at least partly in relation to popular media characterizations of AIDS, especially given the film's opening title: 'The whole world is dying of panicky fright.' Issues of sexual transgression and oppression resonate in 'Horror' and 'Homo', although 'Hero' fits this kind of pattern less easily, even if Ritchie appears to have been a somewhat strange child whose activities included prevailing upon a friend to spank him. It is the absence of too neat or closed a fit between its elements that gives *Poison* its rather unsettling, edgy and distinctly independent quality, hinting at meanings that remain elusive.

Repetition or reworking of events from different perspectives or shifted into different contexts is another strategy adopted by some multi-part narratives in the independent sector, examples including Jarmusch's *Mystery Train* (1989) and *Night on Earth* and Hal Hartley's *Flirt* (1995). *Mystery Train* and *Night on Earth* are exercises in simultaneity, the events of their different components occurring in parallel. Temporal overlap is matched by spatial proximity in *Mystery Train*, the events of which centre around a Memphis hotel and its immediate environs. The protagonists of each of three narrative strands end up at the hotel. First, in 'Far From Yokohama', there is a Japanese couple, in town to visit Graceland and other music-industry landmarks. Then, in 'A Ghost', an Italian woman, Luisa (Nicoletta Brasci), makes an unplanned stop-over after problems with the plane taking her to Rome with the coffin of her deceased husband; she finds herself sharing a room with the non-stop-talking Dee Dee (Elizabeth Bracco), who has just walked out on her boyfriend. Finally, in 'Lost in Space', a group comprising the boyfriend, Johnny (Joe Strummer), his friend Will (Rick Aviles) and Dee Dee's brother, Charlie (Steve Buscemi), drink the night away after the hot-headed Johnny shoots the proprietor of a liquor store.

Johnny and Charlie's relationships with Dee Dee establish a clear narrative connection between the second and third components of *Mystery Train*, although no such link exists between either and the first. Apart from location, the principal linkage is provided through moments of temporal overlap. The couple in 'Far from Yokohama' make love and put on the radio, which gives a 2.15 a.m. time-check and plays Elvis Presley singing 'Blue Moon'. The following morning, as they prepare to leave, a shot rings out. In 'A Ghost', the sounds of lovemaking are heard from a neighbouring room – we are invited to assume it is the Japanese couple – followed by the same time-check and song on the radio. In each case, we also hear 'Blue Moon'

5. Johnny (Joe Strummer) displays the gun that helps to answer a central engima, if downplayed, in *Mystery Train* (1989).

playing down in the lobby, and a repeated exchange between the chief clerk and the bellboy. On the second occasion in the lobby, the routine is followed by a news report about three men, 'armed and extremely dangerous', sought by the police, which turns out to be a foreshadowing of the third narrative strand. A gunshot is heard, again, the following morning in 'A Ghost', after a night in which Luisa sees what appears to be the ghost of Elvis. The same 2.15 a.m. moment is heard on the car radio of the three protagonists of 'Lost in Space', and in a second repetition of exchanges in the hotel lobby. Johnny, Charlie and Will then arrive at the hotel, where it turns out that the clerk is Will's brother-in-law. They beg a room, sleep off the worst of the night and in the morning, after a struggle, Johnny accidentally shoots Charlie in the leg.

The effect of this structure is to create a sense of anticipation and expectation rather different from that provided by more conventional linear narrative. Once the initial overlap is established in the second narrative thread, the viewer is cued to look for other such patterns and to focus on material that might not have appeared to be of great significance first time around. The viewer might or might not immediately connect the sound of lovemaking in 'A Ghost' with the Japanese couple, but is strongly encouraged to do so retrospectively once the time-check is given on the radio. The temporal parallel established, the viewer is then likely to anticipate the gunshot in the morning, changing its status from a surprise event to one that is expected. The gunshot constitutes a more conventional narrative enigma than most of the material presented in *Mystery Train*, although it is handled in an unconventionally non-linear manner. The news announcement of the three men sought by police is likely to be taken as a move towards its resolution – which it proves to be – but is followed initially only by a restatement of the puzzle. The start of 'Lost in Space' comes with strong expectations that the enigma of the shooting will be explained, all the more so when Johnny displays his gun during the initial sequence in a bar. It is a typical Jarmusch move to render the incident as merely an accident, however, downplaying its dramatic significance in favour of an emphasis on formal play.

Night on Earth, comprising five narrative strands set in taxis, has a more openly announced linking structure. Temporal overlap is mixed here with spatial distance. An early image depicts five clocks, showing the current time in Los Angeles, New York, Paris, Rome and Helsinki. We start in Los Angeles, at 7.07 p.m., with the cab driven by Corky (Winona Ryder) and her fare, the Hollywood casting agent Victoria (Gena Rowlands). With the completion of this segment, we return to the clocks, which wind back to their starting times before beginning the second strand, set in New York from 10.07 p.m., and so on. No direct links exist between the sub-narratives, beyond the common frame of the fleeting relationships established between taxi drivers and passengers. A theme of blindness and insight appears to be offered, to some extent, but only implicitly and not obviously in all strands. Four have initially distant and/or hostile drivers and passengers making some kind of emotional connection. The impression is of characters passing in day or night, their lives touching briefly but within a format that does not allow these vignettes to be caught up in any more Hollywood-type conventional/resolved melodramatic fabric.

Flirt follows *Night on Earth* in the use of different national settings, in this case New York, Berlin and Tokyo, although it offers a more radical approach in which the same basic narrative scenario is re-enacted in each. We start in 'New York, February 1993' with a quirky tangled-relationship drama. Bill (Bill Sage) has an hour and a half to provide his girlfriend Emily (Parker Posey) with an answer to the question of whether they have a future together, before she flies off to work in Paris (where she has an ex-boyfriend) for three months. He promptly puts the same question by phone to Margaret, who remains off-screen, with whom he once shared a kiss. Margaret has just left her husband, Bill's friend Walter (Martin Donovan). A routine follows between Bill and Walter in a bar, the latter armed with a handgun that goes off (accidentally?) as the pair eventually embrace. Bill is taken to hospital for treatment to facial wounds. This scenario is repeated, word for word in many details, in the following two segments, 'Berlin, October 1994' and 'Tokyo, March 1995'. The Berlin segment follows most closely, although switching to revolve around gay male relationships. The narrative of *Flirt* becomes something of a formalist game, playing on expectations of repetition to create various subtle changes between one sub-section and another. In Berlin, for example, we do not see the moment of the gunshot and it is unclear, at first, who has done the shooting: the wife of the potential lover of the Bill-equivalent, or her husband, seen entering the building shortly before the shot is heard? The presence of the husband might lead the viewer to expect a shift in the pattern, but that turns out not to be the case. The ordering of events is shifted to a greater extent in the final segment, in which the milieu is that of relationships between dancers, dance teacher and a filmmaker. At first, *Flirt* appears to offer a literal structure of repetition. As it progresses, however, what develops is a subtle pattern of similarity and difference.

Many of the films considered above depart from the classical Hollywood model through the increased importance they give to spatial or temporal systems of narrative organization. Such systems are generally subordinate to linear narrative causality in the Hollywood variety.[20] Unconventional temporal shifts, involving repetitions or overlaps, are probably the most radical and potentially destabilizing for the viewer, so familiar is the dominant pattern of forward-moving narration – even in independent features in which narrative momentum is reduced. Temporal shifts are usually clearly marked and smoothly integrated into the broader narrative thrust in the commercial mainstream, a common example being the conventional flashback sequence. The sense created in *Mystery Train* and *Flirt* of having to backtrack, to revisit material, to identify repetitions and points of difference, establishes a very different dynamic, a structure akin to a spiral in which the ramifications of nuances are explored rather than a linear narrative that offers a single movement towards resolution. The purpose of this can be to unsettle and/or to promote thought on the part of the viewer. *Flirt* invites the viewer to consider the extent to which a different milieu affects the fallout that results from an initial narrative scenario, both underlining and perhaps undermining this by having it spelled out explicitly by a chorus-like group of minor characters who appear in the Berlin strand.

Fooling with conventional narrative ordering can also become a mark of artistically motivated showmanship, as seems to be the case in *Pulp Fiction*, the multiple strands of which unravel in an order askew from that in which they occur. *Pulp Fiction* opens with what becomes a framing device, a hold-up in a restaurant to which the narrative returns at the end, some two hours later. A major narrative strand involving the hit-men Jules and Vincent, who will end up at the centre of the restaurant heist, is established as they begin an early-morning assignment. Next we are introduced to the down-on-his-luck boxer, Butch (Bruce Willis), as he is paid to take a dive in his next fight. Jules and Vincent enter the bar in which this arrangement is being sealed, dressed in T-shirts and shorts. The first-time viewer is unlikely to be aware at this point that we have shifted to a much later moment in the Jules-and-Vincent component of the narrative, a point that comes after events in which they are involved that are yet to be depicted on-screen (an accidental shooting in the back of a car and the subsequent clean-up operation that results in the loss of their usual black-suit-and-tie uniforms). Escaping later after refusing to throw his fight, Butch returns to his apartment and is confronted by and kills Vincent. This makes sense in terms of fabula. Vincent has no further role to play in the underlying sequence of events. But it is disorienting when Vincent appears again, alive and well, when the syuzhet cuts back to the completion of the assignment established earlier. The impression created here is similar to that found in the 'Wise Up' sing-along sequence in *Magnolia*, a celebration of the mastery of cinematic flair and technique that exists as much for its own enjoyment as to be subordinated to any other motivating structure.

A more radical toying with different threads, and with the basis of narrative structure as a whole, is found in *Adaptation* (2002), an independent production given studio distribution by Columbia. *Adaptation* is a highly self-reflexive sequel to *Being John Malkovich* (from the same writer and director), in which the central character is the screenwriter Charles Kaufman (Nicholas Cage), agonizing over the adaptation of a book to the screen. Kaufman begins with a characteristically indie-screenwriter stance, resistant to the imposition of any Hollywood-style devices – guns, drugs, character arcs or the learning of 'profound life-lessons' – on the material. His position is set up explicitly against that of the mainstream, the latter represented by the popular seminar run by the real-life screenwriting guru Robert McKee (Brian Cox). Both Kaufman and the film we are watching play with a number of different points of narrative focus (often expressed in briefly inserted and rapidly cut or fast-motion stylized routines), before eventually settling on the subject known best to the writer: himself. At this point the film goes into reflexive overdrive: Kaufman dictates into a tape-recorder a scene about himself dictating a scene about himself into a tape-recorder. A conversation with McKee leads Kaufman to inject doses of conventional drama into his script, according to the axiom that you cannot lose if you wow the audience in the end. The film shifts as a result into a denouement filled with sex, drugs, kidnap, attempted murder and moments of self-illuminating character insight of the kind against which the screenwriter had previously railed.

How devices that call attention to the narrative process are used and understood depends very much on the way individual features are positioned in the independent marketplace: at the more art-house/specialized end of the spectrum, in which case they might be more likely to be designed to raise questions about various aspects of the nature of experience or its mediation; or at the more commercial/exploitative end, where visceral effects and showmanship might play a larger role. *Adaptation* has a foot in each camp, as both an explicit deconstruction of mainstream narrative design and as a narrative game in which the viewer is encouraged to take pleasure in the style and verve with which it eventually flips its own structure inside out. These are relative tendencies, however, within the indie landscape as much as between the independent sector and Hollywood. Similar arguments can be made to understand independent features that go further into the realms of narrative complexity or enigma.

If viewers have to work to unravel the narrative structures of some independent features, they are likely to be more seriously puzzled or confounded by others that make a point of being 'difficult', opaque or deliberately unresolved. The reversed-order narrative of *Memento* opens with the moment at which the central character, Leonard Selby (Guy Pearce), kills John Edward 'Teddy' Gemmall (Joe Pantoliano), convinced that he has achieved vengeance against the man who raped and murdered his wife. The narrative traces back from this point, establishing the chain of events that leads to this conclusion. As each part of the narrative unfolds, we are unaware of what came before, a strategy motivated subjectively by the fact that an injury has left Leonard with a condition in which he has no short-term memory. At first, the evidence tends to support the conclusion that Teddy was the rapist-murderer, and that he is attempting to take advantage of Leonard's condition to steer him in the wrong direction. Doubts begin to multiply, however, and by the end it seems just as likely that Teddy is what he claims to be, a detective who has tried to help and protect Leonard in his quest. The impression created is that Leonard has decided to lie to himself, in the end, and at Teddy's expense, in order to gain the peace of mind that will come from the illusion that he has resolved the case. Exactly how far Leonard might have deceived himself remains unclear; Teddy accuses him of projecting his own situation onto an invented story – presented to us as a subplot – about another victim of memory dysfunction whose plight had not been believed by his wife, with tragic consequences.

A similar kind of narrative reversal, threatening to pull the rug out from underneath the viewer, although remaining somewhat short of a full or clear explanation, is found in some of the films of David Lynch, a major figure in and around the independent sector since the cult success of the bizarre and surreal *Eraserhead* (1978). In more recent films such as *Lost Highway* (1997) and *Mulholland Drive* (2001), Lynch takes some of the strange qualities of *Eraserhead* into a glossier and higher-budget realm, a particularly dark and grotesque form of film noir. Both *Lost Highway* and *Mulholland Drive* set out to subvert major narrative expectations, principally through transformations in the identities of major characters. *Lost Highway* starts out with strange and menacing goings-on at the house of saxophonist Fred Madison (Bill Pullman) and his wife Renee (Patricia Arquette). These culminate in the murder of Renee, apparently by Fred, although the oddness of some of the circumstances is such that his degree of conscious culpability is left unclear. Fred is sentenced to death, but weird and far from entirely fathomable things happen one night in his cell. Next morning, to the puzzlement of the authorities (and that of the viewer), he has turned into someone else, a car mechanic named Pete (Balthazar Getty). Towards the end of the film, Pete is transformed back into Fred. Lots of dark textures are developed, with plenty of scope for a range of interpretations, but exactly what all this amounts to is left far from clear. Some specific details are deliberately denied to the viewer. Something strange clearly happened to Pete the night he ended up transforming into Fred, and it was witnessed by his girlfriend and parents. 'Tell him' (and us), suggests the former, but nobody does, either at that moment or as a later resolution of the central enigma.

Mulholland Drive offers a similar dynamic, developing a complex narrative around the two principal characters, Betty (Naomi Watts), and an apparent amnesia victim who adopts the name Rita (Laura Elena Harring), only to turn it inside out towards the end. A reasonable hypothesis is that the bulk of what we have witnessed has been an elaborate fantasy generated out of the jealously and envy of the would-be actress Diane Selwyn ('Betty') towards the successful star Camilla Rhodes ('Rita'), but it is far from easy to resolve this entirely without sitting down and working through a great deal of detail in retrospect or on repeated viewing. Commercially, this might be no bad thing, for viewers prepared to make the investment, such films being promoted on the basis of the need to see them more than once. An economy of multiple viewing, of designing films with features that might be understood differently or more clearly if revisited, is particularly effective in encouraging sales on video or DVD. The question 'what does it mean' generated valuable press coverage for *Mulholland Drive* during its release, a phenomenon exploited through the use of print adverts listing a number of details to which attention should be paid in order (supposedly) to unravel the mystery. A disorienting landscape of dream, nightmare and fantasy is an important component of much of Lynch's work, problems of understanding or resolution being part of the 'serious' thematic content. But films such as *Lost Highway* and *Mulholland Drive* are also designed to be enjoyable precisely in their degrees of impenetrability and their abandonment of conventional linear-narrative logic. Suddenly to undermine major narrative premises such as the fundamental identity of leading characters can be disturbing, but it is also the kind of flourish that might be expected, a distinctly 'Lynchian' artistic touch appealing to a particular audience, along with darkly brooding effects on the soundtrack and the presence of strange and manipulative diminutive figures lurking in the background.

An Alternative Narrative Mode?

The point to be made here is that departures from the dominant classical Hollywood form of narrative of the kind outlined in this chapter should not just be defined negatively, as denials, disturbances or subversions. They also constitute an alternative narrative mode in their own right, even if one that contains a number of variations and does not have exact boundaries. A narrative mode, as defined by David Bordwell, is 'a historically distinct set of norms of narrative construction and comprehension'.[21] The classical Hollywood variety is one narrative mode to which a number of alternatives have been offered, including art-cinema narration. The mode of narration found in American independent features of the kind on which this book focuses lies somewhere between the two. In Bordwell's definition, art-cinema narration, 'taking its cue from literary modernism', questions the objective cause/effect definition of reality and identity offered by the classical style: 'the world's laws may not be knowable, personal psychology may be indeterminate.'[22] In support of such a vision of the world, cause-effect patterns are loosened and the symbolic dimension may be enhanced 'through an emphasis on the fluctuations of character psychology'.[23] This is still motivated through a notion of realism, as

Bordwell suggests: a realism based on a different conception of the nature of reality, one that is more contingent and in which events are more open-ended and tenuously linked.

Many films made in the independent sector share some of these qualities with art-cinema narration, along with its tendency towards more self-consciousness about the process of narration, although to varying degrees. Art cinema, or the end of the independent sector that has more in common with art cinema, is likely to pursue such strategies more radically than some independent features. None of these categories are absolute, but they do have particular institutional bases; as Bordwell puts it: 'every mode of narration is tied to a mode of film production and reception.'[24] The notion of a single category of art-cinema narration, embracing a wide range of work, is problematical. But, as Bordwell argues, art-cinema narration gained some sense of coherence by defining itself against classical narrative in a particular social, historical and economic climate: especially that of European cinema during the 1950s and 1960s, building on earlier movements such as 1920s Impressionism and Surrealism. As a distinct mode, an institution, it required the development of a critical-interpretive machinery and its own sphere of distribution and exhibition. To the degree that it can be identified as a more or less distinct entity, an American 'indie' mode has a similar basis in the development of a critical and industrial infrastructure from the 1980s. A test of the extent to which particular narrative strategies constitute a mode of their own might be the degree to which their departures from dominant conventions are likely to be *expected*, as part of the established repertoire of a particular variety of cinema, rather than subverting the expectations of the audiences they actually reach. For the art-house viewer of American independent cinema, a de-dramatized, downplayed, multi-strand or impenetrable narrative structure is likely to be anticipated in many cases rather than a source of disorientation. For the occasional breakthrough hit, the presence of such qualities might be appealing on the grounds of novelty or showmanship, as in the case of *Memento* or *Pulp Fiction*.

If it does constitute an alternative mode – or a series of options – the narrative structure exhibited by some independent features can also be related more directly to the industrial context examined in the previous chapter. Some forms of narrative are cheaper to produce than others, a factor that should never be ignored in the independent sector. Dialogue and character-centred films are generally less expensive than productions dependent on qualities such as major action sequences or exotic locations. More episodic narratives can lend themselves to the pragmatic exigencies of independent production, such as the fact that shooting might take place on many separate occasions over a long period of time, making smooth continuity and tightly integrated linearity more difficult or expensive to achieve. *Slacker* is a good example, its narrative design permitting a process of production in which sequences involving individual characters could be shot separately as time and money permitted. An oblique style in which major events are elided has obvious cost-benefits of a similar kind. The same does not go for the slicker variety of multi-strand narrative, which often requires greater expense in areas such as casting and smoothly mobile camerawork. In some of the work of Jarmusch, however, the existence of strands set in different countries or featuring characters from overseas also makes economic sense. It is not entirely coincidental that *Mystery Train*, with its opening section in Japanese with English subtitles, was financed primarily by Japanese money, or that *Night on Earth*, with segments located in Paris, Rome and Helsinki, was funded in Europe as well as Japan. The connection between settings/characters and sources of funding in Jarmusch films is far from absolute, of course; *Dead Man* (1996) has an American setting despite being funded mostly in Europe. The issue is one of sensibility as well as of financial backing, Jarmusch's influences and style of filmmaking being such that his work has always tended to be received more favourably in Europe than in the USA. The breakdown of *Stranger than Paradise* into three main segments (New York, Cleveland, Florida) can also be related to financial exigency: the film originally existed as just the initial half hour, the limit of what Jarmusch could shoot on a supply of left-over stock donated by Win Wenders. Pragmatic factors can interact productively with the more intrinsic qualities of work, as in the case of *Mulholland Drive*, which started life not as a standalone feature but as the necessarily open-ended pilot for a planned ABC television series. When the network pulled the plug, the film was bought by the French company StudioCanal (part of the Vivendi group that also owns Universal) and restructured, with some additional shooting, as a feature that was picked up for distribution by Universal Focus. While very much in the Lynch mould, some of the qualities of the film can thus be attributed to its unusual production history.

Not all independent features depart substantially from the more familiar and dominant classical Hollywood narrative mode. The aim of this chapter has been to highlight differences rather more than similarities, but it is important to remember that these tend to be relative and variable rather than absolute. The gap between even the more unconventional independent features and work of a genuinely radical or avant-garde cast remains a substantial one, as might be suggested by a comparison between *Memento* and Anne McGuire's experimental video *Strain Andromeda* (1992), in which the science-fiction feature *The Andromeda Strain* (1971) is re-edited to reverse the scene order, starting with the climax and tracing backwards the process of cause-and-effect. The result is far more strange, disorienting and unmotivated than that created by the narrative reversal in *Memento*. Some independent features are more conventional in their narrative strategies than those highlighted in this chapter, but narrative structure is a key defining component of many – along with other formal dimensions to be considered in the next chapter.

3

Form

The specificity of the art film as a mode of production lies in its attempt to bridge the industrial operations of the studios with the artisanal practices of the aesthetic and political avant-gardes, to reconcile commercial and personally expressive functions.

David James[1]

The title character in *Henry: Portrait of a Serial Killer* behaves nicely, politely, with a touch of charm, as he pays the woman behind the counter at a coffee shop. The camera holds on the woman as we hear his footfall heading (we are led to assume) to the door. Cut to a low-angle shot immediately outside, the transition smoothed by an audio-match, in which the sound of Henry's footsteps carries across the cut. We see first his legs, then the rest of his figure coming into frame, as he crosses the road to his car. After a closer shot of Henry entering the vehicle, the film cuts back to a slight pan along the coffee-shop counter, across which the woman is now revealed to lie dead and bleeding (along with another member of staff on the floor), to flashback sounds of gunshots and screams. Murder occurs here in the interstice between two shots, its presence masked initially by the deceptive use of a device familiar from the conventions of continuity editing. The sound-match, along with a consistency in the apparent direction of Henry's movement, creates the impression of a seamless transition in time and space from the moments in and outside the shop. The cut back to the scene of carnage inside produces a startling disjunction, prising open the gap between the two earlier shots and revealing the horrific nature of the action concealed between one and the other. This is a striking example of a subversion of continuity editing devices, the familiarity of which in mainstream and much independent cinema is such that they are not usually noticed. The effect is unsettling, undermining a system of découpage the usual purpose of which is to guide the viewer comfortably and unselfconsciously through the events on-screen.

This brief moment from *Henry: Portrait of a Serial Killer* is one of many examples in which formal devices are used in independent features in ways that depart from the norms of the dominant Hollywood style. It is not a random effect, however, or one that exists only for its own sake. As with most of the cases examined in this and the previous chapter, the departure from mainstream convention is motivated, given a rationale, in the larger context of the film. In this case, a thematic motivation can be established: formally, the killing occurs obliquely, inside the normal, everyday conventions of continuity editing; just as, thematically, the film presents a portrait of a serial killer that is chilling in its suggestion that murder is often concealed within the more banal and ordinary texture of life. Motivations of this kind can go a long way toward repairing or containing ruptures in the fabric of more conventional formal devices, although this might not entirely be the case. Departures such as the misleading continuity effect created in *Henry* are unsettling partly because they can create unease without the exact nature of the departure being immediately apparent to the viewer who does not stop to examine the sequence more closely. Subtle shifts in formal strategies can, as a result, be an effective way of establishing a distinctively offbeat, indie-movie style, without the more overtly radical approach that might be found in art cinema or the further reaches of avant-garde experimentation.

For the purpose of this chapter, 'form' will be defined principally in the following terms, not including the major formal dimension –

narrative – considered in the previous chapter: positioning, movement and framing established by the camera; image quality and textures created through the use of different types of camera, film stock, processing or lighting conditions; sound; and editing regimes. The spectrum of options available within the independent sector is much the same as that found in the realm of narrative, ranging from close to the Hollywood style, at one end, to the margins of the avant-garde, at the other. Departures from dominant convention might be designed to dislocate, as in the example from *Henry* cited above, or to create a more 'showy' stylized effect, such as that associated with some of the films of the brothers Cohen; or just to refresh by avoiding certain overly familiar devices (refusing the conventional use of establishing shots or close-ups, for example; framing off-centre or shooting from slightly unusual angles). If the conventional Hollywood style is taken as the seemingly 'neutral' norm – very much a construct itself, of course – two broadly defined sets of options exist on either side. 'Beneath' the Hollywood style, in the sense that an impression is created of less in the way of smoothly orchestrated fabrication, are those that make claims to the status of greater 'reality' or 'authenticity', as in the realm of narrative, through the use of devices associated with forms such as documentary or *cinema-vérité*. 'Beyond' the classical Hollywood style is a range of more evidently stylized options. As elsewhere in independent cinema, such categories are far from absolute and all-inclusive. The qualities of individual films often bridge the gap between seemingly more 'objective' and expressive styles, and many formal possibilities exist – too many to cover in all aspects here – that do not necessarily fit into so neat a classification.

An Impression of Authenticity

From pioneering films of the 1950s to the latest in digital video production, a strong tendency in one strain of American independent cinema has been towards the creation of a greater impression of reality or authenticity than is associated with the glossier style typical of the Hollywood mainstream. A number of formal approaches have been used to create this impression of verisimilitude. In some cases it can be achieved simply through the rejection of the expensively smooth style of mainstream production, the slickness of which has often been associated with inauthenticity. An impression of authenticity can also be fabricated more directly and deliberately, through the use of devices associated with documentary or news footage. While commercial realities have ensured that theatrically released documentary filmmaking remains essentially a part of the independent sector, techniques associated with documentary-realist forms have often been used in fiction features in an attempt to increase their claims to the status of verisimilitude. Unsteady, hand-held camerawork, inexact framing, restricted views and sudden zooms are among devices that can be used to create an impression that the filmmaker is capturing events as they unfold, unpredictably, before the camera – as is often the case, for practical reasons, in the world of documentary or newsreel – rather than that the events have been planned in advance and carefully staged *for* the camera.

The creation of an impression of authenticity often entails claims to the status of actuality, of something 'really happening' rather than being fabricated, in the pro-filmic reality, the material that unfolds in front of the camera. This can take a variety of forms. It might be a question of the use of real people and/or real locations, both of which were used in a number of independent features produced during the 1950s and 1960s. The development of new, lightweight and more portable cameras and sync-sound equipment gave filmmakers freedom to shoot on real locations with less intrusion than had been possible in the past, much as the advent of digital video was further to enable a later generation. Early exponents included Morris Engel and Ruth Orkin, whose trilogy *Little Fugitive* (1953), *Lovers and Lollipops* (1955) and *Weddings and Babies* (1958) occupies a pivotal position in the independent/art-cinema scene of the decade, influenced by the Italian Neorealism of the 1940s and early 1950s and an influence in turn on the early work of figures such as François Truffaut, John Cassavetes and Martin Scorsese. The films were shot on the industry standard, 35mm film, but using a lightweight camera, designed partly by Engel, that could be strapped to the shoulder. It enabled the filmmakers to work unobtrusively in real locations without any noticeable loss of image stability.[2] The result is highly unmediated-seeming access to the world beyond the studio, the streets of New York and, in *Little Fugitive*, the attractions and crowds of Coney Island, without any of the formal signifiers of authenticity associated with the *vérité* style (based on 'raw' footage unaccompanied by commentary or interviews) that came into prominence during the 1960s in the 16mm work of documentary filmmakers such as Richard Leacock, Albert and David Maysles, Don Pennebaker and Frederick Wiseman. The sheer fact of presence in the real world, capturing the texture of places in *Little Fugitive* such as Coney Island and the streets and empty lots around the Brooklyn home of the central character, seven-year-old Joey (the untrained performer Richie Andrusco), was sufficient in itself to create a strong impression of verisimilitude.

Scenes from real life on the margins are also mixed with dramatically scripted material in *On the Bowery* (1956), shot using studio-scale 35mm equipment, in which three homeless men play themselves. More images of real-life despair form the backdrop to the fictional portrait of a recently divorced woman presented in *The Savage Eye* (1959). A highly formalized and 'poetic' voice-over by a guardian angel figure is combined with footage, some taken with a hidden camera, of the occupants of the netherworld through which she moves, including lengthy sequences at a wrestling match, a seedy club and observing the ministrations of a faith healer. *The Savage Eye* is another example that makes its claims to the status of documentary-authenticity in terms of the milieux to which it gains access, rather than the style of cinematography, most of which remains fixed and static. 'Real life', in the America of the 1950s, tended to be signified, here and elsewhere, by the lives of the marginal and the disadvantaged, the flip side of the world of post-war affluence, suburbia and consumerism.

A number of more mainstream features moved out onto the streets in the post-war years, to create a stronger background texture of reality in thrillers such as *The House on 92nd Street* (1945). Shooting on location rather than in the studio has since become widespread, not in itself signifying any necessary commitment to verisimilitude (and often achieved with the same slick technical apparatus associated with studio production). The use of non-professional performers in place of actors or stars is generally a strategy more likely to be found in the alternative/independent sector, in examples such as the films of Harmony Korine examined in the previous chapter. 'Real' figures appear both in the foreground, as in many of the character vignettes in *Gummo* and *Julien Donkey-Boy*, and in the background, as is the case in a number of scenes in the latter. Shooting using concealed DV cameras enables 'real' reactions to be captured to the antics of the central character, whether in his ramblings on the street or the sequence in which he carries the wrapped foetus of what he believes to be his child home on a bus. The effect is greatly to increase the emotional potency of the material. The response of viewers, aware of the fictional nature of the performance, is likely to be heightened by being mediated through the presence and in some cases the response of real inhabitants of the margins of the diegetic universe.

The central performance is also likely to be heightened by this process, in which the actor is obliged to go out into the real world without the presence of any of the usually visible markers of the fictional status of the action. This brings us to another dimension in which claims to the status of authenticity before the camera can be made, at the level of *performance* itself, even when this occurs within an entirely fictional frame. The pro-filmic reality that matters in the films of John Cassavetes, for example, the 'reality' to be documented by the camera, is that of the unfolding performance of actors and the emotional reality of character to which it aspires. To respect this as far as possible, in what remains a process of fictional construction, Cassavetes favoured long takes, shot in real time with a combination of close, hand-held camerawork and more distanced telephoto coverage from a second camera. Each is capable of creating documentary-style resonances (a camera up-close to and *following* the action or a distanced camera, without privileged access). Vast amounts of footage were expended in the effort to capture the right moment, 'the very instant when a character says the scripted words as if from his or her own heart'.[3] Much was also shot in sequence, to create emotional coherence and continuity of a kind closer to that found in theatre than the usual practice in film, in which shooting is usually organized according to a more economically efficient breakdown of sequences.

Cassavetes' work often has the look of improvisation in front of the camera, but this was not generally the case at the level of basic content and dialogue. Improvisation was usually restricted to rehearsals, although exactly when the camera would shift onto any particular figure was left uncertain during shooting, encouraging the performers to stay in character at all times.[4] Unscripted improvisation within pre-given structures or situations is a source of much of the impact of *Julien Donkey-Boy*, including Ewen Bremner's central performance. In *Gummo*, Korine went so far as to absent himself from the shooting of some sequences – notably a scene in which a group of characters end up ripping apart the furniture, accompanied only by cinematographer Jean Escoffier – producing material of a raw and uncomfortable nature that could not have been created in a traditionally scripted or directed manner. Freedom to pursue such strategies, unencumbered by the apparatus of shooting on film or the cost of allowing the camera to run for long and possibly unproductive periods, is greatly increased by the use of digital video, in which an emphasis is often placed on the authenticity of performance.

The flexible and small-scale nature of the digital production process allows for more concentrated periods of performance, without the long breaks customary when setting up to shoot traditionally on film. Richard Linklater's *Tape* (2001), a heavily performance-centred InDigEnt production based on a one-act play by Stephen Belber, was thoroughly rehearsed in advance before being shot on two digital cameras with little advance blocking of sequences. The performers worked their way through the script in ten-minute chunks, each of which was covered four or five times.[5] The visual style of the film includes dialogue exchanges at several key moments rendered in repeated fast pans from one character to another, a device that maintains the real-time existence of the interaction between performers, for up to four minutes unbroken in one case. The camera also achieves an uncomfortable intimacy in some of the most emotionally charged scenes in the painfully offbeat DV comedy *Chuck and Buck* (2000), the story of the efforts of a 27-year-old suffering from arrested development to recapture a relationship with his childhood best friend. Two cameras were used here, too, in the name of both economy of shooting and integrity of performance. A similar sense of intimacy is generated in *The Center of the World* (2001), directed by Wayne Wang, in which a young computer wizard pays for the services of a woman to join him on what is meant to be an emotion-free version of contractual sex during a three-night trip to Las Vegas. Hand-held

DV camerawork, closely shot, creates a strong impression of presence rather than a more distanced, voyeuristic or aestheticized approach to sequences of sexual activity.

It is not that such effects can never be achieved with larger film equipment and bigger crews. The digital option can make a real difference, however, beyond just being more easy, flexible and viable for those with limited means. The small-scale nature of the low-end digital apparatus makes close proximity to character much less intrusive on performance, and easier to achieve spontaneously, on the fly. It also permits the use of camera positions that would not be possible without time-consuming and expensive alterations to sets or locations; some shots taken from a position flush to the floor in *Tape*, for example, that could not be obtained with most larger cameras without digging a hole. Digital cameras can also shoot much longer continuous takes, a capacity utilized to the extreme by Mike Figgis in the four-way split-screen feature *Timecode* (2000), which was shot in synchronized 93-minute takes, an innovative form of multi-strand narrative in which performers improvise around a predetermined structure and the viewer is challenged to follow simultaneous and often interwoven threads.

If Cassavetes helped to pioneer 'an aesthetic of roughness and imperfection', Ray Carney suggests, he did so inadvertently, in his use of approaches designed to create maximum freedom for his actors and as a result of budgetary constraints.[6] Scenes were lit generally, to enable shots of performances to be taken in any direction at any time, rather than each camera set-up being carefully planned and lit in its own right. Issues such as precise focus and framing took a secondary place to performance and character. It was not unknown for Cassavetes, like many other directors, to manipulate performers, to play on their real emotions or experiences in order to create real responses that could be captured on film. A more extreme example of this kind of approach is found in *The Blair Witch Project*, which shares with Cassavetes' *Shadows* an attempt to blur the line between performer and character by giving the latter the same first names as the former. Part of the impact of *The Blair Witch Project*, and a good deal of its publicity, came from the suggestion that the performers were *really* in a state of some annoyance, fear, tiredness or confusion as a result of the unconventional shooting practice. The three principals, carrying their own film and video cameras, were left to wander in the woods in which the action unfolds, receiving from the filmmakers only occasional messages and instructions and diminishing supplies of food. The directors, Eduardo Sanchez and Daniel Myrick, intervened more substantially on occasion, at one point seeking to tone down the performances when they threatened to peak too early and restaging one of the night-time encounters because of technical problems. But the shooting itself and the dialogue were largely improvised and many of the reactions of the cast appear to have been 'genuine' responses to events of which they had no detailed prior knowledge.

A distinction can be made between the creation of an impression of authenticity in various aspects of the pro-filmic reality and in the use of particular formal devices through which the matter in front of the camera is conveyed to the viewer. In many cases the two overlap, sometimes necessarily. Shooting in real locations or following improvised dimensions of performance might necessitate the use of unsteady hand-held camerawork, awkward zooms or imprecise framing, or might make it difficult or a lesser priority to obtain the range of coverage of angles needed to establish smooth and conventional patterns of continuity editing. Practical and economic factors also loom large in this equation. One of the great appeals of rougher, documentary-style aesthetics is that they are in general more easily achieved on limited financial means than the glossier style associated with Hollywood production. This is one of the strongest examples of the mutual reinforcement of practical-industrial and formal-aesthetic factors in the independent sector. If the distinctive style of the films of Cassavetes was shaped by the priority given to performance, it was also a function of low-budget production. Location shooting was used for the exteriors of *Shadows*, for example, creating much of the film's impression of authenticity, because studios could not be afforded. The exteriors were in most cases shot from a distance, increasing the documentary-type impression of situating the characters in the real world, because of the practicalities of filming inconspicuously in public without permits. The same practical-financial dimension was chiefly responsible for the 'realistic' quality of the sound, which included background noise usually cleaned up in post-production:

what was praised by critics as an innovation had not been intended, according to the director.[7]

The use of formal devices designed to create an impression of documentary-type authenticity remains a contrivance, however, with specific effects, even where it is over-determined by practical and economic factors. Uneven hand-held camerawork in a mixture of 16mm and Hi-8 video made economic sense in the low-budget shooting of *The Blair Witch Project*, the more so in a context in which the film was to be shot by the performers rather than a professional crew. The style was not just a default practical option, however, but a key aspect of what gives the film its particular impact. The combination of the two kinds of footage immediately establishes a hierarchy of degrees of implied authenticity. The black-and-white 16mm footage is, ostensibly, of documentary status, but the video makes greater claims to the status of reality. The video images are marked as looser and more spontaneous, shot in an off-hand manner, in contrast with the 16mm footage, especially in the early stages of the film in which we see some of the preparations that go into the creation of the documentary. Even as a documentary, the film-within-the-film is presented as a construct, producing more carefully fabricated images, while the video is offered as what 'really' happens in, around and beyond the creation of the documentary. By 'containing' the nascent documentary, in other words, the video footage claims access to another level of reality. The impression that the video camera is merely witness to the events is increased by the hostility both Josh (Joshua Leonard) and Mike (Michael Williams) express towards the leader of the group, Heather (Heather Donahue), when she keeps filming at points of high interpersonal tension and anxiety.

A number of other strategies are used to increase the impression of authenticity created by *The Blair Witch Project*. One measure of 'reality' footage is its incompleteness and the existence of prominent absences, the result of the exigencies of attempting to cover unanticipated and unstaged developments. Many such absences are found in the film, whether the result of deliberate confection or the practicalities of the shooting process. The first instance of scary noises in the night is not depicted at all, merely recalled by Josh the following morning. When the camera and sound recorder witness some of what happens on the second night, the sequence is brief and what exactly the characters hear in the woods outside is indistinct, as it continues to be on subsequent occasions. A number of night-time sequences include periods of up to almost a minute in which the screen is black and nothing can be seen. At one key moment, when Heather opens up a bundle left outside their tent after the disappearance of Josh, the precise nature of its bloody contents (in fact, teeth) remains disturbingly unclear. Jump-cuts and elisions, short and long – from just a few seconds or minutes to many hours – are the dominant principles of the editing regime. In some cases, in the 16mm coverage, brief flashes of white/light are inserted between one piece of footage and the next, to create the impression of a rough assembly. Genuine accident was also able to contribute to the effect of the film, most notably in the scene in which Heather gives a tear- and snot-filled apologetic speech to the camera towards the end, the striking off-centre framing of which was apparently unintentional.

Incompleteness is also used as a signifier of reality, at one remove, in *Series 7:The Contenders* (2001), a blackly comic DV spoof of reality TV in which the aim of the game contestants is to kill one another. Two key scenes are missed by the fictional TV cameras, presented instead as 'reconstructions' featuring actors playing the parts of the supposedly real characters. At some other moments the fictional TV show has to resort to footage from surveillance cameras, in a range of different image qualities, all of which have come to signify the presence of the real. A hierarchy of levels of constructed reality is offered, as in *The Blair Witch Project*. The presentation of some events as occurring off-screen, beyond the gaze of the cameras that seek to follow the contenders' every moment, is a rhetorical assertion of their relative degree of reality: that they have an existence beyond that called into being by the presence of the TV camera. At the same time, the fact that some events are seen only in fictional reconstruction implies a greater reality in the rest of the action. The presence of the camera following events, and sometimes getting in the way, is acknowledged. The object of representation claims the status not of unmediated reality but of a reality created principally through media representation. Familiar signifiers of *vérité* coverage are found throughout, as in the first lethal encounter, witnessed at the start of the film. Reigning champion

6. Edgy, hand-held, on the street: *Laws of Gravity* (1992).

Dawn (Brooke Smith) enters a store, closely followed by the hand-held camera. She shoots a victim in the back at close range and again as he lies on the floor. An abrupt cut is made as she starts to move towards the body, a jump in continuity that finds her already bent over the corpse looking for a weapon. A reactive zoom-in catches detail as she pulls a gun from the victim's waistband, another pulling back to keep Dawn's full figure in frame as she returns upright. *Series 7* is an example in which 'reality' is signified not through apparent transparency of representation, as tends to be the case in the use of classical continuity editing patterns, but through its overt pastiche of the repertoire of reality TV shows, including the style of commentary and constant interruptions of the narrative for flashbacks, comments and flash-forwards to the action of upcoming instalments.

Formal strategies that make assertions of authenticity sometimes go hand-in-hand with the kind of downplayed, verisimilitude-claiming narrative structure examined in the previous chapter. A good example is *Laws of Gravity*, most or all of which is shot in a hand-held *vérité* manner that strongly reinforces the line of edgy tension that runs through the film. Right from the start, including titles in plain typewriter-like font, white-on-black, the impression is of scenes grasped on the street and in the neighbourhood. An unsteady camera witnesses Jimmy and Jon in the midst of a typically small-scale heist, taking cartons from the back of a van and running down the street, the camera following behind as if an accomplice in the crime. The next scene has Jimmy, Jon and others in dispute with a fence over the price to be paid for the goods. The camera wheels around behind Jimmy, moves onto Jon and the fence in turn, tilts, swings from one side to another, tilts up and down some more; multiple voices overlap on the soundtrack, throughout, further adding to the impression of hectic ongoing events captured in something like the raw. Long takes are often favoured, increasing the impact of emotionally higher-charged scenes, such as that in which Celia leaves Jon. At the moments of most dramatic action, camera mobility becomes more pronounced and unsteady, signifying the confusion of the moment, as when Jon is arrested on the street and in the finale, which ends in his death. The latter is given the most *vérité*-like treatment in *Laws of Gravity*, the shooting occurring off-screen and the camera given no more privileged view of the events than any of the witnesses within the frame. Immediately after the shots ring out – following a cut to black – the camera-view of the events is restricted, blocked out by the backs of characters milling around the scene. Some moments pass before it fights its way to gain a glimpse and then a full sight of Jon's body, bleeding on the sidewalk. The strategy of cutting to black between scenes is used widely in the film, creating a elliptical pattern akin to that of *The Blair Witch Project*; an impression of capturing episodes from a life that continues to exist in between, as acknowledged by the manifest presence of gaps, rather than the manufacture of a self-sufficiently entire-seeming fictional universe.

Not all recent independent features that lay claim to verisimilitude employ *vérité*-style devices such as wavering hand-held camerawork. *Henry: Portrait of a Serial Killer*, which bills itself in an opening credit as 'a fictional dramatization of certain events', is shot and edited in a generally conventional manner, despite the jarring breach of continuity editing cited at the start of this chapter (one instance of a trademark device in which we tend to see only the aftermath of Henry's handiwork, the body of the victim, accompanied by non-synchronous sound of the moment of killing). Markers of 'authenticity'

– and also of a low budget – include the grainy quality of the image and a harsh sound mix with a good deal of background noise. Devices from more fictional-familiar generic territories are also employed, most notably the music, which tends towards the horror end of the spectrum during or foreshadowing the killings. *Working Girls* is another example that eschews *vérité* forms, even while staking a strong claim to the status of unvarnished and de-dramatized realism. Camera position and editing is generally conventional-classical in a muted, functional and unobtrusive manner, a style that reinforces the message in a manner different from that of *vérité*: as plain and functional as the business in which the central characters are engaged.

The use of *vérité* style can have the effect of drawing attention to the formal qualities of a film, which may or may not be considered desirable. In the case of *Working Girls*, a more neutral and 'invisible' style appears to have suited the purpose of conveying its message about the ordinary-exploitation nature of working in the sex industry. An example in which a *vérité* dimension led to increased profile, and much media criticism, was the release of *Kids*, scripted by Harmony Korine and directed by Larry Clark. As a portrait of a day in the life of a group of sexually active, drinking and drug-taking younger teens, *Kids* was always going to be in controversial territory, but this was heightened by the *vérité* dimension of the shooting style and its concomitant claims to the status of authenticity. The result was that the film was taken more seriously, more readily assumed by many commentators to be an accurate portrayal of the life of a younger generation – whether this was seen as valuable insight or exploitation – than might otherwise have been expected. In the director's view, it was the impression of reality that was responsible for the decision of the regulatory body, the Motion Picture Association of America (MPAA), to give the film a commercially damaging NC-17 rating, after which the film was released unrated.[8] The style adopted by *Kids* is a more smoothly flowing kind of *vérité* than the extreme represented by *The Blair Witch Project* or the more controlled un-steadicam aesthetic of *Laws of Gravity*. Street scenes, including those of two of the main male protagonists walking-and-talking, are shot in a combination of longer shots, as if watching them from a distance such as from the other side of a road, the view obscured on occasion by passing vehicles, and closer and somewhat more conventional footage moving alongside or ahead of the characters. An intercut sequence depicting the conversations (mostly about sex) among a group of teenage boys and a group of girls is constructed through a combination of cuts and pans from one figure to another. The hand-held pans create an effect that is partially *vérité* but that sometimes seems more pre-planned than that would suggest, the camera coming to rest on characters just as they are about speak, as opposed to instances in which the camera seems to *respond* to the action, finding an individual who has already begun to talk.

An Expression of the Fictional World

Many nuances are available within the range of formal devices used to create differing impressions of authenticity. If devices such as unstable camerawork and inexact framing create the strongest impression in some instances, this is far from always the case. Such devices may become too overt and visible in their own right, reminding viewers of the act of mediation that they constitute, and thus the fabricated nature of the material. More subtle variants, and combinations of *vérité* with more smoothly conventional approaches, can be more effective. All such impressions are relative and constructed, even in the avowedly fact-based arena of documentary filmmaking. The line can also blur between that which claims the status of verisimilitude and that which becomes more *expressive*, designed to create effects other than those of an ersatz documentary-realist nature. The point is made above, implicitly, in the case of *Laws of Gravity*: the hand-held, *vérité* style gives the impression of grounding the events in something that feels more real than would be the case if the camera were fixed or moved more smoothly on dolly tracks, but it also has an expressive impact, underlining the edgy and unstable nature of the relationships – beneath all the smiles and banter – between the central characters.

The same formal devices can have multiple functions. The very grainy DV images of *Julien Donkey-Boy*, for example, can be taken as signifiers of rawness and authenticity, of the state-of-the-art in early 2000s formal assertions of harsh, low-budget realism. The extreme nature of the pixelated grain also has a strongly mediating effect in its own right, however, creating something close to a pointillist, impressionist quality. This is not the product of happenstance, but a post-production effect deliberately created in laboratory processing during the transfer of the original footage onto film. A similarly warm colour palate was confected at the same stage to create a nostalgic impression, fitting to the state of mind of the immature Buck (screenwriter Mike White), in the formally more conventional *Chuck and Buck*. Digital video may lend itself very well to the creation of a *vérité* impression, its relatively flattened original image quality being capable of signifying harsh immediacy and presence, but a particular aesthetic is not hard-wired into the medium. Linklater's three-character *Tape*, set in a single motel room, plays on the impression of immediacy in its drama of brooding enmity and betrayal. Although the film was shot in an artificial set built on a soundstage, the glaring and unflattering quality of lighting gives an impression of reality, as if reliant on the kind of available light that might be found in the real equivalent on location. *Tape* also contains a multitude of unusual and constantly shifting camera positions, permitted by the small scale of the technology, that are more expressive in effect. The aim, for Linklater, was to create something akin to a collage effect, thematically motivated by a narrative based on the revisitation, from different perspectives, of a key event in the past of the three characters.[9]

In *Julien Donkey-Boy*, expressive effects are in some instances found in the midst of sequences marked as more *vérité*-realist by the use of mobile concealed cameras and the integration of real people into the fictional material. In one case, material of an ordinary, everyday quality is captured as Pearl hunts in a second-hand shop for baby clothes. When the camera pans a couple of times, however, a smeary-blur effect is created, in keeping with the more stylized parts of the film. Strobing of the image of this kind can result from the process of transferring from 30 frames-per-second American-standard video footage to 24 fps film, the preferred medium of exhibition, a good example of technical limitation that can in some cases be turned to creative effect.[10] Blurry stylization and canted angles are also mixed with signifiers of greater immediacy – hand-held camerawork, glaring light, grainy under-lit sequences – in Hal Hartley's *The Book of Life* (1998). The blend seems appropriate to a narrative that mixes the contemporary/everyday and the religious/supernatural, as a disillusioned Jesus Christ (Martin Donovan), returning to earth on 31 December 1999, declines to unleash the Apocalypse. The faces of both Christ and Satan (Thomas Jay Ryan) are smeared to the point of distortion when in rapid motion, especially in sequences in which each takes to the street, an effect that creates an impression of their otherworldliness. A similar mix seems thematically motivated in the low-budget features of Todd Verow, which occupy a space closer to the underground. In *Little Shots of Happiness* (2000), 'blurrzy' low-grade DV is entirely in keeping with the degrading lifestyle of the central character, Frances (Bonnie Dickerson), living out of a suitcase, drinking heavily and picking up an assortment of men in bars after leaving her husband. A combination of harshly immediate-seeming and more grainy imagery is found in *The Trouble with Perpetual Deja-vu* (1999), an inconsistency resulting no doubt from limited resources, but the effect of which is to underline the impression of fracture and discontinuity that characterizes much of Verow's feature-length work.

Similar shifts between *vérité* and expressive effects also occur in the work of Cassavetes. As Ivone Margulies puts it:

> Cassavetes' composition moves back and forth between an obstructed image (a realist casualness) and a shot design in which focus is used expressively. His cinema-vérité impulse – to record the integrity of performances from a distance – yields an image that is abstract, sensual, and intense.[11]

In *Shadows*, for example, a rough and somewhat uneven impression is created in some sequences, such as Lelia and Hugh in discussion while in the queue at a ticket office. The 180-degree line of action is crossed several times, the camera moving from one side to another of the protagonists and thus reversing their relative positions in the image, to no particularly clear or specific effect. Elsewhere in the film, character interaction is figured in more obviously stylized close-ups, often cut from one to another in sequences that depart from the Hollywood continuity norm – in which some mediating shots might be expected – while maintaining a clear sense of the spatial relationship between characters through consistency of eye-line direction. The stuff of accident or technical shortcoming, often signifying pro-filmic reality, can also have expressive function, as in the case of a number of scenes in *Faces* that were unintentionally overexposed, creating harsh and glaring images that match the emotionally overexposed tone of the piece.[12]

Devices that create impressions of authenticity are also mixed with those of a more expressive character in *Slam* (1998), the story of a young black rap-poet jailed for dealing marijuana. The *vérité* style used in much of the film couples effectively with its message, a documentation of the real cycles of crime, violence and imprisonment afflicting black youths from the ghetto of south-east Washington. Among other formal strategies, the film makes regular use of awkward, slightly jarring zooms, to create its impression of catching the action as it happens. This is often a matter of small touches. In one sequence, the central character, Ray (Saul Williams), is in conversation with his drug supplier, framed mostly in two-shots of the pair, the camera moving slightly to hold them in frame. At one moment we get a closer shot of Ray from which the camera starts to pan back to include the other, at which point the lens zooms out abruptly to re-establish a medium close-up of both characters. Another example of this style comes later, after Ray's supplier has been shot as they conclude a transaction. Too many perspectives on the action are provided for this to be presented in anything like a purely *vérité* style, but the same small device is employed in the detail, to maintain a sense of the camera responding to the events: as a cop bends over the body, the camera lurches up and slightly recentres itself to catch a police car coming into frame, shifting slightly in and out of focus.

Slam combines this approach with a number of expressive devices. Immediately after the first example cited above, we move into a sequence in which Ray is writing in his notebook, composing, and the film itself switches into what might be described as a more 'poetic' mode. Images of neighbourhood people on the street appear in a lower-quality register, created by the use of a different film stock or by processing effects, signifying Ray's subjective consciousness. That this is meant to suggest the thoughts that play into his poetry is made explicit in one image, a blurry pan that ends in a close-up of the page on which he is writing. A series of rapid jump-cuts follows, interspersed with flashes of light (inspiration?), followed by another

montage of stylized images from the street. This is a good example of
the use of non-conventional formal strategies in an expressive manner,
the motivation for which is clear. The *vérité*-realist grammar the film
has previously established is abandoned with the use of images that
could, in themselves, have a more formally radical and experimental
quality, but that are effectively contained by working as an expression
of material related to the consciousness of the character.

Individual subjective experience is the most common motivation
provided for departures from more familiar and conventional formal
strategies such as the framing, editing, synchronous sound and other
audio-visual qualities associated with the classical Hollywood style.
What results can be understood as another form of realism: a *subjective*
realism that seeks to create an impression of individual experience, as
it might seem from the inside, as opposed to an impression of events
seen more objectively. This is not so uncommon in Hollywood itself,
although the scope and extent of formal experimentation – even
when contained in this manner – is liable to be greater in independent
features. Devices that depart from the norm are often used to signify
mental disturbance of one kind or another. Many examples are found
in *Julien Donkey-Boy*. Slowed video and sequences of stills, used on
several occasions, can be read as expressions of Julien's fragmented
consciousness. That they can be located in this way is sometimes made
explicit. The first sequence of stills, featuring his sister Pearl dancing
in a tutu, is preceded by a shot of Julien looking in her direction,
clearly signifying that what follows is his perspective, an impression
increased by what seems to be the roar of his consciousness figured on
the soundtrack. Elsewhere, passages depicted in stills are accompanied
by dialogue that continues as normal, creating a jolting disjunction
between sound and image. Sequences of jump-cuts, including one
that occurs while Julien takes a bath, also suggest the discontinuity of
his subjectivity, a sudden break between one moment of consciousness
and another. In their own right, some of the more expressive strategies
adopted by the film push towards the avant-garde end of the formal
spectrum. A sequence that appears to be from a party, in which Julien
is dancing with a woman, is rendered in slowed video and distorted
music, the camera subjected to whip-pans and movements in and out
of focus, the overall effect of which is disorienting. Taken on its own,

this could be a short piece of experimental video. Here, however, the context encourages us to interpret it as another expression of Julien's mental state. A later sequence, involving an argument and tussle between Julien and his brother, takes the aesthetic of jump-cuts to a similarly avant-garde extreme – again, it seems, in the name of expressing the consciousness of the former – cut hyper-rapidly to the point at which each word uttered in the exchange is cut off before it is completed.

Jump-cuts are also used to establish the disconnected nature of the central character, the socially challenged Billy (Vincent Gallo), in *Buffalo 66* (1998). His posture changes fractionally while the background view out of the window shifts from one location to another in a series of cuts early in the film, during which Billy takes a bus ride after being released from prison. The device can be said to serve purposes of narrative economy, reducing the time spent getting him from one place to another, but the dominant effect is one of dislocation, a departure from conventional editing regimes, that transfers from geographical position to what will be seen to be the relationship between Billy and more 'normal' society. Further sequences of jump-cuts follow when he arrives at the bus station, underlining the intensely agitated state of the character (even if also motivated at this point by his increasingly desperate search for a toilet!).

Shifts in the focal length of lenses and the speed at which the camera runs are combined in both *Julien Donkey-Boy* and Darren Aronofsky's *Pi* to create expressions of subjective mental states. Shooting close to a character with a wide-angle lens creates a distorted perspective in the background, an effect increased by the use of fast or slow motion. At the start of *Pi*, when we are introduced to the obsessive central character, Max Cohen (Sean Gullette), and his theories about the existence of patterns in nature, a slowed wide-angle shot of his head and shoulders is intercut with speeded-up, shakily hand-held footage of the crowded street through which he moves; the former, again, clearly locates the latter as the perspective of the character. The same device is repeated later in the film, with the subjective footage run even faster, to signify Max's deeper immersion in a quest that threatens to lead towards madness. A wide-angle lens close to Julien, combined with slow-motion footage that blurs the background, is used to similar effect in *Julien Donkey-Boy*. In both cases the camera appears to be attached to or held by the character, a strategy used on a number of occasions in *Pi* to create a strong impression of the character's detachment from the environment. A device known as a Snorri-cam, after its inventors Eidur and Einar Snorri, is employed in *Pi*, a camera worn by the performer on a harness. This is used most noticeably in one of several sequences in which Max undergoes hallucinatory experiences in the New York subway. The effect of the Snorri-cam is to produce images that have an unsteady, hand-held quality in the background but in which the character is held in a fixed position relative to the camera. The character thus seems oddly floating and disembodied, moving in a manner that is out of register with movement in the surroundings, a perfect figuration of Max's alienation from the everyday world. A more subtle and subdued version of this effect, created by mounting both character and camera on a slowly moving wheeled dolly platform, is a favourite device of Spike Lee's, used to separate character from background world in examples such as the studio-backed *Jungle Fever* (1991) and the independent feature *Girl 6* (1996).

Long shots and more formal compositions within the frame are used to signify alienation in Todd Haynes' *Safe* (1995). The camera keeps its distance from Carol (Julianne Moore), the protagonist suffering from what appears to be a severe case of allergy to the chemical-drenched textures of modern consumer life. The strategy is in some respects the opposite of that used in the more subjectively expressive parts of *Pi* and *Julien Donkey-Boy*. Both depart from the Hollywood norm, in which editing regimes and camera positions usually establish a careful balance between viewpoints close to those of central characters – giving access to their thoughts and feelings, although not usually through more than fleeting use of directly subjective shots – and more objective and distanced perspectives on the action. *Safe* tends strongly to the latter, denying the viewer the customary proximity to character. When Carol calls at the house of a friend, in her well-heeled San Fernando Valley neighbourhood, we are given a long shot of her at the door of the low, wide modern-style house. The long shot is held when the door is answered and during initial exchanges, keeping us at a distance at a point when, Hollywood-conventionally, we would

7. Distanced, alienating domestic interiors: *Safe* (1995).

expect to be brought in closer, to a more intimate position after an initial establishing shot. We then cut into the middle of an ongoing conversation between Carol and her friend. Exactly what they are talking about is unclear, other than that it involves the death of a relative. The tone of discussion is flat and unemotional, an absence of affect symbolized by the glaring white kitchen in which the encounter takes place and a shift after two medium-long shots to a more withdrawn perspective that situates the two women as part of this cold and emotionally sterile environment. A similar sense of individuals dominated by their surroundings, a formal embodiment of the principal theme of the film, is created in the following scene, in which Carol arrives home. A wide shot is presented of one of the seating areas in her modern-palatial open-plan house, very square-on and with a symmetrical composition of furniture. Carol appears in the right-hand margin of the frame, in the kitchen area and subsequently answering the phone. The shot is held throughout, the camera refusing to privilege the character. The character herself has to move towards the camera, rather than vice versa, to be given more prominence of scale in the image.

   Carol's state of disjunction from her everyday surroundings is also given visual correlative by the use of zoom-dollies, in which an impression of disorientation is created through the simultaneous movement forward of the camera and zooming out of the lens. The effect is to maintain much the same content within the frame (the camera moves forward at the same pace as the zoom moves out) but to shift the depth of field, the result of the change in focal length of the lens. This technique is used to mark two significant occasions in the development of her condition, moments at which her own home becomes no longer a place of safety and security. The way the zoom-dolly is used here is a good example of the difference between the use of such devices in Hollywood and the independent sector. Alfred Hitchcock is usually credited with the invention of the technique, used to create an impression of vertigo in the film of that title. It was also used by Steven Spielberg at a moment of crisis in *Jaws*, and has since become a familiar device used to create impressions of weirdness or disorientation in mainstream cinema. What is different about Haynes' use of the zoom-dolly in *Safe* is the subtlety with which it is wielded. In Hollywood, it is usually used to create a yawning shift of perspective that is clearly noticeable, even if the means through which the effect is created may not be familiar to most filmgoers. In *Safe*, neither the zoom nor the dolly is very pronounced. The precise extent to which the camera moves and the length of the lens changes is not easy to detect, even on close viewing. The impact is not sharp and overt, but quietly dislocating, much like the experience of the central character. A similar sense of subtle dislocation is found in Paul Thomas Anderson's third feature, *Punch-Drunk Love* (2002), a distinctly indie New Line production that gained studio distribution by Columbia on the basis of its star central performer. Wide angles and long shots are used to emphasize the uncomfortable distance created between the viewer and a central character, Barry (Adam Sandler), who seems slightly but consistently unhinged, occupying an awkward space between what would conventionally be understood as either 'normality' or complete 'abnormality'. In one sequence, which begins with Barry characteristically caught in a frame-within-the-frame, between two side walls of his kitchen, the warped perspective of the film is figured literally, the vertical lines starting to bow just slightly as the camera moves in closer.

More temporary states of heightened consciousness can also be suggested by the use of expressive formal devices, most commonly those associated with the taking of drugs, a relatively frequent marker of the alternative worlds explored in independent cinema. In *Pi*, Darren Aronofsky uses a repeated combination of rapid shots each time Max takes the drugs used to keep his terrible headaches at bay. This device is extended to become the central aesthetic principle of his next film, *Requiem for a Dream* (2000), based on the novel by Hubert Selby Jr. Blink-rapidly cut montages, the precise contents of which can sometimes be grasped only subliminally at full speed, are used throughout the film to create an impression of the experience of drug-taking. Shooting-up heroin is signified in the following fleeting images: teeth ripping open a package/a particle of substance viewed under a microscope/a lighter flame/bubbling liquid/syringe-filling/ iris-expanding/ripping open again/a splash of liquid in what appears to be a bottle top/depression of syringe/internal view of flowing blood cells. From single montages of this kind – the contents varied depending on the drug and method of ingestion – *Requiem for a Dream* builds a complex texture of intercut montages. Drug-taking moves on to drug-dealing, for example, as the central character Harry (Jared Leto) and his partner Ty (Marlon Wayans) go into business for themselves.

Into this mix, as the film progresses, is added the drug-taking experience of Harry's TV-addict mother, Sara (Ellen Burstyn). From a brief repeated montage of remote-control-grabbing/on-button-hitting, used to mark the moments when she takes her favourite plug-in drug, Sara becomes integrated into the film's montages of chemical-based abuse, resorting to an array of drugs prescribed by an unscrupulous doctor in her attempt to lose weight in readiness for her desperately anticipated appearance as a TV game-show contestant. She gets her own rapid-montage sequences, comprised of pill-swilling, obsessively being weighed, checking her mail for anything from the TV station, making coffee and being plagued by images of food-related fantasy. It is in this formal dimension, building towards the close intercutting of sequences related to the experiences of mother and son, that the film most effectively makes its case about the comparable nature of addictions located on either side of the legal divide: the use of outlawed substances and potentially damaging dependence on licensed palliatives such as television and prescribed drugs. As the initial impact wears off and Sara ups her own dose of pills, her perspective is figured in an increasingly skewed manner, including the use of an extremely wide, fish-eye lens that at one stage, when she turns inwards towards the camera, distorts her face to monstrous proportions. In the film's latter stages, charting the rapid downward spiral and final detachment from normal reality of all the main characters, Aronofsky employs devices similar to those used in *Pi*, including shifts in the relative speed of action occurring in the same frame (Sara's speech seeming slightly slower than normal while her doctor's words and movement are sped up to cartoonish dimensions; moving slowly on the street, while others buzz past in a blur) and the Snorri-cam, employed in the case of an increasingly frazzled Sara, in the final stages before her admission to hospital and ECT treatment, and Harry's girlfriend, reduced to sexual degradation in return for money and drugs.

Subjective experience provides a major point of anchorage for the uses of expressive formal devices detailed above, but it does not always entirely contain the dimensions of experience signified in these ways. The disorienting or disjunctive qualities created through departures from more familiar varieties of cinematography or editing can also leak outwards, starting sometimes from expressions of individual consciousness but coming to create a more general impression of upsetting the normal textures of the world on-screen. This is one marker of the distinction between the use of such devices in and outside the commercial mainstream. In the mainstream, in general, unless some other very specific motivation is provided, it is more likely that unconventional devices will be restricted to the expression of individual consciousness or experience. In the independent sector, more scope is available for the extension of such strategies. The reason for this is quite simple. Production in the Hollywood mainstream usually aims to avoid unsettling audiences to any great extent. Hollywood cinema tends to be affirmative, ultimately, even when it deals in darker or more serious material, and especially at the basic level of film form, in establishing a broadly comfortable and familiar position from which to experience the subject matter of any individual feature. Part of the advertised appeal of independent cinema is a move away from the Hollywood approach, if only relative, in both content and form, in which viewers are likely to expect or accept the more general use of less familiar expressive techniques. Devices that have some grounding in the subjectivity of character but that are also used more widely in the creation of a fictional world are an effective way of bridging the gap between the mainstream – in which unconventional devices generally require clearer and more fixed motivation – and more avowedly avant-garde or experimental films, in which the whole point might be to use the language of cinema in new ways that are not so easily contained.

On closer inspection of *Julien Donkey-Boy*, for example, it becomes clear that the expressive devices examined above are not used exclusively in relation to Julien himself. Sequences of stills featuring both Pearl and Chris are presented in scenes in which Julien plays no part and is not present as witness. Jump-cuts are also used in scenes in which Julien does not figure, including a highly telegraphic sequence in which Chris climbs up and down the stairs of the family home, part of the exercise regime in which he is encouraged by the crazed father. And the latter features in one of the more avant-garde scenes, in which he talks (rambling characteristically, in this case starting on about an international championship of talking birds) in a scratchy voice-over accompanied by a hypnotic ticking sound and discordant music, to images of Pearl cutting his hair. Sequences such as these are part of the overall aesthetic of the film itself, combined with its moments of *vérité*-style hand-held camerawork, rather than just an expression of the title character. They are grounded in the psyche of Julien to a significant extent, however, and it is not uncommon for subjective states to be signified in ways that go beyond sounds or images that are presented in a more or less directly subjective manner (relatively few images in *Julien Donkey-Boy* are offered as immediately subjective, point-of-view shots, one example being Julien's experience in the confessional, the grill of which is mostly obscured by blackness that appears to signify his own hands held in front of his eyes). It is a familiar convention to accept, as broadly subjective, perspectives generally *associated with* or taken from *close to* those of character, especially if the effect is heightened by devices such as those discussed in relation to *Julien Donkey-Boy* and the other examples examined above. *Julien Donkey-Boy* would certainly be a very different, and formally more radical, film if presented in the same mode without the presence of a central character with a clearly established state of psychological disjunction that motivates in large part, if not entirely, the form in which it is presented.

A similar leakage from lead-character subjectivity into the unsettling texture of a wider fictional world is found in *Buffalo 66*, although in this case it might be contained in terms of collective loopiness. The most unconventional device used here involves the perspective of all four characters in the central movement of the film, in which the somewhat unhinged Billy has randomly kidnapped a young woman, Layla (Christina Ricci), and ordered her to pose as his wife while he visits his parents, to maintain his charade of having a normal and successful life. Director-star Vincent Gallo plays precisely with assumptions about individual point of view and the extent to which it is mapped onto the perspective taken by the camera. He makes unusual use of direct point-of-view shots in sequences around the dining table, in a manner that is odd and more than a little disorienting. When the foursome sits down, before dinner, we are initially given a three-shot looking across the table from one side: Billy is on the far side from that of the camera, his mother and father sitting opposite one another. This could be any ordinary 'objective' shot, but proves to be the perspective of Layla. A quick fade-to-black, and it is replaced by the mother's perspective (the father at the far end, Billy and Layla at opposites). And so on, until all four perspectives have been given. This is a very unconventional usage, directly first-person perspectives being not only relatively rare in themselves, but usually restricted to the viewpoint of a single central figure rather than each member of a group in turn. An uncomfortable silence reigns over the scene – until the mother, Janet (Angelica Houston), speaks in the last set-up in the series – giving the sequence an expressive function, forcing the viewer into the awkward position of each character in turn.

No sooner has Gallo accustomed us to this unconventional approach, however, than he plays around with our expectations. Layla gets up from the table to go to the bathroom, followed by the same three-shot with which the previous sequence began. The shot is much the same, but its location has shifted, into the objective and impersonal realm. A curious gap also exists within the subjective point-of-view shots. For most of the time, all of the characters have their arms resting on the tabletop in one way or another. When we get the first-person perspectives, however, nothing is present immediately before the camera to suggest the arms of the occupant of the viewpoint. The camera position also seems slightly withdrawn, a little farther back from the table than would be the case in the seated position indicated in other shots. This disjunction becomes more explicit in the subsequent sequence in which dinner is served and no plate or any other utensil is ever visible on the table in front of the individual from whose position we are viewing the proceedings, although they are clearly present from the other perspectives. A strange sense of discontinuity is created and another example of dislocation, as if each character becomes disembodied and physically absent, a symptom perhaps of their alienation from one another. Each lives in a very different world of their own making, that of Layla being the only one not clearly established as a realm of self-obsessed derangement.

Some of the films of David Lynch offer further examples in which it is not always clear how far the effects of unconventional and unsettling formal strategies are meant to suggest qualities grounded in the experience of individual characters or the texture of the wider fictional world. *Lost Highway* uses a number of devices to convey the strangely menacing atmosphere of the modern house occupied by Fred and Renee Madison in the first act. Wide-angle lenses, sometimes shooting from higher than usual camera positions, are used to create an impression of slight disorientation, also serving to emphasize the placement of the characters in – and their dominance by – the cool, modernist surroundings, much as was seen in *Safe*. A prowling camera, accompanied by dark music and sound design, creates the impression of a sinister presence in the building. At one point, the location of this kind of perspective seems to shift, disturbingly, in mid sequence. Fred and Renee have just returned home from a party during which the former has a bizarre encounter with a strange man who appears to be present both at the party, standing before Fred, and simultaneously at the Madison house, where he is able to answer Fred's phone call. The camera starts by taking on Fred's point of view, as indicated by shots that tie it to his look in one direction and then another. It then swings around through an arc and moves menacingly in *towards* the character, the dark musical accompaniment being joined by an indistinct distorted vocal sound that implies some kind of threatening disembodied presence (possibly figuring another version of his own self, given the strong theme of doubling that develops as the film progresses).

In some cases, the bizarre experiences of the Lynch universe are conveyed through more conventional styles of shooting and editing, as is generally the case in his debut feature, *Eraserhead*. Most of *Eraserhead* is shot and edited quite conventionally. So strange and nightmarish are the events depicted, that little in the way of specifically formal experimentation is needed to heighten their impact. Quite the opposite tends to be the case. In one (dream?) sequence the title character, Henry (Jack Nance), loses his head. It falls through a strange gap in space and is picked up by a boy who takes it to a workshop where a core sample is taken to establish the suitability of the material to be turned into pencil erasers. All of this is expressed in conventional cinematic grammar: normal continuity, directional matches and matches of scale from one shot to the next; nothing very striking in the positioning of the camera or the kind of image quality produced. The bland, ordinary nature of the style, here and in many other parts of the film, underlines the bizarre nature of the material: to present the weird normally is, potentially, more disturbing than resorting to a panoply of special visual effects.

The same can be said of *Mulholland Drive*. The bulk of the film is shot in a relatively inconspicuous and classical style, its dark mood created largely through music and other aspects of Lynch's sound design. If, as one of the most popular readings of the film has it, most of the proceedings appear by the end to have been the dream–fantasy of one of the central characters, it might have made sense to have shot and edited mostly straightforwardly, to avoid giving the game away. Alternatively, the relatively conventional style, without strong visual signals of dream–fantasy or altered consciousness, enables us to keep our options open as to which parts are and are not meant to be real (returning to the pragmatic dimension considered in the previous chapter, much might have been shot in a particular style, as the original pilot, without the possibility that it would all turn out to have been a dream having been in play at the time). Some localized sequences *are* presented in a heightened manner that invites us more immediately to consider whether they are the stuff of dream or nightmare. In one case, which starts with both characters asleep, Betty/Diane and Rita/Camilla embark on a 2 a.m. visit to a strange club. As they enter a cab, on their way, a mobile camera moves towards them, the image blurring and dissolving into an abstract pattern of unfocused lights. During the journey, the view out of the side windows appears to move a little faster and more unsteadily than would seem to be realistically motivated. When they arrive, the degree of stylization is increased: a low-angle view is given of the cab, from a distance, the parking lot foreground filled with wind-blown litter. The camera then moves fast and low up to the door, a manoeuvre associated with threatening presence in horror films, a distant roar on the soundtrack gaining volume and darker shades. Inside, among other oddities, comes the claim of a magician-type performer that the show is all an illusion.

But this is a relatively rare example of such heightened cinematic grammar in *Mulholland Drive*. Equally effective is the opposite strategy: the use of transparently familiar devices to increase the unsettling nature of shifts between dimensions of reality. In the latter part of the film, we are presented with Betty-now-as-Diane, looking dowdy and depressed in her apartment. She makes coffee. The camera follows closely behind her body, dressed in a dull grey robe, as she carries her cup towards a sofa. She moves out of frame to the left as the camera rises to reveal Camilla lying seductively on the sofa, dressed only in skimpy briefs. A routine cut shifts the angle something more than 90 degrees to a position where we can still see Camilla and look back over the sofa towards Diane. The straightforward and inconspicuous nature of the cut, in formal terms, increases the jolt created by the fact that the Diane who climbs jauntily over the sofa-back is transformed into her previously more glamorous look, garbed only in a pair of denim shorts, the camera moving in to emphasize the detail that her coffee cup has changed into a glass of whiskey.

Relatively small touches – in camerawork, editing, framing, lighting or processing effects – can signify the 'quirkiness', the slight shift from the norm, often associated with indie films. In a carefully orchestrated single-shot sequence that introduces us to various characters at the school attended by the protagonist of the tragi-comic coming-of-age feature *Donnie Darko* (2001), for example, the on-screen action speeds up at two moments, each giving an absurd and somewhat cartoonish impression to the movements of a teacher. The effect is showy, a quality considered in more detail generally below, but can also be given potential motivation. At first, it seems, the device can be understood as indicating the different planes of existence occupied by students and teachers. With the development of the narrative, however, which includes a dimension that invokes the possibility of time travel, the temporal disjunction manifested by the effect might have deeper resonance.

It is not only in the creation of darker and more disturbing effects that shifts from the stylistic norm can be used to expressive effect. The offbeat character of Wes Anderson's first feature, the quirky character-centred comedy *Bottle Rocket* (produced and distributed by Columbia, but very indie-like in style), is established in the visual realm through the decision to shoot the whole film with a 27mm lens. Conventional practice is to use longer lenses with shallower depth-of-field in close-ups, to focus on the plane in which the characters are located. The use of a shorter, wide-angle lens creates a slight distortion of figure, and in the relationship between figure and background, when characters are positioned close to the camera. While disturbing in the context of the sinister spaces of *Lost Highway*, this effect underlines the off-centre nature of the low-key comedy of *Bottle Rocket*, a film in which a hapless would-be criminal trio embarks on unlikely enterprises such as raids on a bookstore and a cold storage depot. Quick and snappy editing contributes towards the effect, as in a sequence in which the three try out a gun before buying from a dealer. A montage presents the arm of each character with the gun in hand, jump-cutting from one to another to a jaunty soundtrack theme, the off-hand levity of the style creating a comic incongruity between the mode of presentation and the potentially serious nature of what they are doing. Subsequent shots emphasize the wide-angle effect, presenting one character half-figure in the foreground and others in the background. The others are not far away, but the lens reduces them disproportionately in stature, to a fraction of the size of the character in the foreground, a quirky impression resulting from the imbalance between this and the conventions of visual perspective with which we are more familiar. A similar effect is created in a number of sequences in David O. Russell's post-Gulf-war action-comedy *Three Kings* (1999), a film much more mainstream in budgeting, star line-up and general industrial location but which uses a range of indie-worthy unconventional formal devices.

In *Bottle Rocket*, the off-beat visual quality seems most appropriate to the character of the naïve, highly strung loveable loser Dignan (Owen Wilson), the architect of the schemes into which he drags or cajoles the others. Wide-angle images of Dignan, close to the camera, give an effective impression of the world as skewed from his perspective. The same visual approach is also used with the other main characters, however, including the more balanced and quietly earnest Anthony (Luke Wilson). His character is also quirky, conducting a romance with a motel chambermaid, for example, that begins with him following her on her rounds, but the visual style seems less specifically attuned to his less solipsistic persona. A different approach could have been used, in which the wide-angle strategy was applied specifically and only in the case of Dignan, confining it to an expression of character. Instead, as in some of the other examples considered above, it is applied more generally, a perspective of most direct relevance to one individual outlook providing anchorage for the shaping of an entire fictional universe.

A good example of the transition between the general and more specific location of images of unconventional quality – of a particularly low-budget, indie nature – is found in two films by Michael Almereyda: *Another Girl Another Planet* and *Nadja* (1994). Both films make use of the murky 'pixelvision' images produced by Almereyda's toy Fisher-Price PXL camera. The former is shot entirely in pixelvision, giving a strange dreamy quality, not very specifically motivated, to a story of the relationship between a couple and their womanizing neighbour. The images are somewhat vague and indistinct, as if shot underwater, figuring possibly the lack of focus in the lives of the characters. *Nadja* is comprised of a mixture of pixelvision and more conventional black-and-white cinematography. In this case, a modern setting of the Dracula story, pixelvision is given a strong measure of motivation through its use in association with the perspective of the central character, the daughter of the vampire. We are first taken into pixelvision in an early sequence, ending in the obligatory neck-biting scenario, in which Nadja (Elina Löwensohn) makes love with a man she has picked up in a bar. Normal footage is resumed until the next vampiric encounter, in which Nadja engages amorously with one of the principals, Lucy (Galaxy Craze). A clear pattern is established. It is complicated somewhat in the second half of the film but, in general, pixelvision is associated with sequences of more explicitly vampire-related action, although in no case is this presented as a directly subjective impression of the world as actually seen through vampire eyes. The use of pixelvision in *Nadja* is, in this sense, less radical or experimental-seeming, because it is more clearly motivated, than is the case in *Another Girl Another Planet*, even if the image-texture of the latter has to be considered to be the product at least in part of economic exigencies.

Foregrounding Form

Unconventional formal devices such as the wide-angle perspective of *Bottle Rocket* can create subtle effects of difference from the norm, effects that play an important part in the constitution of the quirky or offbeat character of indie films. They are often likely to go unrecognized in themselves, contributing to a sense of difference that remains intangible. In some cases, departures from the norm are more overt and noticeable, calling attention to the formal dimension in itself (the line between relatively visible or invisible strategies is not clear-cut, however, its precise location depending in part on the variable perspective of the viewer). This is a practice with a long history in the production of artistic and cultural materials, particularly associated with work in the modernist tradition, in which a great deal of emphasis is often placed on the foregrounding of the forms and materiality of the medium of use. Much avant-garde and experimental cinema can be included in this category, as can some productions that straddle the gap between the experimental and the more conventional-accessible end of the independent spectrum. The foregrounding of form can also be a way of 'showing off', of demonstrating the capabilities of the medium, or often more importantly the creative skills of the filmmakers, in a manner that is more easily integrated into commercially viable parts of the independent sector.

One strain in the American avant-garde of the 1960s and early 1970s was a shift towards an extreme focus on the materiality of the medium, shorn of any substantial concern with issues of narrative or representation. Structural filmmaking, as it became known, emphasised basic qualities of film or of the filmmaking apparatus.[13] In Tony Conrad's *The Flicker* (1966), for example, the entire film content consists of the flickering alternation of single-frame fields of black and white leader. One sub-genre of structural film is organized around basic cinematic techniques such as the pan and the zoom. The former is the structuring principle of Michael Snow's *Back and Forth* (1969), the latter the basis of the best-known work of the movement, Snow's *Wavelength* (1967). *Wavelength* consists of a number of shots cut together, with various changes of stock and filters, to create the impression of one long zoom, lasting 45 minutes, across the space of a New York apartment room. A plot of sorts is enunciated, but only in the margins. Midway through the film, a man staggers into the room and falls to the ground, apparently dead. Rather than stopping to examine this action in any detail, the camera relentlessly continues its zoom, the figure gradually being eliminated from the lower edge of the frame. Towards the end, a woman enters and phones to tell someone about the presence of the body, the call visible only because the phone is located by the wall towards which the camera is pointed. The zoom continues, finally closing in on a photograph of waves fixed to the wall.

This is a particularly interesting example because it is not entirely abstract, but subordinates potentially dramatic material to pre-set and foregrounded formal parameters. The ground between formal abstraction and relatively more conventional narrative-feature-based American independent cinema is quite sparsely populated. In the great majority of cases, formal departures are contained, in whole or part, by the kinds of motivations considered above, especially through the expression of subjectivity. More radical examples are few and far between, largely for economic reasons. The cost of staging character- and narrative-centred events at feature length is such that larger audiences usually need to be targeted, even in the independent sector, than those capable of sustaining outright experiment. One notable exception is the work of Jon Jost, writer, director and editor of a number of films that straddle the line between avant-garde abstraction and more costly narrative-feature production. Jost's films depart in numerous formal respects from the conventional-Hollywood style, and that of most independent features. Motivations for their departures can be identified, thematic motivations and those related to the experience of central characters (the two often linked), as in many products of the heyday of European art cinema in the later 1950s and 1960s, via a pervading sense of disconnection and alienation. Formally, however, they go much further from the Hollywood norm than anything else considered so far in this chapter, with the possible exception of *Julien Donkey-Boy*.

In narrative terms, Jost's films are leisurely and contemplative in style, employing a rhythm very different from anything usually found in the mainstream. Events build slowly and obliquely, the attention of the camera often drifting away from what appears to be the central narrative core. *The Bed You Sleep In* (1993), for example, centres on a crisis in the life of Ray (Tom Blair), whose lumber mill is running into economic difficulty just as his domestic existence is about to be shattered by accusations of childhood sexual abuse from his daughter. The film is focused around and builds to a climax based on these issues, but it also dwells repeatedly on what would conventionally appear to be peripheral material. Where a Hollywood feature would offer a few establishing shots of the work of the mill, in the background or for occasional dramatic emphasis, *The Bed You Sleep In* returns persistently to quite extended sequences in which various aspects of its workings are witnessed. Similarly, when Ray goes fishing, the camera moves beyond the central figure, panning slowly across the flowing water for much longer than would be expected in a more conventional feature, in which such a move might be made briefly to establish the tranquillity of the scene; this is another image repeated on several occasions during the film. In some cases in this film, and in others, sequences such as these are extended further, to a point at which they approach the abstract. In *The Bed You Sleep In*, the camera enacts a series of movements through a café, starting with a slow pan along part of a counter that ends with a perspective looking through a door into the kitchen. By itself, this could be a conventional establishing shot, leading us to the point at which the action of the scene is to ensue. Instead, the movement continues, back along the other side of the counter, developing into a pan around the main seating area and a slow track along a line of tables. This is followed by a further movement, along another section of counter, another pan and a return to the starting point: an unusually elaborate and extended sequence, accompanied by ambient music and background noise, most of which is then repeated again, the entire sequence lasting some five minutes.

No immediate narrative purpose is served by this sequence, or many others during the film, including numerous shots of different buildings in the Pacific Northwest community in which it is set. What is offered instead is a sense of the mood and texture of the place, as something that has an existence beyond the confines of the central narrative thread. If the lumber mill and the jobs of its employees are threatened by closure, this is not presented as merely a device of plot or character, adding to the pressures faced by Ray. A sense is developed, instead, of the materiality of the mill and its work, as a presence that remains in the foreground rather than being relegated to the status of an entirely subordinate function of plot or atmospherics. In Jost's version of a road movie, *Frameup* (1993), one of many extended reveries by the central characters comes towards the end, when the extraordinarily dull Beth-Ann (Nancy Carlin) drones on and on (and on and on!), mouthing banalities about the magnificence of the Californian redwood while the camera performs a very long low movement looking up at the dark trees silhouetted against the sky. Eventually, the colour of the trees becomes distorted into an almost abstract pattern of orange against vivid blue, an image very similar to an extended sequence in *Sure Fire* (1990), in which the colours are more naturalistic, an autumnal golden–orange against the blue skies that feature in the rest of the film.

Conventional framing and editing regimes are frequently abandoned or undermined. A characteristic Jost composition in dialogue sequences is to hold one individual flatly in frame from the side, facing off-screen towards an interlocutor, denying the viewer the usual cut or pan to a reaction shot of the other, whose identity is not always at first clear. When framed together, characters often face away from each other and/or are separated in other ways. In *Sure Fire*, the lack of real connection between two women is suggested by alternately framing one close to the camera and the other facing away, in the background. In some cases the camera lingers, conspicuously, after characters depart from the frame, as at one moment in *Sure Fire* when the authoritarian father Wes (Tom Blair) has been talking to his son, the latter playing out of view on a trampoline: Wes walks out, leaving an empty composition and just the continuing squeak of the trampoline. The meeting of the central couple in *Frameup* is presented in an extraordinarily disconnected style in which neither character is visible apart from their hands: a directly overhead shot focused down onto the section of the coffee-shop counter across which Beth-Ann serves Ricky-Lee (Howard Swain). Alternating monologues constitute one of the basic aesthetics through which the film maintains the sense that each occupies a largely separate universe.

The unconscious familiarity of continuity editing, and the effortless access it appears to grant viewers to events on-screen, makes it one of the most potent domains in which to create alternative and disjunctive effects. Maintaining continuity in one dimension while upsetting it in another is a strategy used by Jost in a number of instances. Continuity of sound is sometimes maintained while that of image is disrupted. In *All the Vermeers in New York* (1990), for example, we see one of the central characters, Anna (Emmanuel Chaulet), coming through a door. The door opens towards the camera and she walks in, and then past the camera out of frame. Cut to a door opening again and the action is repeated, twice, and it becomes clear from the background that it is the same door each time. The action is repeated, in the kind of loop-sequence associated with more abstract works of the avant-garde, fracturing conventional expectations that it will move forward unless there is a strongly motivated reason otherwise (which is not the case in this passing moment), while the background sound, a flatmate's vocal exercises, continues unbroken. A more overt example occurs in *Frameup*. The two principals, each framed standing against a wall, undertake a conversation, a relatively rare quantity in their relationship. The dialogue is sustained on the soundtrack, across a series of discontinuous cuts from one to the other. In each image, the attire of the characters and the décor of the wall is changed, undermining the sense created on the soundtrack of an exchange that exists in the same time and space.

A similar strategy is used in a less marginal part of the independent landscape in *The Limey* (1999), a revenge thriller directed by Steven Soderbergh that offers a useful point of comparison with the work of Jost. Continuity of sound, especially dialogue, is maintained in numerous sequences in which the images suggest spatial and temporal discontinuity. Cuts are made, repeatedly, backwards and forwards in time, between different conversations in which the same threads of discussion appear to be followed. In one example the central character, Wilson (Terrence Stamp), a cockney ex-con seeking to track down the killers of his daughter, is talking to one of her former friends, Elaine (Lesley Ann Warren). The scene keeps switching between two locations: Elaine's home and a nearby waterfront. Continuity of dialogue exists on a word-by-word basis in some parts of this sequence, directly across the non-continuity of location. Wilson, in the waterfront location, says his daughter, Jenny, was always embarrassed by him; 'not embarrassed', replies Elaine. Cut to her home, where Wilson, appearing to follow directly from her interjection, offers 'ashamed'; 'not ashamed' counters Elaine. Cut back to the waterfront, and she adds: 'disappointed', the intonation strongly implying that the two words are part of the same utterance.

This is a radical undermining of continuity conventions. The sequence cannot easily be resolved without an abandonment of the strong expectation that closely continuous face-to-face dialogue has to exist in the same space and time. It is not unusual in the mainstream for a single impression of dialogue continuation to occur across a cut from one scene to the next, in the interests of both slick continuity and narrative economy. But that is not what happens here, where the result is a considerable impression of disorientation for the viewer. Flash-forward insertions are also used in *The Limey*, cuts to moments located later in the narrative sequence, another substantial breach of conventional editing regimes. To flash forward, showing detail for which the viewer has not yet fully been prepared, is to undermine basic conventions of classical narrative progression and editing structure. Motivation for this strategy can be found in *The Limey*, figuring a sense of destiny or fate in the unfolding of events and the determination of Wilson to exact his vengeance. Soderbergh plays with any such expectation established during the early stages of the film, however. In one sequence, Wilson invades a party in the fancy Hollywood hills home of his target, the music promoter Terry Valentine (Peter Fonda). Wilson stands outside, by the pool, staring at Valentine. Cut to Wilson framed from the front, walking, slowly but purposefully, inside. Cut back to the previous shot: his head and shoulders, the stare. Cut inside, Wilson's point-of-view, gliding across the room, followed by a return to the shot that frames his movement from the front. Cut to mid-body shot, as he starts to pull a gun from his waistband. Cut to oblique very low angle as he lifts the weapon clear and points it. Cut back a moment in time, for emphasis, to a side angle of the gun being raised and aimed. Cut back to Wilson outside: a closer shot of his head, the stare continuing. Back inside, camera on Wilson from the front, repeating for a second time the movement in which he raises and aims the gun. Cut to point-of-view shot looking at Valentine, back to Wilson three-quarters from the front as he fires, and back to Valentine as the bullet impacts his chest. We then return to a head-and-shoulders framing of Wilson outside, and watch him walk off alongside the pool towards the building.

At this point, we are liable to read the previous sequences as a flash-forward to the action that is now about to happen. We now get a more complete view of Wilson walking inside followed by the shooting sequence much as before, although without any cuts back to his figure outside. The impression is that the previously witnessed action is now happening in the present tense. Except the outcome is different, Wilson's shot only catching Valentine in the elbow. Cut to Wilson entering again. This time the sequence is coded as more 'real'; party background noise is clear and sharp, emphasizing the extent to which it had previously been muffled. The implication is that the first two versions were works of Wilson's imagination. This time Valentine is shot in the head. But then we cut immediately to a shot in which Valentine is still intact, and to Wilson approaching but being headed off by his helper Ed (Luis Guzman). All three versions of the shooting prove to have been subjective fantasies, but during the sequence the viewer is constantly asked to interpret and reinterpret the status of the action as it unfolds. The temporal location of some textual detail is shifted from start to end of the film. The opening line, Wilson's 'tell me about Jenny', spoken against a black screen, turns out to be a long flash-forward to the question he puts to Valentine in the final showdown. A repeated image of Wilson on a plane, shown from early in the proceedings and assumed to be during his journey from London to Los Angeles appears, by the end, to have been a flash-forward to his return home. The implication, in retrospect, is that much of the unconventional treatment of time and space is the product of his subjective reconstruction of the experience. Further character-based motivation for the strategy of temporal dislocation is suggested in what Wilson reveals to have been the disjunctive nature of his relationship with his daughter, broken by long stretches of imprisonment. Motivation can also be found for many of the unconventional devices found in the work of Jost, in the alienation of characters, the fractured state of relationships and attempts to situate individuals within broader landscapes, both urban and rural.

The Limey remains a more conventional work than that of Jost, for a number of reasons, including the glossy, higher-production-value nature of its cinematography (35mm, compared with the 16mm used by Jost) and its use of stars such as Terrence Stamp and Peter Fonda. Its departures from classical continuity patterns are of substance, but they are also contained to a greater extent by a more conventional, fast-paced Hollywood-style narrative frame. Our attention might be drawn to the use of unusual formal devices, but probably less so than in the films of Jost. The breaks in continuity in The Limey are striking and can be disorienting, but that is partly a function of their fleeting quality, rarely providing enough time for the viewer to unpick or reflect on the precise nature of the less conventionally constructed material. The foregrounding of formal qualities in Jost is partly a function of the extended nature of many of the unconventional devices. Unusual framing of character tends to be held much longer than in the examples considered in the previous section, for example, where it is more likely to be used briefly, to create passing impressions of states of mind. With extension in time comes more attention to the formal qualities in themselves and their difference from the norm. When conventional expectations are frustrated in a sustained manner, a gap is liable to be opened, an awareness of formal mechanisms that usually remain beneath the level of attention. Framing, when held in unfamiliar positions, becomes visible as an effect. Expressive sequences also persist in the films of Jost, often for minutes at a time, gaining a momentum of their own that extends beyond anything motivated by narrative material. Their prominence, as departures from the mainstream norm, is again likely to provoke viewer consciousness of the process itself, as is also the case in the extremely long-held shots in the work of Andy Warhol.

The seemingly endless movement around the café in *The Bed You Sleep In* might establish a sense of some of the broader texture of the diegetic universe, but it is also to some extent *about* the way the camera can explore a space, the integration within the spaces of a narrative feature of something closer to the kind of formal practice manifested in Snow's *Wavelength* and some other structural films. The same might be said of the undermining of continuity in the sequence cited above from *Frameup*. It serves a narrative purpose, along with other devices, in expressing the state of the character relationship. But it is also a demonstration of the way continuity can be both created, cinematically, in this case in the domain of sound, and how it can be undermined. Camera movement and framing in Jost is not always subordinate to the dominant rhythms of the action unfolding in the fictional world. A subtle example from *All the Vermeers in New York* seems to combine an element of the aesthetic of Snow's *Back and Forth* with a more conventional dialogue scene. The camera pans slowly back and forth between the two main characters, Anna and Mark (Stephen Lack), for nearly five minutes during a significant series of exchanges in which he suggests she should move in with him and she asks for what seems an excessive sum of money to help her with her rent. At times, the movement of the camera seems to be attuned to the shifts in importance of who is speaking and who reacting. But this does not always appear to be the case, the almost unbroken series of pans (there are a couple of brief pauses, on Anna) seeming also to have the autonomy of its own formal logic.

What happens in the work of Jost is a shift in the hierarchy that usually exists between the dimensions of film style and narrative-related content. The norm in the classical Hollywood variety is for the former to be subordinated to the latter. Formal devices serve narrative and related purposes, and are not generally meant to claim attention in themselves. If some independent features exhibit the qualities of art-cinema narration described by David Bordwell, as suggested in the previous chapter, the work of Jost extends towards what Bordwell terms poetic or 'parametric' narration, 'in which the film's stylistic system creates patterns *distinct from the demands of the syuzhet system*'.[14] In such cases:'Film style may be organized and emphasized to a degree that makes it at least equal in importance to syuzhet patterns.'[15] Where exactly the lines are drawn between these different categories is open to debate, but they offer a useful framework within which to locate the degree to which style comes to prominence in its own right, alongside or sometimes displacing its role in the service of narrative, character subjectivity or thematics. A film such as Snow's *Wavelength* would clearly be an example of the parametric. As Bordwell suggests, the relative importance of narrative-related and more purely stylistic processes can vary not only between films, and broader categories of films, but also within individual examples. The latter often seems to be the case with Jost, whose films move between passages in which the distinctive stylistic dimension is more or less overtly in the forefront.

The same can also be said of some better-known independent features, including Jarmusch's *Stranger Than Paradise*, the stylized deadpan effect of which is created partly through the use of lengthy sequences during which the camera often remains fixed and static. Style is foregrounded to a significant extent in an example such as this, although not in a rigid structuralist manner – the camera also tilts and pans quite often and framing privileges the important action, such as it is, rather than serving its own ends – or with the degree of departure from more conventional forms found in the films of Jost. A distinctively 'arty' and unconventional stylistic parameter is one of the organizing principles of the film, as is also the case in *The Limey*. Another notable example is Gus Van Sant's *Gerry* (2002), which comes as close to Jost in its near avant-garde foregrounding of form as any recent feature-length product of the commercially distributed independent sector. The film traces the experience of two characters (Matt Damon and Casey Affleck) who become lost in the scrub, mountain and desert landscapes of an unspecified American wilderness. Narrative development is minimal, beyond what appears to be a deliberately arbitrary and unconvincing process in which the pair manage to lose their way after setting out on a wilderness trail to visit a location named only as 'the thing'. They walk around in the heat and engage in a few desultory conversations before one eventually strangles the other and is rescued shortly afterwards by a passing car. The film unfolds in a series of temporally extended shots, an approach inspired by the work of directors such as the Hungarian Bela Tarr and Chantal Akerman. Style is motivated largely by content. The duration of shots in which little happens creates an impression of what might be the real experience of being lost in the middle of nowhere. In one case, the faces of the two characters are framed closely in the shot, bobbing up and down with motion, as they trudge and trudge and trudge and trudge and trudge, seemingly endlessly. The proximity of camera and the holding of the shot for several minutes, combined with a relatively loud sound mix of their footsteps crunching through the sand, create a strong evocation of presence for the viewer, an impression of sharing the experience in something closer to its real duration than formal convention would normally encourage. After a while, however, sound/image combinations such as this come to seem increasingly stylized, formal and abstract – both individually and in the cumulation of sequences as the film unfolds – making the viewer conscious of *cinematic* as much as character-experiential duration.

A similar strategy is used, although veering less towards the abstract, in Van Sant's next film, *Elephant* (2003), inspired by the Columbine and other school shootings. Extended tracking shots, the film's dominant aesthetic, follow the movements of a number of students through corridors and other spaces on an ordinary-seeming day that turns suddenly to under-motivated violence. The viewer is kept both in close physical proximity to characters – as if following their progress, documentary-style – and at a distance, deprived of the brand of emotional intimacy orchestrated in more conventionally Hollywood-fictional découpage. The film has a flatness of texture, a deliberate withholding of any facile attempt to provide an 'explanation' or emotional/interiorized grounding for the extreme violence to which two pupils resort (the only real exception is a moment in which a sense of oppression is implied, in the case of the ringleader, by a heightened volume of background noise in the school cafeteria). The

8. Prelude to a massacre (blame Beethoven?): Alex (Alex Frost), one of the killers in *Elephant* (2003).

impression that results is partly one of faux documentary immediacy, although the extended nature of the shots (and a number of temporal overlaps between one sequence and another) draws attention to the presence of the camera and the extent to which such an impression is always the outcome of a process of active mediation or construction.

The use of formal devices that draw the attention of the viewer can be part of a serious exploration of the medium, but it is also a way of marking the distinctive presence of the filmmaker as *auteur*. Departing from dominant conventions is an effective way for individual filmmakers to lay claim to the attention of critics and other viewers, and thus to establish their own careers. This can involve an implicit critique of forms such as those used habitually in Hollywood and in more formally conservative independent features. It can also involve showier effects, however, as in the artistically motivated examples of narrative structure outlined in the previous chapter. Each has a role to play in the creation of the distinctive character of many independent features.

The line between them may not be precise, but two general tendencies can be proposed. Formal devices that have a critical potential, undermining dominant/mainstream conventions, are more likely to create an uncomfortable and unsettling impression, and are as a result likely to be confined to the economic margins, or used only minimally or in a manner that is clearly motivated. *The Limey* is something of an exception here, although its form is also motivated partly by generic factors, the subject of the next chapter. Formal devices of a showy variety, often located in the exaggeration rather than the undermining of conventional style, are likely to be designed to create pleasurable effects for the viewer, making them more susceptible to inclusion in films designed for a larger indie audience or to cross over into the mainstream. Such devices are also found in the mainstream itself, although usually in works characterized as more quirky or stylized than the norm, or sold on the basis of embodying the distinctive stylistic flourishes of particular filmmakers, including some who made their name in the independent sector.

The question of audience pleasure is, of course, a relative one. For those suitably attuned – in possession of the relevant cultural capital, including an interest in form in its own right – the use of strategies that create disjuncture and undermine the smooth continuity of the Hollywood style can be a source of affirmative pleasure: affirming their own investment in the deconstruction of dominant conventions. Such viewers form one part of the core art-house audience on which the independent sector relies. There are plenty of cases that do not fit neatly into the opposition suggested above. *Stranger than Paradise*, for example, offers the appeal of a stylized and distinctive *auteur*-marked *mise-en-scène* that is neither an explicit undermining nor exaggeration of the mainstream Hollywood style. The same aesthetic might be tediously or magnificently minimalist, depending on the perspective of the observer. The style of *The Limey* undermines some aspects of Hollywood convention more than others. The appeal of indie films on formal grounds is often based, as suggested above, on a sense of difference – the slightly offbeat, quirky, etc. – the exact parameters of which might not be apparent to many viewers. In some cases, though, overt departures from the norm are presented in a manner more likely to be appreciated for their own stylized effect. The extent to which the presence of such devices is recognized, and that they are thus appreciated in themselves, rather than as a contribution to a more diffuse and indistinct overall impression, can play a part in the process through which viewers define themselves as more discerning and cine-literate, a source of pleasure likely to play a greater role in the independent sector than in the Hollywood mainstream.

Showy effects, as used in indie features, range from the exaggeration of conventional formal approaches to the invention or application of other forms of image manipulation. Hyperbolic extension or speed of camera movement is one major source of such effects. Rapid low-level camera movement is one of the distinctive features of Sam Raimi's heavily stylized and semi-parodic *The Evil Dead* (1983) and *Evil Dead II* (1987). A prowling, ground-level camera that makes startlingly fast, assaultive moves towards endangered characters acts as the embodiment of awakened forces of evil. The effect was created, in a classic example of resourceful low-budget indie style, by attaching the camera to a wooden plank carried by two operators running at speed. In *The Evil Dead*, the plank-cam makes its most striking manoeuvre in the closing sequence. It starts out, close to the ground, in the woods behind the cabin in which most of the horror action takes place. It moves off, fast and low, dodging a couple of trees, up to the cabin, in the back door, through the cabin and out the front, all in one seamless move that climaxes in a rush up to the face of the central character, Ash (Bruce Campbell), standing out front, whose scream is followed instantly by a cut to black. Having established itself as one of the sources of the film's cult appeal, flamboyant camera movement of this kind is increased in the sequel. The passage through the cabin is repeated in the early stages, after Ash has decapitated a possessed girlfriend. In this case, the camera rushes up and seems to become attached to the character, carrying him forward at high speed, during which process he executes a number of 360-degree cartwheeling turns before coming to a sudden halt rammed up against a tree and falling into a puddle. Other unconventional camerawork includes a disorienting move in *The Evil Dead* in which the camera starts on Ash, framed from the waist-up from behind and upside-down. The camera pushes in closer to his head and moves around and down, over the top of the inverted head, finishing on a close framing of his face restored to the upright.

All of this is clearly motivated, either by the presence of the invisible evil force or by its effects on Ash, who spends most of his time fighting off the threat of possession. The camera that rotates across the top of Ash's head comes amid a heightened sequence, including numerous alarmingly canted angles, during which the forces of evil are mounting against him for assault. Strange perspectives are motivated by strange and disorienting experiences, but they have also been created here, in works that do not take themselves too seriously, for their own showy pleasure as part of the excessive rollercoaster experience offered by the films. An example in which the kind of perspective offered by Raimi's plank-cam is used without such clear motivation, in the sense of an actual disembodied force, is the first feature by the Cohen brothers, the noir homage *Blood Simple* (1984). The camera makes a very similar low and rapid move in towards the characters in a sequence in which the husband, Marty (Dan Hedaya), struggles with his estranged wife, Abby (Frances McDormand), outside their home. The effect here is a heightening of an important dramatic moment but one in which the device used has no specific motivation. Such stylization largely for its own sake features elsewhere in *Blood Simple*, including a movement in which the camera glides above the polished surface of a bar, drawing attention to the manoeuvre by taking in its stride, with a smooth hop up and down again, the presence of a drunk who lies slumped across the counter.

Fast, low-level hyperbolic camera movement is also used, among other stylized visual effects, in the Cohens' second feature, *Raising Arizona* (1987). Subjective or quasi-subjective ground-level camera position becomes a source of comedy when used to suggest the point of view of quintuplets subjected to a kidnap attempt in their nursery by the hapless recidivist criminal Hi (Nicholas Cage). The most hyperbolic move, directly out of the *Evil Dead* stylebook, comes at the moment when the mother realizes that one of her brood is missing, an emotional shock that appears to unleash into the fictional world the leather-clad comic-book figure of the vengeance-seeking Lone Biker of the Apocalypse (Randal 'Tex' Cobb). The camera moves, hyperfast, up the long driveway of the Arizona household, lifting up over a child's bike, a car and a fountain before flying up Hi's ladder and moving rapidly in on the mother's screaming mouth (a movement broken only by one cut-away to Hi, lying in bed, his face rocking from side to side, and a disguised cut in through the window).

Stylized material of this kind, including plenty of use of slightly distorting wide-angle compositions, is not so much an embellishment as part of the basic visual fabric of early Cohen brothers features such as *Blood Simple* and *Raising Arizona*. More disorienting devices are also used on occasion. At one moment in *Blood Simple*, when Abby is in the office of her now-deceased husband, uncertain what exactly is going on, the camera moves in closer to her face, lifts up and tilts down on her from a higher angle. A shadow passes across her face after which, without the image ever having been entirely obscured, a shift in space has somehow occurred and she is falling backwards onto a pillow in her bed. In similar generic territory, *Bound* (1996), the first film by another sibling pair, Andy and Larry Wachowski, opens with a oddly abstract image, initially difficult to decode, which proves after movement of the camera to have been a directly overhead shot taken from the ceiling of a closet, in which one of the protagonists lies tied and gagged; a similarly abstract impression is created later in an extreme close-up looking down the barrel of a gun lying next to a whisky glass on a table. The effect, in each film, is to contribute to both the sense of duplicitous plotting inherent in the narrative material – everything is not always as it seems – and an aesthetic of self-consciously stylized images.

Sound often plays an important part in the creation of such effects, heightening the sense of stylized play. When the camera performs a showy move in *Bound*, for example, as if following the progress of the signal down a telephone wire, it is accompanied by a whizzy/fizzy electrical-type buzz that is, clearly, in no sense a 'realistic' addition. The effect, as in many of the examples cited above, is further to draw attention to the hyperbolic nature of the camerawork. In the *Evil Dead* films, the subjectivity-of-evil camera plays to a low growly roar for which motivation is suggested in the presence of some kind of unseen beast. A rapid chanting sound accompanies the up-the-lawn camera in *Blood Simple*, creating a sense of breathy panic if not anything more clearly embodied. In some cases in *The Evil Dead* and *Evil Dead II*, however, sound becomes the accompaniment of what is happening to the *camera* rather than just to material within the diegetic world. The flip-over-from-inversion in *The Evil Dead*, for example, is marked and emphasized by a woozy-roaring sound shifting from high to low pitch. One of the strangest sequences in *Evil Dead II*, signifying the latest approach of the evil force, includes an array of creaky, screechy and grinding noises. At first, it seems, some of these are synchronized to the movements of characters: Ash moving his head from side-to-side to a series of brief roaring sounds, for example. But other effects are in synch with the camera, as it whip-pans, zooms and tilts, as if the supernatural force is operating on the means of representation itself.

Much of the expressive material examined earlier in this chapter can be read as showy and formally self-conscious, in addition to serving narratively motivated purposes (the same can be said of some devices used to make claims to the status of *vérité* or to present unbroken performance, as in the whip-pans from character to character in *Tape*). The use of stylized sound effects akin to those employed in the *Evil Dead* films can shift the degree of balance from one to the other. The extended montage sequences of *Requiem for a Dream* are attention-grabbing in their own right in visual terms, for example, but much of the effect is created by the equally stylized and telegraphic snatches of sound that accompany each of the images. In the drug-dealing component, repeated combinations of images of fingers passing money or drugs and notes being thrust into a pocket are set to a cartoonish score orchestrated from sounds including, variously and more or less incongruously, the ring of a cash register, the swoop of a sword through the air and a clashing of blades. Editing, like camerawork, is a major potential source of showy formal effects, from the montage texture of much of *Requiem for a Dream* to more localized usages, such as a dissolve transition in *Blood Simple* from the image of a barman placing his finger on the button of an answerphone to a near-perfectly matched image of one of the main protagonists, Ray (John Getz), pushing his finger down into a blood patch on the back seat of his car. The latter appears to serve little purpose other than its own revelling in the formal potential of the medium, although it might chime with a broader narrative sense of different acts blurring into one another.

Montage sequences featuring characters speaking directly to camera in a manner that breaks the fictional frame, and draws attention to the device, are found in Spike Lee's first feature *She's Gotta Have It*, one of the landmark indie films of the 1980s, and his studio-funded drama of racial-ethnic tensions, *Do the Right Thing* (1989). Character address to camera is one of the guiding principles of *She's Gotta Have It*, featuring the perspectives of the central character, Nola Darling (Camilla Johns), and the three men and a woman who compete for her romantic attentions. One sequence moves into a more stylized and comic register, cutting through a series of chat-up lines used by an assortment of would-be or past lovers. Its privileged position, outside the usual confines of the diegetic universe, is signified by the fact that each is shot against a plain black background. The sequence ends with the line used by Jamie Overstreet (Tommy Redmond Hicks), one of the principals, its shift back into more conventional register marked by its existence in a concrete fictional space, against the background of a street scene. A similar to-camera montage is used in *Do the Right Thing* to give voice to some of the inter-group tensions around which the film revolves: a sequence in which the camera moves in on five characters (the black figure played by Lee himself, an Italian, a Korean, a Puerto Rican, and a white cop) who speak to camera, in turn, mouthing strings of complaints and racially/ ethnically offensive epithets. Serious material is rendered partly comic, through the exaggeration of being piled up in rapid excess and through its extraction, formally, from the conventions that usually locate it as part of a fictional-narrative situation in which the viewer is invited to become socially and/or emotionally involved. On the one hand, playing with form, and drawing it to the attention of the viewer, creates distance and reduces the extent to which we are invited to take seriously the implications of the material, both here and in some of the other examples considered above. On the other, the montage in *Do the Right Thing* neatly encapsulates the multi-dimensional nature of real tensions between social groups.

Among other showy effects used in some independent features is the animation of insert images within the screen. In Gus Van Sant's *My Own Private Idaho* (1991), the figures on the covers of gay magazines on sale in a shop, including the two principals, come magically to life and talk to one another, a clear (and more unambiguously comic) breach of the usual rules of the fictional universe. A similar effect, but extended, typically, much longer in time, is created in Jost's *Frameup*. Two police mug-shots of Ricky-Lee are presented on-screen, the usual full-face and profile images, initially to a voice-over account of his criminal record. One of the images – not stills, but the performer keeping as still as he can – becomes animated and begins to speak. The other erupts into a bout of swearing and complaint and shouts at the first to shut up. The following scene contains an inserted high-school picture of Beth-Ann, which drones on about her background in the same style. An audacious version of this kind of screen-within-the-screen format is used for flashback sequences in *Buffalo 66*, in which video image-manipulation technology is used to create insert screens that grow out from the main image, visually to put the lie to the egregious failures of memory or untruths propagated by Billy's parents. The coherent single time and space of the screen is disrupted. Attention to the surface plane of the image is called more directly by a fictional character in *Pulp Fiction*, and thus more showily, if in passing, when Mia (Uma Thurman) uses her fingers to trace a rectangle (calling Vincent a square) that appears in dotted lines on the screen.

For viewers, the pleasure offered by these kinds of effects, from manic camera movement to various other stylized forms of shooting or editing, might be something like an indie equivalent of the appeal of Hollywood spectacle. In Hollywood, spectacle is quite closely interlinked with narrative material, but it also offers distinctive appeals of its own, often in terms such as a heightened intensity and impact of audio-visual experience. The same goes for some of the showy formal material considered above, especially the more hyperbolic, rapid and exaggerated forms of camera movement or editing. A relative lack of resources for the production of spectacular material staged pro-filmically, before the camera, might put a stronger onus in the lower-budget realms of the independent sector on the use of innovative formal means to create impact, where impact of that variety is sought. *The Evil Dead* is a good example. However impressively and excessively gory the special effects used in its scenes of transformation and death, the impression created would be greatly reduced if it were not for the excesses and inventions of cinematic style. Stylized camerawork and editing can serve narrative purposes while at the same time offering a variety of 'eye candy', pleasurable to watch in its own right, in much the same way as special effects or hyped-up formal devices are used in the Hollywood mainstream. Departures from conventional formal limitations offer a way of refreshing what might otherwise become overly familiar scenarios, as in the very heavily trodden imperilled-teenagers-in-the-woods territory of the *Evil Dead* films.

Much more could be suggested (or speculated) about the precise nature of the appeal of the use of particular heightened formal devices. Qualities such as formal intensity, from plank-cam to hyper-rapid editing, might be appealing partly on the basis of the contrast between the audio-visually heightened fictional experience they offer and the duller realities of quotidian life in the real world.[16] A camera that moves with unusual vigour or that performs unconventionally extended and sometimes seemingly impossible manoeuvres might offer pleasure (perhaps culturally specific) in its embodiment, for the viewer, of less-than-usually bounded kinetic energy, freed from some conventional limitations. An impression of intense energy and a heightened sense of perception, a cinematic 'rush' seeking to approximate that provided by chemicals, is created by the rapid montage sequences in *Requiem for a Dream*. A similar effect is created elsewhere by the use of brief sequences of fast-motion footage, sometimes combined with changes in image quality created through the use of different lenses, stocks or processing. This is another device that has become part of the indie repertoire, used in films such as *L.I.E.* (2001) to create a heightened sense of alienation, both expressive of material related to the diegetic universe (in this case, damaged lives in the commuter belt along the Long Island Expressway) and aesthetically pleasurable in its own right. Devices such as these – and others of a less showy variety – can be understood in a broader context in which one of the appeals of 'art' is the opportunity it provides for formal departures from the familiar/conventional that can create a renewal or refreshing of perceptions, although individual devices can quite quickly become conventionalized in their own realms.[17] More specifically to the indie sector, the appeal of such stylized touches might also lie in novelty itself, experienced with varying degrees of consciousness *as* an act of departure from the dominant norm. Pleasure might result from a sense of freshness and difference, more or less specific or diffuse; of witnessing something that stimulatingly extends the usual/familiar bounds of the form, as in the case of the insert images that grow out from the screen in *Buffalo 66*. Part of the pleasure in this device might lie in the fantastical immediacy – unavailable in real life or, usually, in conventional editing regimes – with which these images, entered into the frame as evidence, permit certain claims made by the unsympathetic parents to be disproved. Rapid cut-away editing to the alternative scene and back can create the same effect, but an added frisson is offered here by both the novelty of the insert device and the fact that it enables both scenes to be kept in view at once.

Witnessing acts of formal virtuosity or showmanship can offer pleasures of its own, in the sheer display of inventiveness and flair, in film as elsewhere. Visual flourishes in the arts might be valued, as E.H. Gombrich suggests, as 'the expression of the joyful exuberance of a craftsman who display[s] both his control and his inventiveness'.[18] An important component of these pleasures for some viewers, as suggested above, might come from their own awareness of the experience of innovation; a form of self-flattery, an activation of accumulated cultural capital exercised by the viewer of independent films or those at the more formally innovative end of the Hollywood spectrum. This is not the case with all independent features, of course, the grounds of appeal for some of which, dating back at least to the work of Cassavetes, is located precisely in an absence of anything that might be understood as being formally ostentatious for its own sake. The foregrounding of showy formal devices is likely to feature most strongly in independent features that owe something to the exploitation school, and often those in genres targeted at relatively younger audiences, rather than in some more serious or 'worthy' varieties, in which it might be considered a superficial distraction – a negative judgement of ornamentation characteristic of the 'classical' western art tradition that can be traced back to the arguments of Socrates against the trickery of rhetorical oratory.[19]

Flourishes of a more gratuitous or audacious nature might be associated especially with the earlier films of independent filmmakers, eager to make their mark and/or working with fewer resources. This certainly seems to be the case in the work to date of the Cohen brothers, whose features have remained stylized but with a tendency in later films toward the development of aesthetics based on the creation of a consistent visual texture rather than outlandish camerawork or editing: the ochre tones created in post-production to create the period impression of the Depression-era *O Brother, Where Art Thou?* (2000), for example, or the contrasty black-and-white (and the grey of the central character played by Billy Bob Thornton) of *The Man Who Wasn't There* (2001). The same appears to be the case with Raimi. In between *The Evil Dead* and *Evil Dead II*, Raimi directed the disjointed madcap comedy *Crimewave* (1985), scripted by Joel and Ethan Cohen and full of excessive sound and visual flourishes. Later studio-backed films such as *A Simple Plan* (1998) and *The Gift* (2000), in generic territory that might lend itself to similar treatment, are far more restrained. *A Simple Plan*, the story of a discovery of money that goes horribly wrong for all involved, is presented in a generally straightforward, matter-of-fact manner, the camera conventionally positioned and often stationary. The style is appropriate to a narrative centred on an escalating series of horrors perpetrated, through what becomes a self-fulfilling momentum, by the otherwise plain and decent accountant, Hank (Bill Paxton). Much the same goes for *The Gift*, another classically smooth production in which occasionally stylized sequences, including jarring cuts, are motivated clearly by the material – manifestations of the clairvoyant visions of the central character – and routine for the generic terrain. The same is not true of all filmmakers, however, as suggested by the highly stylized fabric of Quentin Tarantino's fourth feature, *Kill Bill Vol. 1* (2003), the aesthetic of which is largely founded on showy extravagance for its own pleasurable sake, examples ranging from attention-grabbing overhead camera movement to shifts of register into animé-style animation and a jokey move into high-contrast monochrome at the height of a wildly over-the-top mass bloodbath.

Form and style, like everything else, are related to industrial-economic factors. Low- or ultra-low-budget production creates limitations in areas such as creating smooth movement of the camera. But these can be overcome through ingenuity and invention, as in the case of Raimi's plank-cam or the decision to shoot unsteady and hand-held, making a virtue out of constraint. The latter was the case in *El Mariachi*, one of the most celebrated low-budget achievements

9. Showy, stylized and over the top: mayhem about to break out in *Kill Bill Vol. 1* (2003).

of the 1980s. One source of the energy of the film comes from hand-held camerawork that was originally a necessity rather than a choice because of the poor quality of the only camera-stand available for shooting.[20] Access to greater resources generally permits a more fluid style, as in the numerous crane-shots used in *O Brother, Where Art Thou?*, production backing for which included both Universal and parts of the Disney empire (Buena Vista International and Touchstone), or the choreographed excesses of *Kill Bill*, co-produced and distributed by Miramax. The Cohen brothers have managed the tricky equation of gaining major studio backing for a number of their features, along with independent distributors such as Circle Releasing and Working Title, without surrendering creative control. Such is the value of a successful auteurist reputation: the distinctive mark that results from creative freedom becomes, in some cases, precisely the quality that has a value in the marketplace. Space to pursue more radical formal strategies, such as those of Harmony Korine, is usually premised on lowness of budget, although Korine has also benefited from protection under the wing of Cary Woods, producer of *Gummo* and *Julien Donkey-Boy* as well as *Kids* and more mainstream fare such as *Scream* (1996) and the studio blockbuster *Godzilla* (1998), for which he was co-executive producer. Korine's deal with Fine Line Features for *Gummo*, on a modest (but not micro) budget of $1 million, contained no stipulation other than that it gain an R rating. Van Sant was able to make *Gerry*, after directing a series of more mainstream features including *Good Will Hunting* (1997) and *Finding Forrester* (2000), because he was in the fortunate position of having a guaranteed source of funding ($1 million from a German company) with which to make a film of his choice, with no strings attached.[21]

The point at which the budget *becomes* the aesthetic, 'when the physical limitations of what you can do shapes your *mise-en-scène*', is not easy to determine, as suggested by the indie producer Christine Vachon.[22] In *Swoon* (1992), directed by Tom Kalin, Vachon says, the filmmakers were complimented for forcing the viewer into complicity with the child murderers Leopold and Loeb by using a large number of close-ups. The decision to use so many close-ups was largely an aesthetic decision, reports Vachon: 'Largely. It's also easier and cheaper to light small spaces than it is to light big ones.'[23] The issue was more clear-cut in *El Mariachi*, where close and medium shots were chosen for indoors sequences specifically because of a lack of resources to light larger spaces. Rodriguez also received praise for a stylistic device that was the product of pragmatic limitation rather than aesthetic choice: the fact that faster than usual cutting is used in dialogue as well as action scenes, one of the distinctive features of the film. *El Mariachi* was shot silently because the camera to which Rodriguez had access was not capable of recording sync sound. Sound was recorded separately and matched with the images by hand. Problems of synchronization that affected many sequences were surmounted by cutting at the point where sound and image began to part company, thus cutting into dialogue scenes sooner than might usually be the case.[24] Regular cutting also creates more margin for error than the use of long takes when working with less experienced personnel behind and in front of the camera. It is easier, generally, on reduced resources, to assemble a feature from larger numbers of fragments, a practical consideration that can pay off in the form of energetic visuals.

An important point, made in almost identical terms by both Vachon and Rodriguez, is the extent to which budget limitations can be the source of the creativity and invention that gives some independent features their distinctive formal quality. In Hollywood, problems can often be solved by spending more money. Where money does not exist, creativity often has to step into the breach. As Rodriguez suggests, it is far from always a good move for aspiring filmmakers to seek to create something with the slick formal qualities associated with the mainstream. On limited means, the result is likely to fall short and look like what it is: a cheap imitation. Far better to do something distinctive and a little bit different, which is often a more viable proposition with restricted funds and more likely to catch the eye of the audience for independent features, including distributors and gatekeepers such as festival organizers. The degree of difference, formally, between most independent features and those in the mainstream is open to debate, however. Formal innovation or departure tends to occur against a background of relatively more familiar-conventional material, in the interests of comprehensibility and economic viability, in anything other than work at the avant-garde end of the spectrum.

If spatial continuity and consistency of screen-direction are often undermined in a formally radical example such as *Julien Donkey-Boy*, for example – the relative positions of characters being reversed or rendered somewhat unclear from one shot to another – they are also more conventionally maintained in many sequences, including the extremely telegraphic jump-cut struggle in the kitchen between Julien and Chris. The viewer's bearings are not entirely lost, a marker of the distinction between relative disorientation and outright experiment or abstraction. Spatial continuity is played with on occasion in *Requiem for a Dream*, especially in one sequence in which Harry and Marion lie facing each other on a bed. The sequence is presented in split-screen, the two characters separated by a vertical division between two shots, but positioned as if, more conventionally, in a single shot. At one point Harry lifts his arm to stroke Marion's face and there is only a slight mismatch between the arm leaving frame-right on one side and entering left on the other. At other moments, the division between the two images is more clear-cut, but a disorienting effect is created at the points where they seem both separate and contiguous (an intimation, perhaps, of what proves to be the fragility of their relationship). In most of the film, however, striking montage sequences and distortive effects are balanced by a more conventional découpage in which conventional rules of spatial continuity are obeyed.

More specific industrial factors might also have been responsible for creating an increasingly standardized look in many independent features since the 1990s. In the 1980s, pay agreements generally prohibited the use of union members in low-budget film crews, denying to the independent sector the most competent and experienced technicians. This was changed by the signing of a new agreement, known as the east coast contract, which permitted union personnel to work on low-budget films at reduced rates of pay. Some, seeking an escape from the restrictions of Hollywood, had previously worked on independent features without credit. The result of the new deal, according to indie stalwart Tom Bernard, co-president of Sony Pictures Classics (formerly of United Artists and Orion), has been a greater professionalism, an ironing out of some of the quirks resulting from the use of amateur technicians, which may be a mixed blessing.[25] The increased scale and scope of independent production is also likely to have been a factor in many cases.

Defining independent features on the basis of the kinds of formal approaches examined in this chapter remains a relative rather than an absolute proposition. From creating impressions of *vérité* to the use of outlandishly stylized camerawork, many of these strategies have also been adopted in Hollywood (examples including, respectively, the harshly desaturated unsteady-cam aesthetic of Steven Spielberg's *Saving Private Ryan* [1998] and the ultra-fast or seemingly impossible camera movements flaunted by David Fincher in *Fight Club* [1999] and *Panic Room* [2002]). Of all these, showy camerawork and editing lend themselves most effectively to incorporation in the mainstream, as part of its investment in the creation of increased degrees of audio-visual intensity or bravura effects.[26] There are limitations, however, on the extent to which Hollywood embraces some of the other formal approaches considered above. Touches of *vérité* can be appealing, increasing impact or giving renewed edge to more familiar recipes, but too much edge is not generally what Hollywood seeks, given its strong investment in more affirming varieties of fantasy. Formal devices are often used expressively in Hollywood, but usually in a manner that remains contained. Foregrounded style can be a marketable icing on the cake, but only up to a point, in most cases, and without undermining the centrality of narrative and character.

The same goes for many independent films. Formal innovation usually works with, rather than eclipsing, dimensions such as narrative and character, even in the more showy examples. And a large number of independent features are quite conservative in formal terms, especially those based on the relatively quiet, unmelodramatic depiction of inter-personal drama or those, such as *Working Girls*, in which a transparency/familiarity of style is favoured in the pursuit of broadly social-political agendas. The multi-Oscar-winning *In the Bedroom* is a good example of the former, a Miramax release at the award-garnering classy/prestige 'adult' drama end of the independent spectrum. A couple of unconventional devices are used towards the end, expressing a sense of the dislocation of the central character, Matt (Tom Wilkinson), after he is driven, uncharacteristically, to murder a man who appears certain to get away with a light prison sentence after killing his son. A sequence in which Matt removes his clothes, to wash away any traces, includes two jump-cuts; when he is lying in bed afterwards, just before the close of the film, a slight double-exposure effect is created, a penumbra around the head and upper body, as he turns to lie on his back. These are subtle touches, however, in a film that is quietly and elegantly classical, within a widescreen frame used at times to emphasize the distance between characters.

Top-grossing independent features can be formally innovative, as demonstrated by *Pulp Fiction* (primarily in terms of narrative structure) and *The Blair Witch Project*. In these cases, the conjunction of box-office success and formal departure might be a function of the appeal of the latter, in these generic territories, to a relatively youthful audience. A more conservative style might be more appropriate to indie features that seek to reach demographics such as the relatively older and less 'hip' audience targeted by *My Big Fat Greek Wedding*. The film is very conventionally assembled, with the exception of a modest stylized effect in which one image is manipulated in post-production to 'fold into' its predecessor, a device used on two occasions to heighten sequences in which actions are repeated as part of a series (increasingly amorous goodnight kisses exchanged by the central couple in one case, the downing of ouzos by the staid parents of the non-Greek partner in the other). The boundaries of formal possibility are, in general, more loosely drawn in the independent sector, their precise shape depending on which particular segment of the market is involved. Departing from mainstream convention, if even only relatively or in certain privileged moments, can provide a means of interrogating the classical style and/or offering a frisson of difference that can be sold to audiences seeking an alternative, if not always very radical, to the dominant norm.

4

Genre

Genre is a way of travelling through familiar terrain, but I always
hope to get someplace new.

Michael Almereyda[1]

Strong connections can be made between some of the formal qualities
examined in the previous chapter and their location or impact in terms
of the genre identity of independent features. Formal innovation, or
difference from the qualities usually associated with a genre, can be a
way to either refresh or question and undermine genre conventions.
In the case of horror, for example, the use of forms associated with the
vérité effect can render more real-seeming a territory usually associated
with fantastic qualities, examples including Larry Fessenden's vampire-
oriented *Habit* (1997), considered in more detail below, while showy
stylized devices such as those used in the *Evil Dead* films can be
used to add fresh zip to otherwise potentially stale material. Formal
departures from conventions, including those of narrative, can also
be contained, justified and motivated by genre location, as is at least
partly the case in *The Limey*, the noir-type thriller being a format that

has long offered space for more convoluted and expressive forms than those usually associated with the mainstream, one of the factors in its appeal to a number of independent filmmakers.

If familiar genre location is sometimes abandoned, complicated or undermined in the independent sector, it also forms an important point of orientation in many cases. It can provide a stable base – in terms of both form/content and of economics – within which to offer something different. A regime of difference-within-similarity is also typical of Hollywood genre production, the distinctive feature of the independent sector being the greater potential scope for difference. Some independent features are quite subversive of dominant genre conventions. Others have traded on clearly marked genre location, including the three current all-time indie box-office champions: *Pulp Fiction* (crime/noir thriller, with stylish flourishes), *The Blair Witch Project* (horror, with a clever/inexpensive new twist) and *My Big Fat Greek Wedding* (romantic comedy, conventional but with an ethnic spin). More conventional genre location is also a feature of many productions at the exploitation end of the independent spectrum, films such as the *Nightmare on Elm Street* and *Teenage Mutant Ninja Turtles* franchises that provided the financial security of New Line in the 1980s and 1990s and much of the output of Miramax's profitable Dimension Films label (assorted Screams and other Scary Movies). Its relationship with genre is, therefore, an instance of the pull that exists more generally in independent cinema between the use and undermining of approaches associated with the commercial mainstream.

Genre categories are often more complex than they appear at first sight, in the Hollywood mainstream as well as in the independent sector. The precise boundaries of genres – and what constitutes a genre in the first place – are subject to much debate.[2] What genre broadly entails, however, is a sense of expectations. For both industry and viewer, an identity that can be put in terms of genre, of familiar *types* of films, is to some extent predictable: a type that has attracted audiences with some consistency in the past, or a type that individual viewers have enjoyed (or avoided) and are likely to enjoy (or avoid) again. As such, genre lends itself to either the fulfilling or the undermining or complication of what might be expected. This chapter starts by examining the latter: independent features that, in various ways and to varying degrees, complicate established genre conventions. Such complications can be another way of understanding the specific location of the offbeat or quirky quality of indie features. A set of trajectories-of-expectation exists, against which can be measured various degrees of fulfilment. Expectations are not entirely thwarted, in many cases, but neither are they entirely realized, creating the often-characteristic indie quality of existing in the space between familiar convention and more radical departure. To complicate is not necessarily to undermine or abandon. It still entails the use of genre frameworks, the significance of which to many independent productions, even those of a more innovative nature, remains considerable. Some independent features largely abandon dominant/conventional genre formats, as one of their markers of independence, but this chapter also considers the extent to which the 'indie' film has come to constitute something like a genre, or a group of genres, in itself.

Complicating Genre

The key question at the heart of *Habit*, in which Larry Fessenden stars as well as writing, directing and editing, is whether or not it is *really* a vampire movie, a familiar sub-genre within the horror format. If it is a vampire film, it is one that seems far more 'realistic' than conventional treatments, a quality that puts it in a venerable tradition of independent horror or horror-related features that have sought to revitalize the form by giving its subject matter a harsher or more immediate-seeming audio-visual texture. *The Blair Witch Project* is an obvious recent example, as is *Henry: Portrait of a Serial Killer*, each of which creates its strongest formal impressions of verisimilitude through the use of 'amateurish' video footage. In *Henry*, this occurs in a sequence in which we see the low-grade material shot by Henry and Otis themselves during one of their murderous outings. The film's greatest impression of immediacy is created when the process of mediation is foregrounded in the diegetic world, a reflexive demonstration of the constructed nature of all such impressions. Classic examples of harsh, low-budget horror are George Romero's *Night of the Living Dead* and Tobe Hooper's *The Texas Chain Saw Massacre*, each of which combines grainy, hand-held *vérité* components with more expressive and overtly stylized images – canted angles and lurid music in the former, some excessively large close-ups among other devices creating an impression of claustrophobia in the latter – in a manner similar to some of the examples considered in the previous chapter.

In terms of questioning the reality or not of the supernatural ingredient – although not in visual style – *Habit* has something in common with Curtis Harrington's *Night Tide* (made in 1960 but not released until 1963), a product of the late 1950s/early 1960s conjunction of independent narrative features and formally more radical currents. Dennis Hopper plays a sailor who falls in love with a woman, Mona (Linda Lawson), who wears a false tail to play a mermaid in a sideshow attraction. That she might really be a mermaid, guilty of luring two previous lovers to a watery death and being called to return to the sea, is strongly suggested until a conclusion in which her adoptive father admits to having planted the idea in her mind, and committing the murders, in order to keep her from leaving him. But he claims no knowledge of a mysterious women, speaking a strange language, whose haunting presence unsettles Mona on several occasions. He might just be protecting a women involved in his deception, suggests a detective, but the film leaves open the possibility that something more uncanny is involved.

A more immediate predecessor of *Habit* is Romero's *Martin* (1978), the title character of which (John Amplas) may or may not be a vampire. Martin certainly has a vampiric habit, killing women in order to drink their blood, but one that is given a modern, secular twist. He gains power over his victims not through magic or hypnosis, but by injecting them with a sedative. He pierces their skin not with pointy fangs, but with a razor blade. A gentle-seeming, innocent-looking and shy figure, Martin does not look the part, unlike the elderly cousin, Cuda (Lincoln Maazel), with whom he lodges for the duration of the film. Cuda is the representative of the established genre tradition, in his white beard and white suit, calling his cousin 'Nosferatu' and promising to save his soul before destroying him. His house is filled with garlic and he holds up a crucifix while addressing the object of his antagonism. Martin responds by deflating such familiar generic motifs: pulling down a bunch of garlic and biting into one of the heads, grabbing Cuda's crucifix and pressing it against his face, with no

10. The vampire updated: the title character, with one of the tools of his trade, in *Martin* (1978).

ill effects. 'It's just a costume,' he declares mockingly, later, appearing before Cuda with fangs, whitened face and the obligatory cape.

The viewer is offered either of two alternatives, each making claims to greater verisimilitude than the traditional vampire formula. If Martin is a vampire, as Cuda claims, a number of myths are exploded, including those of antipathy to garlic and crucifixes, and the suggestion that the activity of vampires is restricted to the hours of darkness. It is not like in the movies, as Martin informs a radio talk-show audience, to which he confides his troubles. Even in Cuda's version, the reality surrounding such evil is different from that of the screen fiction, the elderly priest he engages to perform rites designed to free Martin having declared it to have been done 'all wrong' in *The Exorcist*. As a vampire film, *Martin* refreshes the genre by abandoning some of its most hoary clichés and, in grainy low-budget 16mm, giving it a very 'ordinary' contemporary American suburban setting, in which Martin becomes the object of sexual attraction for a bored housewife. Alternatively, we can accept the interpretation offered by Cuda's granddaughter, Christina (Christine Forrest): that Martin is suffering from some kind of illness, maybe related to sexual inexperience, as he himself suggests, and that it is Cuda who is the victim of the insanity said to run in the family. Black-and-white images that intrude on the contemporary action – a younger Martin, from a more Romantic earlier age, involved in amorous pursuit that turns bloody, and subsequently pursued by a burning-torch-bearing posse – can be read as either memories or fantasies.

A similar ambiguity haunts *Habit*, directed less at the central character, Sam (Fessenden), than at the woman with whom he becomes involved after the breakup of a previous relationship. Anna (Meredith Snaider) has a penchant for biting and sucking blood during sexual encounters. Is she a vampire, or are Sam's suspicions the products of his own fragile mental state, the result of excess drinking and emotional upheavals such as the end of his relationship with Liza (Heather Woodbury) and the recent and not entirely explained death of his archaeologist father? Scars on his arms attest to a history of self-harm that provides a source of potential rationalization for the bloodied marks that appear on his body during the film. Fessenden employs a number of devices to create a sense of Anna's potentially supernatural capacities and the influence of her powers on Sam, without, initially, anything to give more explicit guidance to the viewer. Anna has a tendency to appear suddenly and startlingly, as if out of nowhere, an effect heightened by a number of subtle formal dislocations. When the two meet, Anna seems to shift from a position in front of Sam, at a Halloween party, to one behind, in breach of spatial continuity. When Sam meets Anna for the second time, at a festival on the streets of lower Manhattan, the hand-held camera wheels around with him, from behind, as he turns away from a beer counter to find her standing before him, entering the frame from screen-left. He jumps back, startled, an impression heightened by a slightly jolting cut to a close-up of his head. She materializes again, with the same impact on Sam, outside the restaurant in which he works. The camera pans to the left with Sam as he turns, after locking up, and again catches her, already there, standing implacably in a manner that seems vaguely threatening. The formal basis of the effect lies in the intrusion of her figure abruptly into the frame, in sequences in which the camera has been oriented closely around the movements of Sam, a visual correlative to the character's intrusion into Sam's life.

On another occasion, the viewer gradually or suddenly – depending on how closely he or she is attending to the whole image – becomes aware of the presence of Anna standing behind Sam while he is speaking about their relationship on the phone to Liza from his apartment. At first, only parts of Anna's body and limbs are visible, largely integrated into a corner of the background. Framing shifts, after two more shots and a pair of cuts away to Liza, to include more of her body and eventually her face, at which point her presence is drawn most clearly to attention, increasing the sense of a sinister insinuation into Sam's world. Rationalization is provided for this mysterious appearance – which might otherwise support the conclusion that Anna has the vampire ability to materialize and dematerialize at will – in her claim to have had a copy made of his key. Earlier, after Sam has given a speech to a learned society in memory of his father, a trick of editing makes Liza turn into Anna, suggesting in some unspecified manner the displacement of the one by the other. As Sam talks about her to one of his father's former colleagues, Gerry Lyons (Lon Waterford), Liza comes into frame from the left. As she turns to face Sam, a cut is made to the reverse angle and suddenly it is Anna not Liza who stands next to him, the disjunction heightened by being marked at a point that, according to formal convention, should be one of strict continuity. In another instance that questions the status of her existence, Anna sits up in bed early in the morning, after a night with Sam, and her image dissolves away; any impression that this might just be a lap-dissolve, a convention signifying the passage of time rather than anything supernatural, is undercut by the continuation in real-time of an answerphone message left by Liza.

The sense that something is not quite right with Sam is also established formally, as well as in more obvious dimensions such as his increasingly bedraggled appearance. A sequence in which he meets Liza in a café offers a good example of the way relatively minor departures from convention can create an impression of unease or disjunction. The sequence starts with an entirely conventional shot/reverse-shot series, two-shots of Sam and Liza: she facing the camera, seen over his shoulder; he likewise, over hers. A number of cut-away shots disrupt this pattern, creating an uneasy impression motivated by what appears to be his heightened awareness of peripheral detail in the scene. One shot, following the direction of his look, briefly picks up the image of cash being left in payment of a bill on another table. Another focuses on a man sitting behind Sam, talking into a cell phone. Two more give us images of a ceiling fan and a clock, the latter running rapidly backwards. Another starts on a neighbouring table, moving unsteadily, before executing a fast pan back to the man on the phone. The camera is often mobile in these shots, especially at the start, immediately after the cut. The first image of the man on the phone, for example, is caught just as the camera is finishing a quick pan from the left. The same goes for the image of the clock. Cutting into what appears to be the last part of a camera movement creates an impression of catching something fleeting and slightly furtive happening at the margins of perception. To Liza, Sam rationalizes his unsettled state – 'too much coffee', 'just a little hungover' – although it is not clear that he is entirely convinced.

Familiar vampire-movie motifs other than blood-sucking are, for the most part, treated in a low-key manner that does not draw them to attention and requires audience foreknowledge for their activation as potential components of the mythology. 'Aren't you going to invite me in?' enquires Anna on her first visit to Sam's place – an innocent remark, or a manifestation of the convention that the vampire has to be invited into the home of its victim? A bunch of garlic in his kitchen catches her eye, but only in a brief and passing manner. A friend of Sam's, Lenny (Jesse Hartman), disappears early in the film, his health also having suffered after his reports of sexual encounters with a woman who might also be assumed to have been Anna-as-vampire. His role, as Fessenden suggests, is akin to that of Lucy in the original Dracula story, friend of the principal target of the vampire, Mina, and the first to die.[3] Gerry Lyons, with white hair and beard, is, like Cuda in *Martin*, the Van Helsing figure, the knowledgeable vampire hunter, although his role is kept very much in the margins; Sam fails to return what might be interpreted as a crucial phone call offering help. Like *Martin*, *Habit* offers some more explicitly supernatural-seeming material, especially towards the end. Some sequences might be explained-away, to some extent, as the feverish dreams of Sam: the ghostlike apparition of Anna with mottled skin who appears in his room one night (he seems to have a puncture mark on the belly the following morning, but could that be the result of self-harm?); a strange sequence in which Sam, running naked through

the street at night, shot at an extremely canted angle, comes across a
ship containing coffins, one of which contains a conventional vampire
figure complete with fangs, white face and red-rimmed eyes (the ship,
approaching Manhattan, is seen at the start of the film and again at
the close, and, as the favoured conveyance of the classical vampire,
is another point of contact with the source narrative). Sam's friend
Nick (Aaron Beall) becomes the spokesperson for the rationalized
account, making a speech in which 'vampirism is everywhere', used
as a metaphor for the influence of drink, drugs, television, advertising
and the myriad 'insidious Faustian bargains we make very day.' On
balance, however, and especially towards the end, *Habit* seems to lean
towards the literal account, unless Sam is assumed to be in the grip of
a major psychosis the subjective fantasies of which are shared with the
viewer. Anna is seen, in a climactic showdown, as a fanged antagonist,
somehow capable of opening the window of an upper-floor room
from the outside before a struggle that ends in both falling to their
death below.

Habit, like *Martin*, can have it several ways: as an edgy new take
on the vampire format; as a merging in some respects of vampire
and secular experiences; or as a film that leaves space to question
the reality of vampirism in its literal/conventional shape. Vampirism,
or some secular/obsessive equivalent, is brought into close proximity
with a relatively ordinary-seeming world, the latter figured in part
through the use of formal devices associated with the *vérité* tradition.
It is thus made more unsettling. The denial of certainty about the
location of the events – supernatural or not, or some combination
of the two – challenges viewers to come to conclusions of their
own, rather than to slip into the comfortably familiar and contained
routines of a more conventional treatment of the generic mythology.
The fact that a supernatural force such as that of the vampire might
invade a recognizable contemporary world carries more potential
for discomfort than its presence at greater distance in time or space.
The removal or questioning of some of the familiar trappings of the
form reduces the extent to which its more disturbing features are
likely to be taken as merely part of a separate world of genre-based
fantasy. Horror encroaches on a world closer to that of the viewer,
merging at times into a texture more like that of potential everyday

experience. As a result, it makes claims to being taken more seriously, and positions itself as a cultural form of a 'higher' status than that usually associated with the genre. This is an important issue in the value judgements involved in distinctions between independent features and Hollywood/mainstream production, although horror is a territory in which elements with 'higher' and 'lower' cultural associations are sometimes mixed.[4] Distributors consigned Harrington's *Night Tide*, for example, to the exploitation and drive-in circuit, despite the fact that its resonances blended classic low-key studio chills, in particular *Cat People* (1942), with more avant-garde work, such as Harrington's preceding short films and Maya Deren's enigmatic *At Land* (1944), in which the director herself plays a woman who emerges from the sea.[5]

A similar effect to that of *Habit* is achieved in Abel Ferrara's *The Addiction* (1995), in which overt parallels are suggested between the vampire's craving for blood and addictions of a more conventionally narcotic nature. Ferrara uses hand-held camerawork to create a *vérité* effect at times, combined with a more expressionist use of high-contrast black-and-white images, charting the experiences of a doctoral philosophy student, Kathleen (Lili Taylor), whose academic study of evil is taken into new dimensions after she is bitten in the neck by another woman. Kathleen's own first taste of blood is presented precisely as a fix, a dose taken from an addict's syringe. Evil of a mythic or fantastic nature is blended with images from real atrocities such as the My Lai massacre in Vietnam, Nazi concentration camps and contemporary news footage from Bosnia, the latter playing on a television while – off-screen – Kathleen is claiming another victim. That Kathleen becomes a vampire in the literal sense is strongly suggested – she cannot eat or sleep, cannot bear strong sunlight, covers up her mirrors and possesses what appears to be superhuman strength – but the parallels drawn with both drug addiction and historical evils suggest that this experience is not so easily separable from its more earthbound equivalents. The challenging, independent status of the film is marked by its mixture of more familiar genre tropes with such material, and a script laden with references to the work of figures such as Nietzsche, Sartre, Becket and William Burroughs.

Connections between horror-genre material and real-life issues of a more contemporary political nature are also made in Fessenden's two other contributions to the form, his first feature *No Telling* (1991) and *Wendigo* (2001). *No Telling* is an updated take on the Frankenstein story, in which Geoffrey (Stephen Ramsey) conducts animal experiments to the increasing suspicion and horror of his wife Lillian (Miriam Healy Louise) during a summer retreat on a military-owned complex in the countryside. The film's style is a mixture of some hand-held, awkward-zoom *vérité* and a number of more stylized and genre-indicating devices, matching its blend of real-world and horror-genre content. Exaggeratedly high and low camera positions and a tendency to cut into scenes in close-ups (rather than using establishing shots) are among devices used to create a threatening and slightly claustrophobic impression from the start. Fessenden makes liberal use of a Raimi-style plank-cam, most notably in a long and low rapid pull-back from Lillian, as she lies sunbathing in a field. The plank-cam functions not simply as a crude lift from Raimi, as some critics implied. It and many other formal signifiers are those of stylized horror, but the expectations they encourage, of some kind of horror-conventional monstrous presence, are largely undercut. Horror is located, instead, in secular-political issues of corporate involvement in animal experimentation in search of dubious procedures to exploit on humans, along with the use of chemicals in farming and more general issues of scientific/environmental probity. If anything tangible, other than just a signifier of life-out-of-balance, the plank-cam perspective might be taken as representative of some kind of presence of nature. It catches Geoffrey in the act, on more than one occasion, most explicitly in a wheeling motion around the front of his car and towards him in the middle of one of his more nefarious acts – continued in an edgy series of jump-cut shots – as he removes from a trap a dog destined to be conjoined to a calf in the culmination of the horrors enacted in his laboratory. Some direct nods to the gothic original are included, for the horror cognoscenti, including a shot in which Geoffrey's shadow falls threateningly across the figure of a young girl, but the focus is on issues of strongly contemporary relevance.

Much the same goes for *Wendigo*, which again places characters from the city in the countryside, this time a couple and their young son, and follows *Habit* in opening up a gap between explanations of a rational and a horror-mythical nature for some of the events that ensue. Space is created to question the reality of the Wendigo, a shape-shifting Native American spirit creature that appears to intervene in what becomes a deadly conflict in the Catskills between New York weekenders George (Jake Weber), Kim (Patricia Clarkson), their son Miles (Erik Per Sullivan) and a dispossessed and resentful local, Otis (John Speredakos). Visual evidence for its existence is provided, much of it fleeting, although rationalizations are also supplied aplenty. Nods are made to the possibly mixed-up nature of Miles, the figure with whom the Wendigo is primarily associated. George offers a heart-to-heart in which he tells Miles about the nature of mythology, the ways people make up stories to make sense of the world. As in the case of *Habit* and *No Telling*, the film itself employs a number of formal devices that imply the existence of something more than just the usual quotidian dimensions of reality. Events surrounding the characters are intercut with stylized images of nature including rapid-motion shots of river flow, of trees and clouds, of cloud-shadow shapes passing over snow-covered ground. Some shots seem to embody the perspective of the Wendigo itself, one of the manifestations of which is a figure constructed from branches: most clearly, a rapidly moving camera, with bits of twig appearing before the lens, that pursues Miles immediately after the shooting of his father, and also a number of sequences that create a rapid stuttering quality of image through the use of either fast inward-moving jump-cuts or blink-montages of still frames. It is possible to read as blurred the line between that which suggests the actual existence of the Wendigo, as natural spirit, and a more diffuse impression of the presence of natural forces. The film suggests, more subtly than *No Telling*, that the latter have been disturbed, through developments such as the flooding of a nearby valley to create a reservoir of drinking water for the metropolis.

A sense of proximity to something like the real world is created in *Habit* through both narrative material – the way lines are blurred between vampirism and more earthly obsessions and addictions – and formal qualities that create an impression of verisimilitude. The same kind of combination is found in John Cassavetes' *The Killing of a Chinese Bookie* (1976), a rendering into typical Cassavetes territory of material associated with the crime/gangster genre. The narrative scenario is recognizable generic stuff. The owner of a rather sleazy nightclub, Cosmo Vitelli (Ben Gazzara), owes $23,000 in gambling debts to the mob. When he cannot repay other than in instalments, Cosmo is presented with the alternative of carrying out the killing of a mob adversary, a figure known as the Chinese Bookie. He does the deed, reluctantly, getting wounded in the process, only to find that he has been set up and is next in line for a bullet. This is all given a generically unconventional Cassavetes-style treatment. The film is very low-key, in most cases lacking the usual markers of heightened melodrama or suspense. Key moments tend to be underplayed and often oblique in their manner of presentation. Cosmo's figure is often obscured, for example, in the sequence in which we first learn of his gambling debts. Shots of a card game are overlaid with general dialogue about the level of a raise, none of this focused especially on Cosmo. A shot of Cosmo blowing out his cheeks is the first hint that he may be in too deep. He says he needs more credit, is told this is not possible, and asks to see the man in charge. The sequence is rendered from two set-ups, each of which marginalizes Cosmo in the frame. The first is centred on the character he asks for more credit, who stands behind him, our view of Cosmo restricted to part of his head appearing in a lower corner of the frame. The second is taken from Cosmo's side, as if the view of a player at the table, but another player intrudes between Cosmo and the camera; all that is visible is part of his chest and one arm, until he leans more fully into the picture at the end of the last shot taken from this perspective. This is a key dramatic moment, introducing what will prove to be the mechanism that drives the narrative, but it is decentred and underplayed rather than given the heightened treatment that might be expected. Exactly how Cosmo comes to be so deeply in debt is not shown, just a transition to the scenes the following morning in which he is confronted with the problem of how to pay.

Formally, the impression created in the card-table sequence leans strongly towards *vérité* – towards action 'caught', inexactly, rather than seeming to be the product of pre-established cinematic choreography. The same goes for much of the rest of the film, shot hand-held in variable and often harsh or murky light, far from always in the sharpest focus. It is only afterwards, when Cosmo is called in to discuss his debt, that the full significance of the card-table sequence – and the depth of his predicament – is brought to light. A similar kind of effect, in which the viewer is denied a full view of what is developing at crucial moments, is created in two other important sequences: the killing itself and the deployment of the mobster Flo (Timothy Carey) to finish the job. In the killing sequence, Cosmo finds his way into the bookie's home and observes him bathing with a woman. The bookie wanders into a pool, whistling quietly, at which point Cosmo's precise position in relation to his target is unclear. The elderly man keeps walking, seeming calm but perhaps slightly disturbed; he looks off-screen to the left, looks forward, and continues on his way across the pool, the camera panning slowly with him into a closer shot. He looks out of frame to the left again: cut, this time, to follow his look. The camera pans slowly to the left, along a length of wall, before revealing Cosmo, framed head-and-shoulders. Our awareness that Cosmo is the object of the bookie's look is delayed, and an unusually oblique quality given to the sequence, through a denial of what might have been an earlier eye-line match shot – after the bookie's first look in what proves to be Cosmo's direction – and the slow pan across the wall, rather than a direct cut to Cosmo himself. A cut back to the bookie is followed by another tightly framed shot of Cosmo as he cocks the gun, lifts it into the foreground and fires, the loud report of the gun shattering the silence in which the encounter has been played out, except for the low whistle of the bookie. The absence of non-diegetic music (music not produced from within the fictional world), here and in the rest of the film, is another significant reduction in the degree of information supplied to the viewer, musical accompaniment often performing an important role in the precise delineation of how a situation is developing moment-by-moment on-screen. The dramatically important fact that Cosmo is wounded during a subsequent exchange of fire only becomes apparent some time after his escape.

Missing from the killing sequence is an establishing shot that would clearly set out, in advance, the spatial relationship between the two characters at the critical moment. Instead, Cassavetes chooses to draw out the process of realization in a manner that is more character-centric and slow burning than would usually be expected in a central set-piece action sequence. The reluctance of the *mise-en-scène* to cut more quickly to the chase might be taken as a reflection of Cosmo's own reluctance to commit to the act. A form of suspense is created, but one that seems off-centre: we know Cosmo is around somewhere, and that the bookie is in imminent danger, but not exactly where he is during his quarry's moments of greatest exposure to the camera. Something similar happens when Flo turns up at Cosmo's club. Cosmo is seen mooching around the bar area during a performance of his girlie show, accompanied by the doleful rendition of a song by his resident MC/singer, the tragi-comic figure Mr Sophistication (Meade Roberts). The camera lingers for quite extended periods on the show itself, as it does on numerous occasions during the film. Cosmo's attention appears focused on the act until a shift in the direction of his gaze and a cut to a higher angle reveals the threatening presence in the audience of Flo, who was seen being allocated the task of killing Cosmo in the previous scene.

If the attention of the viewer is often directed to the stage show in *The Killing of a Chinese Bookie*, rather than to the gangster-related plot, the same goes for Cosmo himself. One of the distinctive features of the film, and its unusual take on generic material, is the extent to which the central character's life is *not* taken over by the dangerous and dramatic intrusion into his normal routine. Ordinary life, in his particular milieu, is not put on hold for the duration. He remains preoccupied with his business and the everyday problems of managing his performers. Even while *en route* to carry out the killing, and faced with the complication caused by a puncture that forces him to call a cab, he is sufficiently distracted from the mission to ring the club in what proves a frustrating effort to ensure that all is proceeding smoothly in his absence. He returns to the club again later, after escaping the attempt to kill him, using his diplomatic skills to assuage the doubts of Mr Sophistication and to get his performers belatedly on stage, despite the fact that he is still bleeding from his untreated wound (maybe fatally; the ending is ambiguous) and that the club is the obvious place for the gangsters to find him. The sequence backstage and when Cosmo addresses the audience, to silence their slow handclap, is extended, the attention of the film to this dimension equalling that of its central character. The effect, along with some of the other formal strategies detailed above, is to decentre the generic components in the mix. Normal routines and preoccupations are maintained – for both Cosmo-as-character and Cassavetes-film-as-Cassavetes-film – despite the intrusion of material from the world of gangsters. The usual kind of show must go on, for both Cosmo and Cassavetes: at the risk of his life, for the one; at the risk of undermining what might be more commercially attractive genre material, for the latter (Cosmo is likely to end up dead, one way or another; the film, appearing in the wake of the success of *A Woman Under the Influence* and intended by the director to be a more commercial proposition than his previous work, met a dire fate at the box office).

Similar generic territory – a world of what initially seem to be standard-issue greying, middle-aged Italian American mobsters – rubs up against a typically quirky Jim Jarmusch approach in *Ghost Dog: The Way of the Samurai* (1999). The title character (Forrest Whittaker) works as a hit-man for the mob, but one of unconventional character: a bulky, taciturn African American figure, in hooded top, who lives in a rooftop shack, keeps in touch by carrier pigeon and seeks to live according to the Samurai tradition enshrined in a book, quotations from which are presented as a form of punctuation throughout the film. Ghost Dog sees himself as loyal retainer, in traditional fashion, to the mobster Louie (John Tormey) who once saved his life. Problems ensue, not dissimilar to the central narrative dynamic of *Chinese Bookie*, when complications in one job lead Louie's bosses to order the hit-man's death. Unlike Cosmo, the protagonist of *Ghost Dog* is perfectly at home in a world of professional assassination; presented as a cool, stylish and highly accomplished figure, his long, silenced handguns even making the swooping sound of a sword when he wields them single-handedly to wipe out most of the mobster gang in one set-piece sequence. If he is an incongruous figure to the mobsters, as evidenced by the reaction of Louie's colleagues when told about their unconventional relationship, they are also given a number of quirky touches that suggest a life beyond their generically dictated characteristics. During a discussion of Ghost Dog's unusual name, one lapses into a rap routine – as he does later, shortly before his demise – while the man in charge, Vargo (Henry Silva), who has a predilection for children's cartoons, does an impression of the noise made by an elk.

Many of the conventional pleasures of the gangster/hit-man genre are supplied by *Ghost Dog*, including no shortage of aestheticized violent death. But they are combined with the offbeat sensibility of a typically indie cast, ingredients that would not usually form part of the recipe such as the central character's relationship with his 'best friend', the French-only speaking operator of an ice-cream van. The overarching narrative dynamic is familiar-conventional enough: hired assassin performs a hit, becomes a target, is given a grievance (the trashing of his home and the massacre of his pigeons) and exacts revenge. Along the way, however, the unhurried pace leaves room for a number of departures, and the climax obeys the logic of Ghost Dog's Samurai-inspired code, rather than that of more conventional expectations: faced with the prospect of a western-style shoot-out with Louie, he draws an unloaded weapon and allows himself to be killed.

The death of the central character is structured more centrally and inevitably into Jarmusch's engagement with the western genre, as suggested by the title, *Dead Man* (1995). William Blake (Johnny Depp) is an accountant who heads west with the promise of a job that fails to materialize. He becomes a wanted man, with a price on his head, after killing a man in self-defence and getting a bullet lodged next to his heart. Familiar western tropes – the naïve easterner's initiation into the ways of the west, his unjust treatment as an outlaw – blend with eccentricities such as the assumption of the Native American character, Nobody (Gary Farmer), that Blake is the poet of the same name and a typically leisurely Jarmusch style in which narrative development is punctuated by cuts or fades to black and a jangly/reverberating guitar accompaniment by Neil Young.

The western genre has also been given treatments claiming the status of greater verisimilitude, examples including the National Endowment for the Humanities funded *Heartland* and *The Ballad of Gregorio Cortez*, both of which are associated with the 'regional cinema' strand of independent production in the late 1970s and early 1980s, the sober 'granola movie' tradition associated with the early years of Sundance. *Heartland* is the moving, low-key account of the experiences of Elinore Randall (Conchata Ferrell), a widow with a seven-year-old daughter, Jerrino (Megan Folsom), who takes up employment with a rancher living on the remote Wyoming frontier of 1910. Existence is hard and spartan, the film shot in a style as quiet, unfussy and matter-of-fact as the lives of the central characters. Events that might elsewhere be presented with melodramatic flourish are treated as just another part of the practical routine. The fact that Elinore is to marry her employer, Clyde (Rip Torn), emerges obliquely and only barely stated, in the gap between two scenes; a product not of romance but of pragmatic necessity if she is to gain the degree of independence she craves. Her pregnancy is revealed in a similar manner, as an already-established fact within the diegetic world, when Jerrino is invited to feel the movement of the baby. The baby's subsequent death, in the middle of a harsh winter, is handled without sentimentality.

Traditional frontier values are celebrated in *Heartland* – especially endurance, often silent and dialogue-free – but not those usually to the fore in the western genre, in which such scenes of domestic fortitude are likely to be restricted to marginal characters against which more romantically heroic figures are defined. *The Ballad of Gregorio Cortez* focuses on a character cast into the more generically favoured role of outlaw, pursued by a posse. Gregorio Cortez gains mythic connotations during an 11-day pursuit in the Texas border country, but he is identified as an ordinary man, a farmer with young children, forced onto the run after what proves to have been a misunderstanding of language that led to the death of his brother and a sheriff. The focus of the film is on inter-cultural tensions, specifically the racist attitude of many Texans towards their Mexican neighbours, the images including but not dominated by a number of sequences shot in *vérité* style.

Material suggesting a greater degree of 'reality' within generic territory can also be inserted into films that are not remotely committed formally to the creation of impressions of authenticity. *Pulp Fiction*, for example, could hardly be more distant stylistically from *The Killing of a Chinese Bookie*, despite overlaps at the level of genre. But part of its distinctive character also results from the integration of relatively more real or ordinary-seeming detail into familiar generic routines. The much-cited discussion of the names and qualities of particular varieties of burger both before and during the sequence in which Jules and Vincent wipe out the occupants of an apartment is one example. The discourse, like the exchanges about the meaning of a Madonna lyric and the cases for and against tipping waitresses in the opening of *Reservoir Dogs*, has become an identifiable stylistic quirk associated with Quentin Tarantino. But it also functions to ground the characters, to some extent, as suggested in the previous chapter, to give them preoccupations more akin to ordinary, everyday life, suggesting that even central gangster protagonists, like those of *Ghost Dog* – as opposed to the inadvertently involved Cosmo – are more than just functions of the generically defined world they inhabit.

A dilemma of a quotidian variety also overtakes a lengthy sequence in which Jules and Vincent are required to clear up the bloody mess created in the back of their car after the latter accidentally shoots a confederate in the face. Household cleaning products take centre stage, rather than the usual accoutrements of a pair of hit-men. A number of shifts occur from what might usually be expected in the generic terrain. The cause of concern is the messy aftermath of a killing, the kind of real consequences that are not usually given extensive treatment. At first, the narrative tension that results is created – as might be expected, in terms of conventional antagonist – by the prospect of the state of the car's interior being spotted by the police, the incident having occurred some distance from Jules and Vincent's home territory. Once their employer finds them a emergency refuge, however, the suburban home of Jimmie (Tarantino), the factor giving deadline urgency to the clean-up shifts, incongruously, into the domestic realm: Jimmie's acquiescence in the operation is conditional on its completion before his wife arrives home from work. The prospect of an angry wife – much more a part of the vagaries of 'ordinary' life – becomes as great, and more immediate, a threat as that posed by the more generically coded fear of discovery by the police.

Incongruity, in a case such as this, and many others in *Pulp Fiction*, creates a comic effect that lies in the difference between the two very different registers brought into conjunction: that of the bloody aftermath of death and that of domestic routine. This is another marker of the offbeat quality of *Pulp Fiction* and *Reservoir Dogs*, and of a number of other independent features: a shifting of tone that can create a destabilizing effect for the viewer. Comedy, as I have argued elsewhere, is best understood strictly as a *modality* rather than as a genre, an inflection that can be given to any kind of material rather than a body of substance in its own right.[6] Material presented in a comic mode is generally assumed not to be meant too seriously. We

11. Mixing modalities: painful violence and comedy intermingle in *Reservoir Dogs* (1992).

are not supposed to invest too much in such events or in the possible implications they might have, either for components of the fictional world or for what they might imply of the world beyond the text. More serious modalities *do* ask us to consider such implications, to greater or larger extents, depending on the precise nature of the material (by the same reckoning, opposing qualities such as those of realism and genre-based fantasy, as found in some of the horror examples considered above, can also be understood in terms of differences of modality as much as of genre location). Elements of comedy are often worked into more avowedly serious material, functioning as a form of 'comic relief' for the viewer, a relaxing of dramatic tension, suspense or whatever qualities are dominant in the rest of the film. This is as true in many independent features as it is in Hollywood. The presence of comedy is often ameliorative, especially for films that tread in sensitive areas. It was considered vital to the marketing campaign of Robert Townsend's *Hollywood Shuffle*, for example, that the film was clearly identified as a comedy – as well as the product of a black filmmaker:

> This was the only way to avoid confusion over the delicate issues that were at the very heart of the film: a black filmmaker's view of the discrimination of blacks in the Hollywood movie industry, and his view that blacks are sometimes complicit in this discrimination.[7]

The comic dimension, although unpalatable to some, was also played up in publicity for *Pulp Fiction* and credited for much of its ability to appeal beyond its anticipated core audience.[8] The balance between more and less serious moments can be a subtle and shifting one, even in relatively straightforward mainstream productions. In some cases, however, the blending of comic and non-comic modalities can create an unsettling effect in which the viewer is denied a clearly and consistently offered position of orientation: whether to take on-screen events seriously, to become 'caught up' by or implicated to some extent in what is happening, or to remain in the more detached position often characteristic of comedy. This is a quality more likely to be heightened in the independent sector, or other alternative cinemas, precisely because of its refusal of the more settled and comfortable routines favoured, for commercial reasons, by the Hollywood-style mainstream.

Comedy is mixed with difficult and painful material in some independent features, a notable example being Todd Solondz's *Happiness*, a portrayal of lives of quiet desperation, the comedy of which is never far from a sense of the suffering of characters, suffering from which it is not easy to remain detached. Comedy and pain often occur simultaneously, rather than one offering relief from the other. This is the case in a number of pointed lines of dialogue. In the opening scene, for example, in which Joy Jordan has just ended her relationship with Andy (John Lovitz), the latter asks if the break-up is because of someone else. 'No,' Joy replies, earnestly, 'it's just you.' The line has a comic edge because it seems to be pulling in two different directions, comedy emerging from the gap between the two. From the tone and context, Joy's answer appears intended to be ameliorative, assuring Andy that she is not seeing someone else. The effect, however, is to drive home the more hurtful alternative, that she is simply rejecting him, because of his own nature, rather than that some other factor has intervened for which he is not to blame. In this and other examples, comedy is created through the creation of distance between viewer and characters, the viewer being made aware of ironies or levels of meaning less accessible to the character. *Happiness* usually leaves the viewer to linger on the immediate consequences in the scene, however, in a manner that maintains a sense of implication in the emotional pain that results. Another example is found during a sequence in which Joy's mother, Mona (Louise Lasser), visits a property agent in search of new accommodation after being told by her husband that he wants to separate. The agent is going through the formalities, typing Mona's details into her computer. Does she have a husband, children, pets? No. 'So really then just you alone all by yourself,' she concludes, cheerily and blithely unaware of the devastating quality of the remark, underlining in triplicate the lonely state of Mona's life.

Similarly double-edged comments come from the mouth of Joy's sister Trish. 'Somehow you always seemed so doomed to failure,' Trish beams to Joy, in the aftermath of her break-up with Andy. 'But now I see that's not true… there's a glimmer of hope for you after all,' she continues, nodding, beaming again, and failing entirely to engage honestly with the unhappiness of her sister's life or the discomfort created by her remarks. And there is also the most painful irony, in Trish's airy, taking-everything-for-granted observation about Joy to her husband, Bill ('You know, she's not like me. She doesn't have it all'), coming as it does shortly after his paedophilia has been indicated to the viewer. Viewers are, again, distanced from the character, in their superior knowledge of the side of Bill's life that will bring her world crashing down, and in their awareness of the brittle irony that underpins her comment. If Trish is, generally, a relatively easy comic target, in her smug suburban satisfaction, the steady, serious undermining of the foundations of her life creates a counter-dynamic in which we are encouraged to care more for her fate than might otherwise be the case.

The most distinctly 'alternative' and unsettling uses of comedy in *Happiness* come in more direct relation to Bill's acts of paedophilia, a taboo territory in which any hint of comedy would not usually be considered acceptable. A number of discomfortingly comic nuances are worked into a sequence in which Bill plots the rape of Johnny Grasso

(Evan Silverberg), a friend of his 11-year-old son who is sleeping over for the night. Bill is at first frustrated, when Johnny turns down the offer of ice-cream served with a chocolate fudge sauce that has been laced with sleeping tablet powder, designed to ensure that Bill can proceed uninterrupted by Johnny or any members of his own family. He eventually finds something Johnny will agree to eat, a tuna-salad sandwich, which is suitably doctored. Bill takes his son Billy (Rufus Read) up to bed, leaving Johnny downstairs to eat his sandwich. Upstairs, Bill performs a series of funny-seeming quick little steps as he nips about, checking everyone else is asleep, steps that give his antics a slightly comic impression that is disturbingly incongruous in the context. On his return downstairs, another comic effect is created by the way he comes bounding eagerly into the frame, only to halt at the edge of the picture when he sees the sandwich still lying untouched on the floor, a comically coded deflated look on his face. Intruding any hint of humour into scenes such as these – otherwise treated quite seriously, rather than part of a broader instance of 'bad taste' comedy – is an extremely unconventional and high-risk strategy, part of a non-judgemental approach to the character of Bill to which we will return in the next chapter when considering more generally the social/cultural stance taken by some indie features.

The mixing of comic and non-comic modalities is found in some films that offer an indie-style twist on the conventions of more familiar comic genres, such as romantic comedy. Hal Hartley's *Trust* (1991) has many of the ingredients of the form, but in a somewhat different flavour. The opening scenes introduce us to the oppressive domestic circumstances of the two principals: the pregnant high-school drop-out Maria (Adrienne Shelley), blamed by her mother for the heart attack that killed her father, and the bookish, intense and idealistic Mathew (Martin Donovan), bullied by his father and prone to random explosions of violence against others. Convention leads us to expect that their paths will cross, and that a romantic relationship will develop. This does prove to be the case, although in an eccentric manner. Mathew's proposal of marriage, and to father the baby Maria plans to abort, is offhand, the relationship lacking the usual signifiers of 'romantic love' or sexual attraction. One of the key dynamics of romantic comedy, the reconciliation of differences between the protagonists, is initially sustained. The undereducated Maria takes an interest in words, a domain established as one in which Mathew is well schooled. In a reversal of romantic cliché, Mathew encourages Maria to wear her glasses, rather than to remove them in order to appear superficially more attractive; 'I like librarians,' he replies to her objection that they make her look like one. She begins to tame her hair in a ponytail. Mathew, for his part, tries to live in a more conventional manner. He accepts a job he had previously rejected, repairing television sets despite his strong aversion to the medium, and eventually swallows pride to ask to return to his previous employment – and the accompanying welfare benefits – with a company that knowingly turns out substandard products. He even ends up watching television himself, at the end of a hard day of compromised principles.

This dynamic is eventually upset, however, rather than leading towards domestic bliss. A succession of events and misunderstandings leads Maria to have her abortion, after all, during and after which her glasses are removed, and Mathew quits his job. The film ends with their relationship re-established in spirit (including a final move in which Maria puts her glasses on once again), but with Mathew being hauled off by the cops after bringing out a hand grenade – a talisman of his ready-to-explode character – at work. One of the central tenets of romantic comedy is maintained, the sense of some kind of essential inner belonging between Maria and Mathew, isolated together against a dishonest and superficial world. No clear indication is given of how this might be sustained beyond the final credits, although that is not unusual in conventional varieties of the format. *Trust* shares a sense of the fragility of relationships with the more questioning of Hollywood romantic comedies,[9] but departs principally in an uncertainty of tone that makes it hard to establish unequivocally as either romance or comedy.

What exactly represents a more or less conventional ending to a romantic comedy of distinctly indie character is a question raised by *Secretary* (2002), in which a relationship of mutual sado-masochistic satisfaction develops between Lee Holloway (Maggie Gyllenhaal) and her employer, a lawyer known only as Mr Grey (James Spader). Lee, fragile, prone to cutting herself and freshly released after a short stay in a psychiatric hospital, appears to be the perfect match for Grey.

What might otherwise seem an abusive relationship turns out to be the satisfaction of her desires. When she seeks to move closer to Grey, however, beyond a controlled masturbation ritual, he pulls away, dismisses her, and seeks a new recruit. To end the film at this point would be a good example of resistance to genre convention, to the reconciliatory dynamic so central to Hollywood romantic comedy (and many other Hollywood productions). It would seem to adhere more plausibly to the logic of the situation, rather than confecting some fantasy/movie-type way of keeping the central characters together. The latter is what ensues, however. Lee performs a vigil to declare her love, in which she refuses to move from Grey's desk, and we are left with the pair setting up home together, continuing the relationship into the domestic sphere. On the one hand, this can be read as a cop-out, a shift in favour of conventional reconciliation. But conventional reconciliation of such a bizarre variety is perhaps just as offbeat/unconventional as its denial, an introduction into genre-familiar space of sufficiently alternative material to undermine as much as it reinstates.

In some cases, an alternative stance towards genre frameworks is taken further, to a point at which familiar conventions are undermined or deconstructed rather than merely complicated or mixed with other qualities. The western, for example, is subjected to a number of indignities that leaves little intact in *Lonesome Cowboys* (1968), directed by Andy Warhol and Paul Morrissey. The film opens with a characteristically extended pre-credit sex sequence, in mid and close shots, an outdoor location including rock and underbrush the only indicator of generic location other than the title song on the soundtrack. A conventional western street-setting is established soon afterwards, but undercut by the camp and halting nature of the narration provided by one of the central characters. A posse of cowboys approaches, to comments such as 'maybe they're real men' and 'I think he's got mascara on'. Two of the cowboys, established as a group of brothers, proceed to talk about haircuts and clothes, one demonstrating a series of exercises needed to build up the thighs sufficiently to support a gun-belt. The film is filled with deliberate anachronisms, including the flaunting of items such as ring-pull beer cans, sunglasses and jockey shorts. The texture of the piece is familiarly Warhol/Morrissey: roughly shot and assembled, with plenty of flash/jump-cuts, clumsy camerawork and an emphasis on talk over action, both often desultory. *Lonesome Cowboys* exists in the orbit of the 'Warhol/Morrissey film', as its prime identifier, more than that of the western genre. But there is some substance to the act of genre deconstruction that results from the intrusion of the Warhol/Morrissey approach into the generic territory, particularly in the overturning of the constructions of masculinity usually associated with the western.

Jon Jost's *Frameup* is another example that offers an implicit critique and a denial of the usual pleasures associated with the generic terrain on which it treads, in this case the outlaw/couple-on-the-road format. The opening images seem conventional enough: shots of bleak, open landscape, roads, a few rural buildings, even if they are perhaps held a little longer than is usually the case in the establishment of place. Then comes a typical Jost shot, a flattened straight-on view of a freight train passing in the middle distance, which functions almost as an in-joke; held for a long, long time, abnormal for anything like a conventional fiction feature although motivated, in this case, by the extreme length of the train itself. From this point onwards, any of the usual celebration of freedom and movement associated with the form is replaced by an overwhelming impression of stasis, in the holding of images that come to verge on the abstract and in the interminable ramblings of the principals, Ricky-Lee and Beth-Ann, even though they complete a conventionally structured journey from the Midwest to the fantasy attractions of California. Eventually, towards the end, comes some genre-conventional action: Ricky-Lee holds up a store, kills three people in the process, is arrested and tried, and the pair are executed by lethal injection. These events are all handled, however, in a manner that robs them of any hint of the cinematic, dramatic or romantic glory often associated with the violent activities and fates of outlaw protagonists. The killings are presented obliquely, Ricky-Lee held in close-shot from the neck upwards as he shoots; we see neither the gunshots nor the impact on the victims, only the noise of the gun and the sound of bodies falling. The process of execution is rendered both matter-of-fact and pathetic. A split screen offers a view of both characters, first during the preparations, rendered abstract in a series of close-ups of detail, and then in side-by-side head-and-shoulder shots, harnessed to the table; he swearing and protesting, she whimpering, as their lives slowly ebb pointlessly away.

Using Genre

To complicate or to undermine genre conventions is still to mobilize them to some extent, even in the more radical departures. The line between use and abuse is not clear-cut but a question of balance, to be argued in specific cases. How far complication has to be pushed to reach the point of more substantial undermining is likely to remain subject to debate. The difference might be that between *Lonesome Cowboys*, as a refusal of key conventions of the western, and the 'Warhol presents' Paul Morrissey horror films, *Flesh for Frankenstein* and *Blood for Dracula*, produced back to back in Italy in 1974. The world of *Flesh for Frankenstein* and *Blood for Dracula* is still identifiably a corner of the Warhol/Morrissey universe, with its stilted performances and the presence of familiar faces/bodies such as those of Joe Dallesandro. But the pull of familiar genre-based narrative routine – and with it, more conventional découpage – is much stronger than anything found in *Lonesome Cowboys*, even if it dips into semi-parody and excesses of blood and sex. The fact that examples such as *Lonesome Cowboys* and *Frameup*, in which genre is radically undermined, are found at the more underground/experimental/art end of the spectrum says much about the influence genre continues to exert in many independent features.

The distinct signifiers of vampire-horror are still important to genre-complicating films such as *Martin, Habit* and *The Addiction*, for both the effect they offer the viewer and their status in the industrial landscape of the independent sector. As films more likely to be read largely or exclusively in secular terms, as accounts of mental incapacity, addiction or disintegration of one kind or another, they would not be as dramatically charged (with as much at stake, if the pun can be excused) or as likely a commercial prospect. The same goes for the raising of issues such as environmentalism and animal experimentation in *No Telling* and *Wendigo*. The horror components provide a stable base from which to explore questions that might not be so easy to sell, and that might seem overly 'preachy' to many potential viewers, in their own right. Genre functions as a marketing device, a way of selling a package for which the existence of an audience has already been demonstrated, even in the case of productions such as these that exist at the economic margins. It is for this reason that films such as *Flesh for Frankenstein* and *Blood for Dracula* continue to be more available on videotape or DVD than most other works from the Warhol and/or Morrissey stable: their familiar horror genre basis gives them an angle perceived as marketable to an audience wider than that for works identified only as part of the underground/avant-garde. Working within existing genre frameworks, even if complicating them, has always been an important way of making independent production possible, because of the greater likelihood of securing an audience to ensure financial viability; or, at least, of convincing backers that this is likely.

Horror has been a particularly attractive niche from this perspective because of its potential economic grounding in the exploitation sector. If indie filmmakers want to do something a bit different, edgy, political or stylish, their best bet is often to work within a genre such as horror, where a viable audience has existed for low-budget fare of varying kinds, from the drive-in of the 1950s and 1960s to the 'midnight movie' of the 1970s and the video market from the 1980s. Horror tropes have proved hospitable to a wide range of options starting from outside the mainstream, as we have already seen: from the *vérité* aesthetic of *The Blair Witch Project* to the stylistic and other excesses of *The Evil Dead*; from hokey exploitation pictures such as those of Morrissey and the Troma studio (home of the Toxic Avenger) to the arty minimalism of J.T. Petty's virtually dialogue-free 16mm feature *Soft for Digging*, an eye-catching offering at the 2001 Sundance festival. *Soft for Digging* provides a good example of the potential play between similarity and difference that can be found within particular generic or sub-genre frameworks. The film is usually discussed at least partly in connection with *The Blair Witch Project*. The two films were shot at around the same time and in much the same place, in the woods of southern Maryland and northern Virginia. Both trade on a creepy quality of motion through landscapes of thin but densely packed woodland, and play on a broader mythic heritage: notions of unearthly presences in wooded wilderness areas that have resonances in American culture (from early settlement religious doctrine to the likes of *Twin Peaks* and *The X-Files*) and elsewhere. Both were made on initially very low budgets, less than $6,000 on 16mm for *Soft for Digging*, Petty's New York University final thesis production, and gain much of their impact from factors linked to their limited means. From these points of similarity, however, they depart quite radically. *Blair Witch*, with student-age characters oriented towards a youth audience, was clearly designed with serious commercial exploitation in mind, even if the full extent of its success could hardly have been envisaged. *Soft for Digging* is very different, with its elderly central character Virgil Manoven (Edmond Mercier), who stumbles obliquely upon the murder of a child while wandering through the woods in a striking burgundy robe and white combinations, and its hypnotic use of very long stretches without dialogue.

Apart from the degree of commercial insurance they can offer, certain genres also lend themselves particularly well to the kinds of qualities sought in some independent production. Horror has an intrinsic potential to create unsettling impressions that, as we have seen, can shade from more obviously generically motivated and fantastic components into areas closer to those of everyday life. The genre lends itself to formal innovation, as a way of figuring such impressions, in examples such as the subtle dislocations of *Habit* and the minimalist aesthetic of *Soft for Digging*; in the latter, a sense of unease located in the quotidian is created through the use of expressive sound motifs involving agitated water (noisily boiling in a pan, a kettle, the stream flowing outside Virgil's cabin and a screaming shower faucet that provides background to the film's violent climax). Horror is also well suited to exercises of showy stylistic excess such as those found in the *Evil Dead* films and the flourishes of camerawork and rapid-editing found in a more commercially established exploitation-sector production such as *The Convent* (2000), the first feature from the previously straight-to-video Alpine Pictures to gain a theatrical release. Some of the same goes for film noir and related crime/thriller formats hospitable to indie-favoured qualities such as tangled narrative structure and the more-than-usually expressive use of form. The noir/thriller tradition provides grounding and motivation – a context for audience understanding – for some of the narrative complexities and inversions of films such as *Memento*, *The Limey* and Lynch's *Lost Highway* and *Mulholland Drive*.

The Cohen brothers have achieved much of their impact through working within and revisiting established genre frameworks, starting with noir in *Blood Simple*. If *Blood Simple* is, essentially, a stylish and brooding updating of the crime/noir world of films based on the work of writers such as James M. Cain, *Fargo* and *The Big Lebowski* offer more eccentric departures. Maintaining central tenets such as greed and dishonour-among-thieves, *Fargo* swaps the darkness and shadow of classical noir for a whitened-out *film blanc* setting in the snow-covered flatlands of Minnesota. Urban paranoia is traded-in for a distinctly offbeat regional setting characterized by the deadpan delivery of the local Scandinavian American accent (the ubiquitous 'yaaah' instead of 'yes') and the presence of central figures such as an insightful sheriff, on the trail of the crooks, who happens to be heavily pregnant. *The Big Lebowski* is in territory closer to that of the Raymond Chandler school, playing specifically on the title of *The Big Sleep*, although with an equally unconventional pivotal character, the ultra-laid-back and semi-permanently stoned 'Dude', Jeff Lebowski (Jeff Bridges), caught up in a sprawling plot revolving, like *Fargo*, around a staged kidnapping. The Cohens have also offered updatings of screwball comedy, as a format that lends itself to the development of wacky characters and nutty plotlines, in *Raising Arizona* and *The Hudsucker Proxy* (1994, produced and distributed by Warner), the latter a homage to the worlds of Preston Sturges and Frank Capra.

The more alternative the perspective offered by independent features, the more useful familiar generic terrain can become, as a basis from which to judge distance from or proximity to the mainstream norm. A good example is the use of the conventions of romantic comedy in films about gay or lesbian relationships, an issue to which we will return in the following chapter. Alternativeness or independence might seem to be measurable by an avoidance of established/mainstream genre structures, although this proves to be less common or clear-cut than might be expected. We are returned here to the wider difficulties involved in the business of defining genres or the boundaries between one genre and another. Classic 1990s indie features such as *Clerks* and *Slacker* might be said to exist outside any obvious genre category, but genre-belonging of some kind can be found for many others. *Stranger than Paradise*, for example, might be considered to become a road movie after the first third, even if a distinctly eccentric one. Some generic categories seem more clear-cut, and are more widely recognized as such, than others. 'Emotional-relationship drama' is a category that might fit a substantial number of independent features, but tends not to be seen as a genre, except when labelled 'melodrama', a term that has plenty of complications of its own (essentially a mode of presentation found across a wide range of genres). Issues of taste-judgement come into play here, as in many systems of classification. 'Genre' has often connoted a culturally 'lower' form against which supposedly non-genre films are distinguished, although this is a loaded judgement, dependent on the prevailing cultural values enshrined at one time or another.

'Independent cinema' is itself a term that asserts a distinction from the Hollywood mainstream, as suggested above, and one that has sometimes, if loosely, implied the status of something like a genre – or collection of genres – in its own right. If we ask what category *Clerks* and *Slacker* primarily belong to, in working classifications, the answer might be 'low-budget, first-feature indie production', one part of the wider independent landscape. Whether such a category merits the term 'genre' is open to question. Individual films can be subject to the gravitational pull of more than one category, depending on which aspects of their characteristics are being highlighted. *Laws of Gravity*, for example, might join *Clerks* and *Slacker* in 'low-budget, first-feature indie production', but is also under the influence of the 'small-time street-hood' sub-genre. None of these categories should be seen as fixed, absolute or mutually incompatible. That all independent features of the kind on which this book is focused cannot be subsumed to a single category should already be clear, but many continue to offer workings *in* and reworkings *of* generic identity that constitute some of their most rich and diverse qualities.

5

Alternative Visions

Social, Political and Ideological Dimensions of Independent Cinema

A light, airy romantic refrain wells up on the soundtrack as Bill Maplewood catches sight of the object of his desire. Yearning strings play over images of his gaze; a more playful flute trills over two medium close-ups, giving us his point of view. This is a very familiar movie confection, and just a passing moment in *Happiness*. But it is situated in a context that makes it, in its quiet way, extraordinarily transgressive, beyond the bounds of anything that could be conceived in a product of the Hollywood mainstream. The object of Bill's desiring gaze is, of course, a young boy, 11-year-old Johnny Grasso, who he will proceed to drug and (off-screen) anally rape in the following scenes. What makes the brief sequence described above so unusual is precisely the extent to which it relies on cinematic devices of such banal conventionality: the use of music, especially romantic music, to indicate emotional states, and editing based around eye-line match shots to reveal the object of desire and to heighten (progressively closer shots of both protagonists are used) the implied degree of yearning. The effect, normal enough in other situations but extremely uncomfortable here, is to implicate the viewer, to some extent, in the economy of desire that is on display.

Point-of-view shot structures do not entirely force viewers into particular perspectives, and all the baggage that comes with them, an issue that has long been debated in theories of cinema spectatorship. But they do encourage viewers to allow themselves to be drawn into events on screen, to share vicariously, from the security of their seats, some of the emotions experienced in the fictional world, including those of characters with which they might consider themselves to have little in common. The very idea of offering viewers the discomfort of some implication in the activities and desires of an active paedophile immediately marks *Happiness* as something out of the mainstream. The impression is continued during the scenes described in the previous chapter in which Bill attempts to drug Johnny. The structure of the sequence generates suspense. Will he or won't he succeed? Will he, at last, get Johnny to eat something into which he can mix his sleeping draught? The *at last* is given some emphasis, and contributes to the sense of painful comedy examined in Chapter 4. Bill's repeated initial frustration encourages the viewer to will his success, at least partially, and even while being appalled at the enterprise in which he is engaged. Again, to offer even a sniff of this kind of allegiance with a paedophile in the middle of his manipulations is something that would usually be well beyond the pale of what is deemed acceptable in 'normal' mainstream cinema or society.

Happiness presents Bill Maplewood as an exceedingly ordinary, banal figure, even if his job as a therapist makes him far from typical. Bill is quiet, grey, recessive, middle-class and apparently successful in his career. He is presented as an ordinary man who is also a predatory paedophile, rather than in the dominant tabloid/Hollywood guise as some kind of monster. And it is here that a serious point is being made: that paedophilia tends to be found close to family and friends, in ordinary life, rather than in the form of an exotic threat from outside. The latter is far more comfortable to imagine than the former, which has the potential to undermine a number of generally conservative investments in the supposed sanctity of the 'traditional' family unit. *Happiness* refuses the kind of strategies that would, more conventionally, demonize Bill and leave him safely distanced from the viewer. It encourages instead an uncomfortable degree of proximity: a proximity to character that implies the social proximity of paedophilia.

The result is likely to be a double sense of discomfort for the viewer: not the full cinematic degree of identification or allegiance we would expect to experience with a more obviously sympathetic character, but something awkwardly in between; and discomfort in raising the difficult issue of the extent to which paedophilia is a part of the everyday fabric of our society, one example of what the film presents as a spectrum of sad, often abusive forms of relationship. On both counts, this is quintessentially independent territory, restricting the likely audience and inviting attack from the forces of conservatism.

An important aspect of any definition of independent cinema, in addition to the industrial and formal dimensions considered so far, is the space it offers – potentially, at least – for the expression of alternative social, political and/or ideological perspectives. Formal departures from mainstream convention often have socio-political implications, as has already been suggested in some cases. The American indie sector has also provided an arena hospitable to a number of constituencies generally subjected to neglect or stereotypical representation in the mainstream, the most prominent cases in recent decades being black- and gay-oriented cinema. Greater scope has been found for more liberal, open or radical treatment of contentious issues such as paedophilia, freed to a significant extent from the relatively narrow moral economy typically operative in Hollywood. Independent features have in many cases been able to avoid the kind of ideologically loaded imaginary reconciliations used in Hollywood features to smooth away any awkward social or political issues that might initially be confronted.

Whether independent production of the kind examined in this book more than occasionally constitutes a radical cinema in an explicitly political sense, rather than in the implications of a broader treatment of particular social issues, is more questionable. Independent cinema is certainly not immune to implication in the reinforcement of dominant ideologies (including those of patriarchy, capitalism and racism), and is as far from being a single entity in this as any of the other respects considered so far. Even in its more openly alternative or radical incarnations, the art and business of reaching an audience often necessitate a number of compromises, including the use of some of the genre frameworks examined in the previous chapter.

If independent features such as *Happiness* attract attention – often of a critical variety – for the controversial territories onto which they stray, this might not always be accidental. Controversy often sells, as was seen in Chapter 1 in the case of the marketing strategy favoured by Miramax. Figures such as paedophiles, and others defined as sexually deviant by mainstream society, turn up disproportionately often in indie films, partly because they raise issues independent cinema is more capable than Hollywood of treating with any complexity but also because they offer the potential for a *frisson* that can be marketable, as was demonstrated by the landmark box-office success of *sex, lies, and videotape*. What results might, in some cases, be defined in part as a kind of exploitation cinema for those who situate themselves as more culturally/educationally discerning. The problem of what sells, and to whom, remains a central one for independent filmmakers inspired by strong social, political and/or ideological agendas. Independent features offering alternative social perspectives are often dependent on the existence of niche audiences, rooted in particular social groups, capable of sustaining a particular level of production. But, as was suggested in Chapter 1, there is no guarantee that audiences defined in terms of one specific attribute according to which they are denied adequate representation in the mainstream (such as race or sexual orientation) are likely to have radical or alternative tastes in other respects.

Independent filmmakers are sometimes caught between seeking to cater to the tastes of audience groups defined on social-cultural lines (black or gay, for example) and those defined as likely to frequent more marginal alternative/art-house productions. The strongest alternative visions are likely to combine challenging socio-political material with formal innovation, but in doing so they risk limiting the size of the potential audience within a particular constituency; the appreciation of radically unconventional formal strategies usually requires the mobilization of resources of cultural capital that are unequally distributed in society. To maximize the potential audience tends to entail compromise, in formal innovation and in the extent to which political or otherwise uncomfortable issues are raised in an explicit manner. This is partly a matter of what is likely to be palatable to audiences themselves and partly a question of the economically crucial perception of financiers and distributors, whose notions of the bounds of what is likely to prove viable are often likely to err on the narrow side. At one end of the spectrum lies material that is radical in both form and content, in aesthetics and politics, while the other shades into the Hollywood mainstream. As in other respects, however, much ground exists in between the two extremes, the precise contours of the landscape varying from one alternative movement to another.

Black Independent Cinema

Films by new black filmmakers were an important component of the indie upsurge of the late 1980s and early 1990s. By far the best-known figure of the period was Spike Lee, the success of his debut feature *She's Gotta Have It* being credited with inspiring a generation of others. The degree of celebrity enjoyed by Lee, who went on to build a career moving between studio and more independent work, is in some ways symptomatic of the dilemma that has faced independent black filmmakers. Lee's has generally been a brash, stylish and marketable variety of indie or studio-based production that contrasts with the much less commercially oriented work of his immediate predecessors in what became known as the LA School, based at the University of California in Los Angeles in the 1970s. The LA School, whose leading figures included Charles Burnett, Haile Gerima and Julie Dash, was an avowedly radical grouping, fuelled by the currents of 1960s struggles such as the civil rights movement, the Watts uprising, the anti-Vietnam-war campaign and support for wars of national liberation in Africa, Asia and Latin America.[1] In its portrayal of the lives of black Americans in the 1970s and after, it stood in opposition to Hollywood's wave of blaxploitation pictures, a primarily action-oriented format used to target urban black audiences at a time when the studios were in economic difficulty.

One of the films that started the blaxploitation trend was, in fact, a more radical independent feature, Melvin Van Peebles' $150,000 *Sweet Sweetback's Baadasssss Song* (1971), a work that can be situated between that of the LA School and mainstream, mostly white-directed blaxploitation. *Sweet Sweetback* makes a number of inflammatory political gestures of a kind unlikely ever to be found in a Hollywood production. The central character, Sweetback (Van Peebles), named for his prodigious sexual abilities, is arrested as part of a charade by two police officers seeking to give the impression that they are making headway in a case. Diverted on their way to the police station, they pick up a young black radical, Moo Moo (Hubert Scales), who is subjected to a severe beating. Sweetback at first attempts to ignore what is happening, but eventually responds, rescuing Moo Moo by hitting the officers repeatedly with the handcuffs attached to one of his wrists. A shift of consciousness is implied, in which the previously passive and decadent stud becomes emblematic of an assertive black spirit fighting back against oppression. Sweetback goes on the lam, montage sequences in which he runs through various parts of a decaying urban landscape forming a substantial part of the texture of the film, eventually killing two cops before escaping across the border into Mexico. Along the way, the film suggests that Sweetback has the support of the Los Angeles black community, evidence including a sequence in which he escapes arrest when a gathering crowd torches a police car.

Sweet Sweetback was a radical intervention on more than one level. The presentation of a strongly sexually active male figure was itself in breach of the constraints within which black representation had been held since the furore created by the racist image of a sexually threatening black male caricature in *The Birth of a Nation* in 1915. Black male figures had, for decades, been effectively emasculated, in roles ranging from those of comic buffoons to the idealized and 'safe' middle-class characters played by Sidney Poitier in the 1950s and 1960s.[2] It was this confident, sexually active black figure that was to be celebrated in a number of blaxploitation features from *Shaft* (1971) onwards. Adding to this a provocatively radical stance, a depiction of routine police brutality that seems to provide justification for the killing of officers in self-defence and the heroic escape of the offender, made for a controversial mixture, and box-office impact that led to a domestic gross of $15 million. The insurgent impression created by the film was increased by its unconventional stylistic approach, an uneven but potent mix of *vérité*-style hand-held and often oblique camerawork, disjunctive editing and expressive effects including multiple exposures and colour-tinted negative images.

As an alternative to prevailing movie representations of black

Americans, *Sweetback* provoked widely divergent responses, both celebrated and dismissed as offering little more than romantic myth.[3] The rhetoric of the film is one of collective resistance, but the central dynamic remains a more familiar individual rebellion and across-the-frontier escape. If the film was a striking departure in its open endorsement of fighting back against blatant police oppression, the figure of Sweetback maintains many stereotypical features. The spectacle of the black male as generously endowed super-stud is the stuff of racist cliché, even if it had been repressed in Hollywood. Here, and in mainstream blaxploitation, the principal emphasis often remains on urban ghetto mythic-fantasy figures – whether as figments of the white or black imaginations – and a narrow range of black experience. In their different ways, independents ranging from leading figures of the LA School to Spike Lee and others who emerged in the 1990s sought to provide representations that accounted more adequately for the realities and complexities of black American life.

The LA School drew upon a rich heritage, including a mixture of documentary-style realism and contemporary developments towards a politically radical 'Third Cinema', associated initially with post-revolutionary Cuba and the Cinema Novo movement in Brazil. The influence of realist schools, including Italian Neorealism and the British social documentary movement of the 1930s (one of the leading figures of which, Basil Wright, taught at UCLA), is particular apparent in films such as Charles Burnett's *Killer of Sheep* (1977) and Billy Woodberry's *Bless Their Little Hearts* (1984). *Killer of Sheep*, shot for less than $10,000 on black-and-white 16mm as Burnett's master's thesis, is a low-key portrait of the Watts ghetto of Los Angeles. Forward-moving narrative drive is replaced by a series of lingering sequences that create an understated impression of the texture of daily life on the margins, focused around the family of the title character, Stan (Henry Gale Sanders), who works in a slaughterhouse. Much time is devoted to the slow unfolding of action within the frame, including many documentary-seeming sequences of children playing in and around their homes and in a dusty wasteland near the railroad tracks. Typical of the film's style is a scene in which Stan and a friend invest in a used car engine and carry it, laboriously, down the steps from the apartment of the seller. The carrying of the engine is shown in full, a sequence that halts forward-moving narrative progression and would be likely to be skipped in a mainstream feature. Characters and viewers are obliged to see the action through, without ellipsis, creating an impression of the real, sustained effort involved, both in this particular enterprise and in the keeping together of life more generally. That it ends in futility – the engine falls, broken, from the back of a pick-up truck as soon as it moves off – is also characteristic of the numerous offhand disappointments charted by the film. *Killer of Sheep* avoids sentimentality, however, more so than some of the classic works of Italian Neorealism that also give a central presence to the plight of young children (most famously, *Ladri di Biciclette/Bicycle Thieves* [1948]). The play of the children is sometimes mean and harsh, and extremely naturalistic. Moments of pain and disappointment are mixed with happier interludes, depicted with equally unsentimental detachment, including a sequence in which a single shot is held on Stan and his wife in a slow dance to a blues theme. The film resists pressures for any major/melodramatic plot developments or crises. Stan rejects the overtures of a gangster-type pair who seek his involvement in a killing that might give the film a turn into more generically coded territory, and the film ends in a spirit of endurance, of life continuing as it is rather than being subject to any classical narrative arc or any individual-centred solutions to social problems.

The aim of the filmmakers involved in the LA School was not, generally, to achieve crossover success into the mainstream, but to create a separate and politically more radical version of independent cinema, a project that often put it at odds with the industry-oriented aims of the UCLA film school.[4] Few of its films received any conventional cinema distribution, although *Killer of Sheep* won prizes in 1981 at the Berlin and US (to become Sundance) film festivals, before most of the key developments in the building of the independent infrastructure examined in Chapter 1. It is in its separation from mainstream circuits, as well as in some specific approaches to form and content, that the LA School has significant points in common with the Third Cinema movement. A more direct connection existed in the person of Gerima, an Ethiopian-born member of the group who contributed a number of key works produced from the USA. A thematic connection between Third World struggle and the Watts landscape of films such as *Killer of Sheep* and *Bless Their Little Hearts* is introduced in Gerima's *Bush Mama* (1976).

Bush Mama creates from the start a sense of the oppressive nature of impoverished black life in the ghetto. The opening images are accompanied by what builds to a cacophony of overlapping sounds representing the various state forces arrayed against the central character, Dorothy (Barbara O. Jones): the repeatedly questioning voices of welfare and unemployment officials, the crackle of a police radio, the constant overhead presence of helicopters. Third-person shots of street scenes, including a car pulled over by the LAPD, are mixed with hand-held, subjective, first-person sequences that combine with the oppressive soundscape to give the impression of taking the viewer inside the experience. A number of character voices, including that of Dorothy's imprisoned husband, offer more or less radical interpretations of the situation and prescriptions for action. The key turning point, however, is her engagement with a poster featuring an African woman holding a baby in one hand and a gun in the other, an image she comes to recognize as emblematic of her own embattled position. A sequence is edited to create the impression of an exchange of looks between the two, followed by the latest in a series of apparently arbitrary shootings of black men on the street outside her home. When her daughter is raped by a motorcycle cop, Dorothy fights back, killing (it appears) the officer and making a speech that implies a political awakening after being arrested and beaten in a police cell.

The implied link between the situation of black Americans and Third World liberation struggles becomes more explicit in *Ashes and Embers* (1982), Gerima's evocation of the experiences of a black Vietnam veteran still struggling to come to terms with his life eight years after the end of the war. Ned Charles (John Anderson) is angry and alienated, haunted by actuality-footage flashback memories of Vietnam, but a figure employed to ends very different from those associated with Hollywood's contemporary version of the (often psychopathic) disaffected Vietnam vet. Parallels are suggested between the lives of black Americans and those of the Vietnamese, building on a connection implied in *Bush Mama* through the figure of Dorothy's husband, T.C. (Johnny Weathers), a veteran whose Vietnam nightmares feature the helicopter noise that is also ever-present in the ghetto.

Ned's elderly rural Grandma (Evelyn A. Blackwell) is gradually losing the land she toils, forced to sell up to pay taxes and keep herself alive. A thin, bony figure in a wide-brimmed hat, she resembles a Vietnamese peasant, in both appearance and emotional investment in the land; a parallel suggested at first implicitly, later in editing that juxtaposes her in Ned's consciousness with Vietnamese women and children. At one point Ned takes flight, running through trees, a sequence intercut with shots from the perspective of a helicopter machine-gunner shooting down into a green jungle canopy. Directional matches and the sound of gunfire carrying over into the present create the impression that Ned himself is the target of attack. At another point he collapses in pain in the street, projecting onto himself the impact of a beating given in flashback to a Vietnamese captive.

Ashes and Embers achieves an effective balance between individual-character-centred melodrama, focused on Ned, and broader contextual material. The former leans often towards the expressionist, a range of cinematic devices including inversion and spinning of the camera combining with dissonant music to create an impression of his disordered state of mind. The latter is provided largely through group discussions by members of his activist girlfriend's study group, from which Ned usually remains withdrawn, on subjects such as Vietnam and the prospects for unity within the black community. One of the strengths of the film, as a narrative fiction, is its ability to provide some analysis, through such discussions, and the didactic implications of the montage linkages considered above, without favouring abstracted political-ideological commentary over a version of the experience as lived by a central character. *Ashes and Embers* is thus able to offer emotional impact – in a narrative framework that is evocative and circular, rather than forward-driving – as well as ideological intervention. By the end, the film implies, Ned has changed and escaped his alienated state, learning lessons of history through stories of slave rebellion from his Grandma, and others, and being brought to a new, empowered stage of consciousness.

The notion of revisiting the past in order to provide lessons for the present is the guiding thesis of Gerima's later and probably best-known film, *Sankofa* (1993), a joint production with backing from the USA, Burkina Faso, Ghana, Germany and the UK. A black American model on a photo-shoot at a fortress in Ghana, West Africa, in which slaves were held before being shipped to America, is transported back into the past. Mona (Oyafunmike Ogunlano) is then reincarnated as Shola, a timid plantation house slave who eventually fights back and joins a rebellion of the kind memorialized by Grandma in *Ashes and Embers*. The relationship between history and the depicted present plays an important role in a number of the works of the most prominent figures associated with the LA School, in terms of both narrative material – lessons, hauntings or understandings from the past, a reclaiming of history from its official, white versions – and, in some cases, alternative narrative structure. This is one of the principal formal respects in which links can be suggested between this variety of black independent cinema and conceptions of Third Cinema.

For Teshome H. Gabriel, one of the major theorists associated with Third Cinema, who was based at UCLA, a key characteristic of Third World cinema is its tendency to draw on qualities found in folk art, such as non-linearity and repetition of images, qualities found in some of the work of the LA School.[5] *Sankofa*, in its journey into the past, has a texture filled with symbols – especially birds in flight – and creates an impression of magic and ritual incantation, both beyond and as part of its narrative momentum. *Ashes and Embers*, similarly, mixes narrative progression with an emphasis on repeated images that establish a spatially oriented symbolic geography. It opens in a Los Angeles sequence in which Ned and a would-be actor friend are subjected to routine oppression by the police, images that recur periodically throughout the film, along with the Vietnam flashbacks, the evocation of Grandma's rural landscape and semi-abstract images of the oppressive memorials and statues of Washington, D.C. The American indie film most celebrated for such qualities is *Daughters of the Dust*, directed by Julie Dash, an evocative portrait of the Gullah community, descendents of African captives living on the Sea Islands off the coast of South Carolina and Georgia in 1902. Geographically, the Gullah live in a state of limbo, displaced into a history of slavery from their original homelands yet not in America proper, an in-between state that can be read as a heightened version of the status of African Americans more generally. In their isolation from mainland America, the opening titles inform us, the Gullah created and maintained a distinct, imaginative and original African American culture. Temporally, the film looks in two directions: forwards, from the perspective of members of the Peazant family, about to cross to the mainland and travel north; and backwards, to African traditions embodied in the shape of the elderly matriarch, Nana (Cora Lee Day), who is to stay behind.

In its own textual strategies, *Daughters of the Dust* favours the perspective of Nana, focusing on a single day, that of a picnic held to mark the imminent departure, around which is woven a complex web of memories, associations and character relationships, including the narrating voice of an unborn child. The non-linear style is a conscious attempt to evoke the traditional West African oral culture of the *Griot* storyteller, according to Dash: 'The *Griot* will come to a birth, wedding or funeral and over a period of days will recount the family's history, with the stories going off at a tangent, weaving in and out.'[6] The impression created by the texture of the film, in which one sequence passes to another in an order not driven by forward-moving narrative, is that of an overlapping of cultural influences and heritages. The paraphernalia of modernity – a photographer brought in to record the departure, newspapers, a kaleidoscope that offers a perspective akin to that of the film – are juxtaposed with those of ancient ritual, tradition and the presence of ancestral spirits evoked through the use of chanting voices on the soundtrack. The message, conveyed by Nana and embodied in the film, is the importance of maintaining a connection with tradition, a carrying forward of her spirit, as a source of strength and renewal amid the hardships of life in white-dominated America.

Another quality shared by some examples from the LA School and the advocates of Third Cinema is narrative open-endedness, in which situations are left unresolved rather than being subject to the kinds of closure and resolution typical of Hollywood and other mainstream cinemas. To offer closure, as Gabriel argues, is to separate the events of the work from the ongoing business of everyday life or from the possibility of a range of alternative outcomes.[7] The endings of films such as *Killer of Sheep* and *Bless Their Little Hearts* leave the central characters to continue their existence, with little prospect of any significant point of climax or closure. Their individual fate is no more subject to facile change than the broader social fabric of which they are a part. States of altered consciousness are implied in *Bush Mama*, *Ashes and Embers* and *Sankofa*, in which we can assume the central characters to have learned and progressed as part of a collective process of resistance, although this is much less clearly the case for the family members who move north, to an uncertain future, in *Daughters of the Dust*. The emphasis of Third Cinema, for Gabriel, is also on collective consciousness and experience, rather than that of the individuals who form the almost exclusive focus of Hollywood-style production, a quality very much to the fore in the multi-vocal *Daughters of the Dust* and implied in the other examples considered above, in which the problems faced by characters are the outcome of social forces rather than individual foibles.

The aim of advocates of Third Cinema was to create a cinema removed from the Hollywood model of passively consumed entertainment. Third Cinema, as a guerrilla cinema that cannot be assimilated by the dominant system, is designed to act as a pretext for politically oriented audience discussion in underground venues, rather than to enter into official channels of distribution. This may have happened to some extent with films associated with the LA School, partly by default, given that they have largely been ignored by both mainstream and independent distributors. Beyond their more immediate constituency, however, these films have achieved recognition as forms of 'art' as much as for their value as tools for directly political agitation and intervention, even if the two are not entirely separable. For Fernando Solanas and Octavio Getino, the difference is that between Third Cinema, as part of a revolutionary process, and 'Second Cinema', as a cinema of artistic expression (each being distinguished from the dominant, commercial-consumerist 'First Cinema').[8] As Paul Willemen suggests, products of Third Cinema have often been consumed outside their region or country of origin in Second Cinema terms, 'bracketing the politics in favour of an appreciation of the authorial artistry'.[9] The same can be said of much of the recognition given to the better-known filmmakers of the LA School, especially Burnett and Dash, each of whom has to date produced one feature that achieved major critical success at the commercial art-house end of the indie spectrum: *Daughters of the Dust* and Burnett's *To Sleep with Anger* (1990).

Daughters of the Dust has a number of qualities that enabled it to find a niche-marketable place in the independent landscape of the early 1990s, although it took a year to find a distributor after its premiere at Sundance. Its 'exotic' qualities, including beautifully photographed landscape, African-influenced music and elements of period-costume drama – young women at the beach picnic, in long, flowing white dresses – give it a lush visual and aural texture likely to be appreciated by art-house audiences. The film's rhythms, and its explorations of time and space, as Ntongela Masilela suggests, are not only 'consonant with the lived experience of time and consciousness by Africans in the Diaspora', but also akin to aspects of the work of earlier international art-cinema directors such as Andrei Tarkovsky, Michelangelo Antonioni and Miklos Jancsó.[10] *Daughters of the Dust* also had a potentially existing niche market in the readers of black women writers such as Alice Walker and Toni Morrison. With *To Sleep with Anger*, Burnett achieved $1.4 million in investments and crossover from the margins to commercially distributed art-house independent cinema (Samuel Goldwyn) by gaining the services of a Hollywood star, Danny Glover, in the central role as the disruptive figure, Harry, who inveigles his way into the hearth of a middle-class Los Angeles black family. The film is another exploration of the relationship between the past and the present, Harry being the product of the old South, the heritage of darker forces, a character based on a figure from Georgia folklore. The film exhibits a number of qualities that mark its indie status – winner of the Special Jury Prize at Sundance in 1990 – including its ambivalent attitude towards a central character who may or may not be the incarnation of an actual demon. It performed disappointingly at the box office, handled primarily as an art-house production and doing better with white audiences than black;[11] like *Daughters of the Dust*, however, it is distinguished from most other products by filmmakers associated with the LA School by continuing to maintain an existence in mainstream channels of video distribution.

Neither Dash nor Burnett has yet been able to match the combination of critical acclaim and theatrical release achieved by *Daughters of the Dust* and *To Sleep with Anger*, being forced either into work for cinema of a more conventional nature or into television-funded and/or documentary production. A suggestion of the compromise needed to remain viable in the theatrical business is offered by the film with which Burnett returned to the cinema after *To Sleep with Anger*, *The Glass Shield* (1995), co-produced and distributed by Miramax. The central character is a rookie cop, the only black officer in his precinct, the plot concerning the framing of a young black man who was stopped illegally, simply because he was black. But, these race-themed elements aside, *The Glass Shield* is a mostly conventional and formulaic tale of a young idealist's blunder followed by an earnest attempt to uproot corruption, albeit with a partially downbeat ending. Box-office prospects were intended to be improved by casting the rap singer Ice Cube as the wronged man, but the film was not a success.

Movement into the mainstream-indie, genre-oriented territory of *The Glass Shield* might be seen as a mark of retreat for Burnett, an indicator of the difficulty of sustaining a more radical project in anything other than a marginal existence. The opposite is the case with the career of Spike Lee, for whom low-budget 'guerrilla' production was a necessity rather than a virtue in the case of his first full-length feature, *She's Gotta Have It*. The film's success at the box office (a US gross of more than $7 million that demonstrated the existence of a significant audience for black indie features) enabled Lee to achieve his goal of gaining access to studio finance for his next film, *School Daze* (1988, Columbia Pictures) and a relationship with Universal that saw the production of *Do the Right Thing*, *Mo' Better Blues* (1990), *Jungle Fever*, *Malcolm X* (1992), *Crooklyn* (1994) and *Clockers* (1995). Since the end of his affiliation to Universal, Lee has also made a number of more independently financed, lower-budget features, including *Girl 6* (with Fox Searchlight), *Get on the Bus* (1996), partly funded by a group of black investors, and the 16mm and DV production *Bamboozled* (2000). Even when backed by major studio finance and distribution, Lee has claimed the status of an independent filmmaker, maintaining creative control over key areas such as script, the hiring of cast and crew, and final cut, although he has often had to struggle to obtain anything more than modest budgets. A continuity of style and approach to issues can certainly be identified across the studio/independent bases from which he has worked.

12. The film that inspired a generation of new black independents: *She's Gotta Have It* (1986).

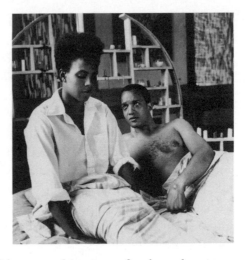

Lee's work is characterized by a combination of style and content that is generally bright, sassy and accessible, an entertainment cinema, marketed as such, that has also sought to take on board a number of issues specific to the concerns of black communities. *She's Gotta Have It* may be a low-budget, black-and-white production, for example, but it is designed to be of far more popular, commercial appeal than the likes of *Killer of Sheep* or *Bush Mama*. The tone is generally light and pointedly comic, with some exceptions, the emphasis on sex an obvious selling point at the more mainstream/crossover end of the indie sector. The film was sold as a fresh, stylish example of independent production, the suggestive title a blatant borrowing from the tactics of exploitation cinema. At the same time, *She's Gotta Have It* is a contribution to the questioning of simplistic racial stereotyping, sharing with many of Lee's films the portrayal of a diversity of central black characters, none of whom are offered as definitive representatives but as ordinarily flawed individuals.

Many of Lee's films focus on complexities and divisions within the black community that undermine any racist ideologies based on notions of essential black or African American characteristics. *School Daze* revolves largely around splits between the darker and lighter skinned students at a black college, for example, and between middle-class black students and local working-class black youths. The dark vs. light skin issue recurs in *Jungle Fever*, which starts out by setting up what appears to be a Hollywood-conventionally reconciliatory trajectory in the cross-racial affair between a black architect from Harlem and an Italian American secretary from Bensonhurst, two New York areas noted for a history of mutual hostility. Each, predictably, faces opprobrium from within their own family and community, but the film resists the conventional individualist line that the central couple can overcome such obstacles. A strong, un-Hollywood sense is created of ingrained and embedded communal tensions, a baggage that drags down almost every character in the piece.

A similarly complex and ambiguous portrait of inter-communal relations is found in *Do the Right Thing*, this time during a hot summer's day of rising tension in the predominantly black Brooklyn neighbourhood of Bedford-Stuyvesant. None of the characters is offered as an easy subject for unambiguous audience allegiance, a quality rarely found in the Hollywood mainstream. On one level, the film leans towards the position represented by two black 'radical' characters who campaign against an Italian American owned pizza restaurant, leading a protest that ends with the death of one at the hands of the police and the torching of the business by an angry crowd. They are both presented as caricatures, however, while a more rounded picture is given of the restaurant owner, proud to have fed the community for decades, despite the overt racism of his elder son. The pizza delivery boy, Mookie (Lee), who acts as a narrative intermediary linking a number of different threads, is the nearest thing the ensemble production offers to a central consciousness, but he is presented as essentially lazy and irresponsible. A multiplicity of characters and perspectives are on offer, including a conclusion that juxtaposes conflicting quotations from the writings of Martin Luther King and Malcolm X. The impression of a black community united in some respects, while diverse and divided in many others, is maintained in the independently black-funded *Get on the Bus*, in which a number of conflicts are played out among a group of black men *en route* to Louis Farrakhan's Million Man March in Washington.

Lee's commercial successes have owed a good deal to his personal ability to make the headlines, through both the subject matter of his films and his reputation for self-publicity and outspoken media comment. The deliberate provocation of controversy that generates media coverage, including attacks on the racism of his own studio employers, has served to make up for the limited scale of promotional budgets allocated to films perceived by Hollywood to be profitable only within particular specialist confines.[12] The high profile enjoyed by Lee created a burden of expectations, however, his work tending to be subjected to intense scrutiny by critics with a variety of agendas who in some cases make the mistake of expecting/assuming the characters and events portrayed to be perfect paradigms of one quality or another, rather than representations of something closer to a flawed, ambiguous and/or messy reality. This is a problem of excessive expectations that often results when the work of one or a small number of individuals is taken to represent an entire community. In the case of *She's Gotta Have It*, for example, Mark Reid castigates Lee for having 'inadequately constructed Nola as an independent woman',[13] as if she or any of the other characters in the film are meant to be representatives of some ideal. *Do the Right Thing*, for Reid, 'suggests that to celebrate black empowerment, African-Americans must deny an Italian-American small businessman his property rights'.[14] But only if what the film offers is assumed to be simple, positive endorsement of what happens, rather than a more subtle and complex unfolding of events from which no one emerges clearly as a winner.

A difficult gap exists here, between work that aspires to the complex and ambiguous qualities often celebrated in art-house/indie-style production – which might sometimes be a question of positioning in the marketplace but can also be read as honouring the complex texture of lived reality – and the more didactic approach advocated by those seeking to use film as a more immediate vehicle for socio-political intervention. Lee's films are often placed explicitly in socio-historical-political context, but they do not offer detailed analysis of the underlying causes of structural racism or conflict between different ethnically defined communities. A typical Lee strategy is to provide marginal reference to the history of black oppression or struggle, sometimes through photomontage sequences such as that running from slavery to the civil rights era in the opening titles of *School Daze*, or through dedications to real victims of racial conflict or controversy.

Explicitly political issues are raised in the body of a number of Lee's films, from a campaign against black college investment in South

Africa in *School Daze* to the presence of Martin Luther King and Malcolm X as exemplars of different courses of action in *Do the Right Thing* and the specific focus on issues raised by the latter in *Malcolm X*. The emphasis, however, is on symptoms and responses rather than underlying causes, the latter being far harder to square with a cinema in which an important emphasis remains on the commercial imperative of providing entertainment rather than education or analysis. Emotional melodrama generated from close proximity to the experiences of individuals remains the primary mode of presentation, rather than the more distanced modality required for sustained causal analysis, even in a case such as *Do the Right Thing* that provides a larger than usual number of perspectives. A focus on effects rather than causes is one of the key grounds on which Third Cinema advocates Solanas and Getino criticize mainstream, consumer-oriented cinema, although this is a quality that remains even in the more radical socially/historically conscious films of the LA School considered above, none of which makes any real attempt to investigate the causal factors leading to phenomena such as slavery, black poverty or the Vietnam war.

The scale of Lee's success, commercially in some cases and in gaining access to projects of the scale and conspicuous nature of *Malcolm X*, might have proved a mixed blessing for others. He demonstrated that black filmmakers could generate profits without simply reproducing white-oriented cinema, to the immediate benefit of black directors in both the indie and studio sectors in the late 1980s and early 1990s. But, as with 1990s crossover indie profile more generally, the result was also to raise the bar of expectations, potentially making it harder to gain investment or distribution for independent black filmmakers seeking to operate at a lower or less commercially marketable threshold. Lee himself came to work on a smaller, more niche scale by the latter half of the 1990s, however, after a number of films that failed to meet studio box-office expectations.

The early 1990s saw a veritable explosion of black filmmaking, following the breakthrough represented by *She's Gotta Have It* and the equally low-budget *Hollywood Shuffle*, a direct assault on Hollywood racism. A satire that grew out of director Robert Townsend's own years of frustration as an actor faced only with racist-stereotypical parts, *Hollywood Shuffle* is a loose assembly of skits in which Townsend stars as a performer caught between the desire for a career and his objections to the narrowly racist range of parts on offer. The film, although uneven in quality, is a good example of the balance that can be achieved between the explicit making of serious points and the use of a more marketable framework – in this case, light comedy – within which to do so. The issue of racist stereotyping in the entertainment media, and the complicity of some black performers, is taken up more acerbically in Lee's *Bamboozled*, in which a black middle-class television executive attempts to get back at a crass boss by inventing an appallingly racist black-face minstrel show that turns into an unexpected hit.

Some fifteen American films with black directors were released in 1991, according to Emanuel Levy, 'more than in the preceding two decades', even if this remained a small proportion of total output.[15] If Lee remained by far the most prominent single figure, black filmmaking gained its most solid industrial base elsewhere, in the coming-of-age-in-the-ghetto/gang sub-genre, a format that straddles the studio/independent divide and that offers useful examples of points of similarity and difference between work produced in the two sectors. If the social context of the early years of the LA School was the political radicalism of the late 1960s, Ed Guerrero suggests, that of the early 1990s came out of a period of black frustration, nihilism and anger, in which black rage was often turned inward, 'expressed as gang and drug warfare'.[16] The malaise affecting the black ghetto was a symptom of wider processes including economic restructuring that resulted in the export of jobs from the inner city. For conservative commentators, however, blaming the victims was a convenient way of short-circuiting any analysis of the structural roots of the problem. The ghetto landscape and its disaffected young black inhabitants featured prominently in a number of social and political discourses of the time, giving it the kind of popular currency on which film industry production cycles tend to draw.[17] The portrayals of black youth in the ghetto that played into this context had another strongly marketable component in the form of gangsta rap, an element of black hip hop that had crossed over with great commercial success into the white youth culture of the period.[18] It is unsurprising that this territory was one in which Hollywood felt confident to dip a toe in the early 1990s, the Columbia production *Boyz 'N' the Hood*, directed by John Singleton, appearing alongside Matty Rich's indie feature *Straight Out of Brooklyn* in 1991. The textures of rap music and its predominant reference points of macho posturing, as a particular form of black youth assertiveness, play a role in both, and in the independently produced *Menace II Society* (Allen and Albert Hughes, 1993), although the combinations of qualities vary considerably from one example to another.

The main emphasis of *Boyz 'N' the Hood* is on the 'cautionary tale' and the imparting of (patriarchal) moral lessons about the importance of responsible fatherhood in keeping black male youth away from a downward spiral into gun-culture and mutual killings. The 'street' culture of violent macho bonding is kept primarily in the background, especially in the first half of the film, although it serves as a key narrative device in the latter stages. *Menace II Society* is in fact the most exploitation-oriented of the three films, more so than the earnest studio picture, in keeping with the usual strategy of its producer and distributor, New Line Cinema. The film mixes a morality tale – the central sympathetic character becomes mixed up in the drug culture from childhood, eventually falling victim to a cycle of violence that he instigates – with a sizeable dose of violent exploitation *frissons*, gangsta rap and ghetto/homeboy atmospherics. A shared strategy of *Boyz 'N' the Hood* and *Menace II Society* is the use of an essentially good-hearted central focus of allegiance, pulled into the life of crime by irresistible environmental forces in the case of the latter, to offer a comfortably touristic route into the exploration of ghetto life, a more distanced perspective being kept on what are presented as its more exotic/violent/out-of-control species.

As an independent portrait of youth in the ghetto, *Straight Out of Brooklyn* is very different from *Menace II Society*, the difference that might be expected between the exploitation-happy New Line and a feature with the credentials of the former: co-produced under the non-profit Public Broadcasting Service's American Playhouse label and distributed by its partner in the early 1990s, the art-house oriented Samuel Goldwyn. The lower-budget ($450,000) *Straight Out of Brooklyn* offers an unvarnished impression of life in the projects; a strong feeling of rootedness in the place, shot in a

13. Life in the projects, unvarnished: *Straight Out of Brooklyn* (1991).

plain style, and with no textural romanticization of guns, drugs or youth/gang mythologies; no effort, really, to sell the film through the marketability of rap-oriented crossover black youth culture (rap itself appears only minimally on the soundtrack). The friends with whom the central character, Dennis (Larry Gilliard Jr.), eventually holds up a drug courier, one of them played by the director, come over as ordinary and somewhat foolish, shorn of much in the way of macho ghetto theatricals. The crime comes late in the proceedings and as an anticlimax, easily performed, although it leads to a tragic conclusion, an ending accompanied by a closing title calling for change that shifts the film, like many other black independent features, into a more urgently didactic register. Rather than focusing almost exclusively on youth – clearly a commercial decision in most examples of the format – *Straight Out of Brooklyn* also devotes more than obligatory background space to the situation of the parents of Dennis: a broken and defeated father, who takes out his frustrations in drunken assaults on his own wife and property, and a wife struggling to find low-paid employment to keep the family together.

Other examples of independent black filmmaking have looked elsewhere for generic ground that permits a mix of commercial appeal and scope for the inclusion of specifically black-oriented material, including a revisionist approach to the Western in *Posse* (1993), directed by Mario Van Peebles. Frontier racism and the efforts of black people to create and sustain their own community in the west figure centrally in one of the two main plot devices, while the issues are addressed more didactically in a prologue and the closing titles. In a number of cases, independent black filmmaking has replicated conventionally white-centred formats without any reference, central or marginal, to black-specific social or political issues. *Love Jones* (1997) and *Hav Plenty* (1998) are good examples of this tendency, two slick romantic comedies featuring young, middle-class, black characters and clearly targeted at a similar demographic. The existence of such relatively 'ordinary' films demonstrates, from one point of view, the status of black-directed/oriented films as an established part of the indie landscape. The fact that black characters and their relationships can be represented in essentially colour-blind terms represents a victory over a long history of racist stereotyping. It comes at the cost of an absence of any engagement with the realities of continued structural racism in the United States, however, a middle-class focus generally being required if such issues are entirely to be avoided, although that is no more than is the case for a great deal of non-black independent and mainstream production. Neither *Love Jones* nor *Hav Plenty* exhibits any narrative or formal qualities that would, in themselves, be marks of indie status, a fact that underlines the extent to which merely to be black written and directed and to feature an all-black cast remains, in most cases, to be restricted by definition to one or another part of the independent sector.

Institutions of the kind that were central to the expansion of independent cinema more generally have developed to offer additional help and support to black filmmakers. The Black Filmmaker Foundation (BFF) was created in 1978, offering facilities such as workshops, seminars, conferences and a skills bank and employment listings for members.[19] Other organizations include the African American Filmmakers Association and the Organization of Black Screenwriters. Bodies focused on the crucial areas of marketing and exhibition include Blackfilm.com and UniWorld Films. The latter produces events such as the Black Cinema Café, a showcase for indie films targeted to potential audiences in cities such as New York, Los Angeles, Atlanta, Detroit, Washington and others with high-density African American populations. Black-oriented film festivals have played something of the role that events such as Sundance perform for the wider indie movement, examples including the Acapulco Black Film Festival and New York's Urbanworld Film Festival, which also has a distribution arm.

Gaining other than very minimal distribution remains difficult for most black filmmakers, however, a fact that has driven some into doing the job for themselves. Director Robert Hardy's student-coming-of-age drama *Chocolate City* (1994) was shot for $20,000 while Hardy was studying for an engineering degree in Florida.[20] It was not shown in theatres, but gained a national home video release and was distributed independently over the internet. Hardy and producer William Packer created their own company, Rainforest Productions, during the process and raised the $200,000 budget for their next feature, *Trois* (2000), from 50 African American investors. Much of the package was put together at the 1998 Acapulco festival, where the film premiered as a 'work in progress' in 1999. Rainforest then marketed and distributed the film by itself, grossing more than $1 million in some 90 cities after securing openings in mainstream rather than art-house venues, an achievement based on the racy nature of the material, which centres around a *ménage à trois* relationship that turns into a lurid *Fatal Attraction*-style melodramatic thriller.

Self-distribution and other alternative approaches, including grassroots marketing targeted at ethnically or hyphenate-American defined constituencies, have also been used by filmmakers from other non-white communities, including a number of examples cited in Chapter 1. The independent sector remains the only viable option for most non-white American production that seeks to challenge dominant stereotypes – the implicit function of which is to legitimate inequalities – whether African American, Chicano, Asian American or Native American. Examples of independent Chicano production include Gregory Nava's *El Norte*, the distribution campaign for which is examined in Chapter 1, and Nava's larger-budget *My Family* (1995).

Each offers a distinctively Hispanic perspective, the former more obviously political in its sympathetic treatment of illegal migrants into the USA, the latter charting three turbulent generations of a Mexican American family in East Los Angeles. The dominant modality in both cases, however, is heightened emotional melodrama more than emphasis on the specific social conditions facing different parts of the Chicano community. An effort to create a spiritual dimension, rooted in the exoticism of Latin America, is found in both films. This is oddly at variance with any more politicized perspective in a sequence in *My Family* in which one character, who narrowly escaped death in a fast-flowing river as a young child, is deliberately and unnecessarily shot by the police. The spirit of the river came back to claim him, concludes the narratorial voice of the film, a reading that pulls into the orbit of myth what otherwise appears to be a simple act of racist murder.

A low-key, de-dramatized narrative style of the kind analyzed in Chapter 2 characterizes the early films of Hong Kong born director Wayne Wang, a style that produces a commitment to subtle and insightful portrayals of the textures of Chinese American life. Wang's first feature, *Chan is Missing*, is, nominally, a detective story in which a cab driver and his nephew search for a friend who goes missing with $4,000 of their savings. The emphasis, however, is on a leisurely exploration of various facets of the San Francisco Chinatown community rather than any resolution of the central mystery. The more Jo (Wood Moy) and Steve (Marc Hayashi) investigate, the more complex and contradictory the case becomes. Conventional ingredients of the detective genre, including Jo's voice-over and hints that Chan might have been involved in a number of dramatic incidents, including a murder, are combined with sequences in which a documentary-style impression is created as the often hand-held, black-and-white photography dwells on an assortment of background characters and their environments. The portrait that emerges, in contrast to conventional one-dimensional stereotypes, is of a community marked by various shades of opinion, from political rivalries between supporters of the People's Republic of China and Taiwan to varying grades of allegiance to the cultures of China, the United States or a combination of the two.

A similar sense of the rival pull of two cultures, characteristic of recent-generation immigrant populations, is found in Wang's second feature, *Dim Sum: A Little Bit of Heart* (1984). A few lines of intra-family conflict are engaged, gently, principally the tension between a mother and her unmarried daughter, but the primary emphasis is on the evocation of a slice of life. The character-based narrative dimension is bracketed by interludes in which quietly contemplative, static shots – images of empty rooms, trees, hanging washing, reflections on water – create the impression of an alternative sensibility, reminiscent of the style of the Japanese director Yasujiro Ozu. The main narrative hook, the effort of Mrs Tam (Kim Chew) to see her daughter Geraldine (Laureen Chew) married before the former reaches her 62nd birthday, the age at which a fortune teller predicted her death, is abruptly dropped towards the end, demonstrating the extent to which the investment of the film lies elsewhere, with the revelation that the fortune teller's view has now changed and the pressure on Geraldine is removed. Tensions reflecting the different experiences of succeeding generations are an important source of material more generally in films from representatives of more or less recent immigrations to the United States, including *Dim Sum*, *My Family*, and films by Ang Lee such as the Taiwan/US co-productions *The Wedding Banquet* (1993) and *Eat, Drink, Man, Woman* (1994).

Gender: From Independent Women Filmmakers to New Queer Cinema

If black filmmakers or those from other ethnically defined communities have often struggled to get their voices heard, even in the independent sector, the same has generally been true for women, and doubly so for women of colour. *Daughters of the Dust* is by far the most critically high-profile production by an African American woman but the density of its texture did not make it a vehicle by which Dash could readily gain access to funding for future theatrical releases. Black women directors have, generally, been given a lower profile and have to struggle harder than their male counterparts to get their films funded, produced and distributed, suffering from the dual burden of prevailing gender and racial inequality. Relatively few have been able to produce feature-length fictional narratives. Of those produced, many have been denied anything other than marginal exhibition, as in the case of Kathleen Collins' *The Cruz Brothers and Miss Malloy* (1980) and *Losing Ground* (1982), films credited with paving the way for *Daughters of the Dust* to become the first narrative feature created by a black woman to gain commercial distribution.[21] A few other independent films directed by black women also gained distribution during the early 1990s upsurge, the best-known of which, *Just Another Girl on the IRT* (1993), written and directed by Julie Harris, is a portrait of an outspoken teenager coming of age in the Brooklyn projects. The emphasis on family, and especially mother/teenage-daughter relationships, is a central feature of other features by black women, including *Alma's Rainbow* (1993) and *Love Your Mama* (1993). The difference of dynamic often found in films made by women is evident in the treatment in *Love Your Mama* of the narrative thread relating to the older son, Wren (André Robinson), the familiar figure of the inner-city black youth drawn to a life of crime, in this case stealing cars. Wren narrowly escapes death after being shot repeatedly during a police raid. The emphasis is not on Wren himself, however, or the criminal subculture into which he is inducted, but on the impact of this and a series of other crises on the matriarch, Mama (Audrey Morgan), around whom the film revolves.

Like black filmmakers, male or female, women are often given little choice but to operate in the independent sector, either because they seek to go beyond the confines usually permitted in the mainstream or because it is the only place where any options are open. Even in the indie world, women face persistent inequality. Where opportunities are created, women filmmakers tend to receive lower budgets and find it harder to gain distribution or to build a sustained career after making the initial breakthrough. A number of groups have sought to help women film- and video-makers, the best known being Women Make Movies, created in 1972, which operates a distribution service, providing copies of many titles unavailable through mainstream channels, and a Production Assistance Program offering various forms of training and assistance. As with the products of those from particular racially or ethnically defined backgrounds, there is no necessary connection between the gender of the filmmaker and the material produced, no essentially 'female' aesthetic, although there are some identifiable tendencies. Independent films made by women range from more or less overtly feminist work to productions that can be seen as women-oriented in a general, culturally defined sense (often through focusing on relationship-based issues, a quality conventionally associated with women) and others that are gender non-specific.

Contemporary feminist currents fed to varying extents into a number of films produced in the 1970s, both in and outside Hollywood. An example in the independent arena is Claudia Weill's *Girlfriends* (1978), an $80,000 feature which focuses on the break-up of the relationship between two New York college graduates. A more overt and militantly feminist vision of a kind that could only have been produced in the independent sector is offered by Lizzie Borden's *Born in Flames* (1983), set in a near-future New York, ten years after a social-democratic war of liberation that was supposed to have led to equality but has left women with many grievances. A number of scenes depict women routinely being hassled on the street, while protests are made about cutbacks in day-care, the ending of free abortions, the forced sterilization of minority women and discrimination against single women and lesbians in housing and employment. A montage sequence depicting women performing various forms of menial work points forward to Borden's next film, *Working Girls*: the image of hands placing a condom on a penis is inserted between shots of food-packing and washing-up, implying an equivalence between sexual and other forms of labour. A guerrilla Women's Army plans armed intervention, the murder of its founder leading to the unification of some of the diverse women's voices heard in the preceding scenes.

Born in Flames is an unusually radical and directly political intervention for a feature-length production. Some of the protests voiced are specific to the fictional scenario, but many have obvious relevance to the world beyond that of the screen, a dimension emphasized by the fact that no effort is made (partly because of budgetary constraints) to create a projected future world different in texture from that of the time the film was made. In advocating an insurrection that includes both physical violence and media interventions, the film takes a political stance that seems as radical today as when it was made. It also departs from the norms of fictional narrative style. Instead of emotional proximity to central characters, in the conventionally character-centric dynamic maintained by most independent features, the fabric of *Born in Flames* is woven from a mixture of strands including television news reports, broadcasts from rebel radio stations, footage and voice-over commentary from FBI reports and activities, and numerous brief scenes of comment and analysis from various perspectives. The effect is to create a modality closer to that of politically oriented documentary, in which the viewer is encouraged to remain emotionally distanced and receptive to analysis.

A more general sense of foregrounding the experiences of women is found in many other independent features, including the work of two figures prominent in the indie scene of the 1980s and 1990s, Susan Seidelman and Allison Anders. A good illustration of the way marginal, low-budget qualities can be mixed with more established formats is provided by Seidelman's first two features, *Smithereens* and *Desperately Seeking Susan* (1985). The $60,000-budget *Smithereens*, shot soon after Seidelman finished film school, is set on the edges of the New Wave culture of New York's Lower East Side, a hip but seedy milieu that gave the film a cult appeal at an early stage in the development of the contemporary independent movement. The film's narrative is limited to a series of abortive engagements between the central character, the abrasive and self-centred Wren (Susan Berman), and two males: a sensitive-artist type, who lives in the back of a van, and a narcissistic sometime New Wave singer (played by the punk singer/writer Richard Hell) into whose life Wren seeks to inveigle herself. The success of *Smithereens*, which became the first low-budget American indie to be accepted into competition at Cannes, led to Seidelman being hired to direct *Desperately Seeking Susan*, a more mainstream independent production budgeted at $4.5 million and featuring stars such as Madonna and the upcoming Rosanna Arquette. *Desperately Seeking Susan* foregrounds a world similar to that of its predecessor, but one into which the viewer is led by more generically familiar and plot-oriented devices. A dull, timid housewife from New Jersey (Arquette) becomes mixed up in aspects of Lower East Side culture, along with a background crime-thriller plot, after being knocked out, losing her memory and being mistaken for the more exotic Susan (Madonna). The result is a contemporary version of classical screwball comedy-of-mistaken-identity, a more conventional/commercial re-packaging of some of the elements of *Smithereens* that grossed $24 million in the USA.

Allison Anders' second feature, *Mi Vida Loca* (*My Crazy Life*, 1993), is an example of a distinctly women-oriented take on generically familiar, male-dominated territory, in this case the world of Los Angeles gangs. By the age of 21, we are told, most of the men in Latino neighbourhoods such as Echo Park, where the film is set, are either disabled, in prison or dead. In response, considering their men essentially unreliable sources of support, the group of women around which the film revolves begin to establish their own, rival operations. Conventional gang-related material, a world of deadly rivalries and revenge killings, is given a fresh spin, the primary focus being on the women left to bring up fatherless children, figures usually pushed to the margins of the text.

A central focus on relationships between women is a defining characteristic of many independent features made by women, including *Mi Vida Loca* and Anders' first feature, *Gas, Food, Lodging*. The enduring nature of such bonds is often celebrated, amid the assorted pressures of life, as in Nicole Holofcener's quirky comedy of romance and relationships, *Walking and Talking*, a low-key portrait of the stresses put on the close friendship of Amelia (Catherine Keener) and Laura (Anne Heche) when the latter announces her engagement. *Walking and Talking* was generally critically lauded, if not a box-office hit, but the problems often faced by women filmmakers were highlighted by the difficulty writer-director Holofcener faced getting finance for her subsequent feature, the more biting (but award-winning) *Lovely and Amazing* (2001). The project, developed by Holofcener and Good Machine, was rejected everywhere it was offered and only went into production after Holofcener's agreement to shoot in high definition video on a budget lower than that for her debut.[22]

An emphasis on the close texture of relationships often comes at the expense of narrative momentum, as is the case in both *Walking and Talking* and *Lovely and Amazing*. A stronger investment in narrative drive is consonant, generally, with more goal-oriented dominant western male gender constructions. Any such distinctions on gender lines have to be qualified, however, especially in the independent sector, where there is a wider tendency to focus on character and life-texture rather than plot. A significant overlap may exist between two forms dominant in their own spheres: forward-moving, linear narrative and a wider, male-oriented culture. To eschew plot-centric forms in the cinema is, in many cases, to choose or suffer operation on the limited resources available in the independent sphere, to be relegated to what some would consider a secondary position akin to that generally offered to women in society. The corollary should be that women are more likely to be at home in the indie sector, which may be true in some respects as far as sensibility is concerned but is clearly not the case in terms of equal availability of opportunities or resources. A critical bias often exists in favour of narrative resolution and marked character development, dimensions taken for granted by some critics as markers of quality, even in works such as *Lovely and Amazing* and some of the films examined in Chapter 2, to which they are of less relevance.[23] An impression of closure is created in *Lovely and Amazing* in one dimension, for example, when the mother (Brenda Blethyn) is released from hospital after complications during her liposuction treatment, a narrative core emblematic of a wider engagement in body-image insecurity issues. Few of the myriad personal/emotional problems faced by the major characters appear in any way resolved, however, a fact that seems central to the edgy and uncomfortable nature of much of the material.

One of the most striking manifestations of the early 1990s boom in independent production, and a contributor to its wider and sometimes controversial public profile, was the movement that became known as New Queer Cinema, a term coined by the critic B. Ruby Rich to mark the appearance of a group of fresh, provocative and formally inventive lower-budget gay- and lesbian-oriented features including Todd Haynes' *Poison*, Gus Van Sant's *My Own Private Idaho*, Gregg Araki's *The Living End* and Tom Kalin's *Swoon*. In its original incarnation, New Queer Cinema was very much a product of its time, in terms of both the developing state of indie cinema and alliances and organizations formed in the gay and lesbian communities in the wake of the impact of the AIDS virus; 'a more successful term for a moment than a movement', as Rich was to put it on reflection at the end of the decade.[24] It also had deeper roots in American independent cinema,

14. En route to murder-as-bonding-ritual: *Swoon* (1992).

however, and, whether or not the term is still merited, contributed to the creation of one of the most successfully institutionalized parts of the indie sector, with its own well-established network of festivals and distributors.

New Queer Cinema can be read as a revisiting, in a more commercially viable, feature-narrative form, of the radically gay element that was an important constituent part of the American avant-garde cinema of the 1960s, the work of filmmakers such as Kenneth Anger, Jack Smith and Andy Warhol. It is testament to how much had changed in gay and lesbian communities by the 1990s – and in the scope for independent feature production – that a similarly polemical stance, if not exactly similar material, was translated into a much less marginal form of cinematic production. The underground cinema of the 1960s received little if any coverage in the gay and lesbian press of the time, a period in which its flaunting of transgressive sexuality ran contrary to a prevailing strategy of seeking to project a 'respectable' image of homosexuality.[25] A drive for assimilation and 'acceptance' continued to mark the dominant strain of gay and lesbian activism in the 1970s and into the 1980s, its correlative in cinema being the use of restrained and largely conventional approaches. As with products from other marginalized groups, films from gay or lesbian perspectives were confined to the independent sector initially through necessity – the fact that they could not be made elsewhere – rather than through the adoption of formally innovative strategies.

Early examples include *Desert Hearts* (1985), a lesbian-themed feature that adopts an otherwise very conventional narrative framework in which an uptight New York English professor, Vivian (Helen Shaver), ending a lifeless marriage in Nevada in 1959, is reawakened by the erotic attentions of Cay (Patricia Charbonneau). Cay is figured as a representative of earthier, rebellious forces, challenging Vivian's excessively ordered existence. The underlying dynamic buys into broader notions of the western frontier experience as one of awakening from the inauthenticities of existence in the metropolis, the Nevada desert offering a zone of freedom and potential regeneration. This is another example of the way genre-related frameworks can both contain and provide a space within which to develop unconventional material. The frontier dynamic is schematic and conventional, reducing somewhat the impact of the material, yet given a different content when the principal representative of its hallowed virtues is a lesbian.

Desert Hearts is clearly sympathetic towards the couple's burgeoning relationship, and the dilemma faced by Vivian, and proved successful at the box office, providing a rare instance at the time of an affirmative portrait, in which a lesbian relationship does not end in either death or despair.[26] Cay remains coded somewhat as an 'outsider', however, and the plot device ensures that lesbianism is visited only via a character who begins as unambiguously heterosexual. The structure is that of a lesbian awakening/discovery or coming-out story, an alternative to dominant gender narratives but less radical than those in which the non-heterosexuality of the principal characters is taken as a given. The principal novelty of the first two gay male indie features to appear in this period, *Parting Glances* (1986) and *Longtime Companion* (1990), lay in the simple fact that they presented gay characters in a world in which their sexual orientation was taken for granted from the start, rather than an issue or problem in its own right. *Parting Glances* explores a triangle of relationships that functions much the same as any other, gay or straight, even though one of the central characters is suffering from AIDS. AIDS itself is treated as an established fact of gay life rather than a major plot device. A restrained, matter-of-fact approach to AIDS is also found in *Longtime Companion*, which traces the ravages of the virus on a group of gay men during its spread in the 1980s. The tone is quiet and undemonstrative, without great flourishes of emotion, an impression heightened by the use of an elliptical narrative framework, in which the characters are visited at different moments between 1981 and 1989. The illness and death of some individuals are dwelt on, while others are passed over. The contraction of the virus or death often occurs in the narrative interstices, a device that creates a strong impression of the implacable nature of the threat, and the resilience of the gay community, while minimizing any tendency for melodrama.

The tenor of these films, whatever their individual differences, creates an implicitly assimilationist stance that stakes claims for the common humanity of gay or lesbian characters. Some of the problems they face may be specific to their particular gender identity, most obviously the level of threat from AIDS, but form and character/relationship/emotional content create an impression marked as 'ordinary' or 'normal' rather than exotically alternative. To treat gay or lesbian characters in this way, rather than as a 'problem' or source of amusement of some kind, was itself a not insignificant step, in comparison with prevailing tendencies in Hollywood. The style of filmmaking that gained the label New Queer Cinema went further, however, in keeping with a contemporary shift towards a more confrontational brand of gay and lesbian campaigning. The term 'queer', formerly part of the lexicon of homophobic abuse, was adopted as a positive signifier by groups ranging from activists to academic theorists. The activist group Queer Nation was born in New York in 1990, with its slogan 'Queers Bash Back', in response to attacks on gays and lesbians in the East Village. The more aggressive, in-your-face stance of groups such as this was a response to both the AIDS crisis itself, which prompted new forms of community activity, and the increased level of homophobia it created. In American independent cinema, and some examples elsewhere, including the work of the British directors Derek Jarman and Isaac Julien, the same climate encouraged an equally bold and assertive burst of activity.

Two of the distinguishing characteristics of New Queer Cinema are portrayals of gay or lesbian characters that make fewer concessions to notions of what might be palatable or especially accessible to straight audiences and, very much in keeping with this in many cases, a more radical approach to form. If previous gay- or lesbian-oriented productions belonged to the independent sector largely by default, the works associated initially with New Queer Cinema are more wilfully and assertively independent on a number of counts. The overtly gay-oriented prison narrative strand of *Poison*, for example, offers no outside perspective, no compromise to any other sensibility, sufficiently so to have provoked howls of outrage at the fact that the film received funds from the National Endowment for the Humanities. Queer or otherwise sexually deviant subtexts also exist in the two other strands of the film, most obviously in the potential for 'Horror' to be read as a metaphor for AIDS. Little effort is made to offer 'positive images' of gay characters, or of any other homoerotic activity, in the prison strand, the polarities of which range between hazy romantic nostalgia and anal rape. The same goes for *Swoon*, which could hardly be imagined as a plea for sympathetic understanding of gay characters, given its focus on the relationship between Nathan Leopold (Craig Chester) and Richard Loeb (Daniel Schlachet), the notorious real-life pair jailed in Chicago in the 1920s for the murder of a 13-year-old boy. The crime is committed solely for kicks, the film suggests, playing a part in sexual bonding rituals between the two protagonists. The viewer is thrust into uncomfortably close proximity to their actions, the killing being performed in a claustrophobic sequence inside a car. Little of the conventional sense of access to the interiority of central characters is provided, however, despite alternating voice-over commentaries from both. The presentation of the pair remains as cool and detached as the characters appear to be from many of their acts. *Swoon* reinstates the gay dimension of the Leopold and Loeb story, an aspect glossed over by earlier films inspired by the case, most notably Hitchcock's *Rope* (1948), and does so in a manner that seems deliberately provocative, focusing on precisely the kind of material that might otherwise be used to support homophobic perspectives such as those manifested by the voices of authority within the film. The rejection of an approach based on the creation of positive images is taken to more disturbing extremes in Todd Verow's first feature, *Frisk*

(1996), an adaptation of the novel by Dennis Cooper in which both gay sex and a connection between sex and murder are presented in a far more explicit manner than anything found in *Swoon*, in a narrative based on a series of letters from a character whose desire for greater sexual knowledge and possession leads him beyond the surface of the skin, in acts of increasing violence and mutilation.

One of the most sustained bodies of provocative, in-your-face queer indie filmmaking is found in the work of Gregg Araki. From the opening titles, *The Living End*, *Totally Fucked Up* and *The Doom Generation* announce their intention to incite, with possessive credits reading, respectively, 'An irresponsible movie by Gregg Araki', 'Another homo movie by Gregg Araki' and 'A heterosexual movie by Gregg Araki' (the latter far from entirely true!). The Araki style here, and in *Nowhere* (1997), is a lurid, sexually polymorphous version of the mainstream youth/teen-angst movie, shot through with a strong vein of anger. The teen world imagined by Araki is one in which a fluidity of gender orientation is largely accepted by the slacker-generation principals, against a background of sporadic and often violent homophobia. The latter reaches its highest pitch in the climax of *The Doom Generation*, in which a homophobic assault against the three main characters, caught during a *ménage à trois*, culminates in a shocking, blood-spattered sequence – shot in strobe-effect lighting that creates a nightmarish impression – in which Jordan (James Duval) is killed by having his penis amputated with a pair of shears. The fact that the assailants bring out an American flag and conduct the attack to the accompaniment of *The Star Spangled Banner*, one mouthing from the Oath of Allegiance, creates a political subtext present on occasion in other Araki films (in *The Living End*, for example, one of the principals proposes infecting President Bush with the AIDS virus, suggesting that it would prompt a magic cure to be found the following day).

Araki obliges the viewer to confront the existence of virulent AIDS-era homophobia, employing AIDS itself as either a foregrounded narrative device or a persistent subtext. It provides the romantically doomed impetus for the lovers-on-the-run, road-movie structure of *The Living End*, in which the introspective Jon (Craig Gilmore) saddles up with the violently inclined and rootless hustler Luke

(Mike Dytri), the latter needing to escape Los Angeles after killing a cop. Both are HIV-positive and, as Luke declares, have nothing to lose. The romantic-nihilist attitude struck by the film is expressed in background textural detail such as the 'Fuck the World' graffiti viewed at the start and in Jon's 'Choose Death' bumper sticker. Jon does have something to lose, however, and maintains an attachment to his settled existence through telephone contact with a girl friend in LA, eventually deciding he wants to return to the relative comforts of home. The contrast between Jon and Luke is typical of a dynamic that offers a bridge between violently rebellious figures such as Luke, and Xavier in *The Doom Generation*, and 'safer', more domesticated or 'easily led' representatives of gay or potentially gay/bisexual youth such as Jon, Jordan in *The Doom Generation* and Andy in *Totally Fucked Up*, the latter both played by Araki regular James Duval.

AIDS discriminates against no one, intones a TV public information announcement in *Totally Fucked Up*, a point immediately contested by one of the characters, who describes it as government-sponsored genocide, 'a born-again Nazi republican wet dream come true'. Araki's work supports José Arroyo's suggestion that, even when not mentioned so directly or provocatively by name, AIDS can be understood as the 'political unconscious' of New Queer Cinema, as both an 'absent cause' and an important interpretative context.[27] An impression of doom and pending death is pervasive, from the emphasis on high levels of gay teen suicide in *Totally Fucked Up* to literal signifiers of imminent apocalypse in *The Doom Generation*, which opens with flaming letters in a nightclub reading 'Welcome to Hell' and throughout which the number 666 is a recurring motif. *Nowhere* is set on what is supposed to be Armageddon Day, with the approach of the biblically predicted Rapture; it also offers a student milieu in which classes to which casual mention is made include Thermonuclear Catastrophe and History of Lethal Epidemics (not to mention the notes from Human Sex Orgy requested by one character). Jordan pulls back from intercourse with Amy (Rose McGowan) in an early scene in *The Doom Generation*, commenting, 'I'm afraid of catching AIDS', a fear he later overcomes, although his subsequent involvement in a three-way session is a precursor to violent death. The AIDS-era conjunction of sex and death, especially gay male sex – seen at its most disturbing in *Frisk* – is given stark figuration in *The Living End*, in the image of Luke fucking Jon, after the latter's decision to return home, while holding a gun to his own head. He pulls the trigger, as he climaxes, but the gun proves to be out of bullets, leaving the pair alone in a bleak expanse between highway and the sea.

Araki's films are clearly products of an assertively queer sensibility, mixing social-political resonances with more marketable and exploitation-oriented youth genre dimensions, the latter including plenty of opportunities for the display of nubile, scantily clad bodies, male and female. The emphasis on a generation of angst-ridden or doomed teenagers comes over as both seriously coded AIDS-era material or metaphor, specific to a particular constituency, and as a more familiarly romantic alienated-youth posture. Formal departures from convention also play an important part in the location of Araki's films within the independent landscape, as both arty-alternative and as 'cool' youth-oriented indie productions. If Araki's films, and other examples of New Queer Cinema, are often provocative at the level of content, in their treatments of the lifestyles and actions of gay or lesbian characters and issues such as AIDS, the same can be said of some of their stylistic features. Formal qualities are often drawn to the attention of the viewer, through a range of devices including direct reference, parody and stylistic excess.

Reminders of the existence of cinema or video, as constructs, rather than transparent windows onto versions of reality, are found in a number of Araki's features: Jon writing an article on 'the death of cinema' in *The Living End*, with a Godard poster among other cultural reference points in his apartment; the video-maker Steven (Gilbert Luna), whose interview footage with other characters forms part of the texture of *Totally Fucked Up*; the central character, Dark (Duval), with a video practical assignment to be completed in *Nowhere*. Self-conscious devices embedded more firmly in the structure of the films include the chapter-title headings of *Totally Fucked Up*. Headings such as 'more teen angst', 'lifestyles of the bored and disenfranchised', 'the young and the hopeless' create a distanced, ironic perspective on the film's own stance. The same effect is created by various statements in the form of graffiti and other signs found elsewhere in Araki's work. 'God help me' reads a large sign next to one character in *Nowhere*, a part of the diegetic background that, because of its excessive appropriateness and role as non-diegetic commentary, draws attention to the constructed nature of the film's fabric. As he declares his desire to leave towards the end of *The Living End*, Jon comments on the 'hackneyed, romantic fantasy we've been having', another self-conscious gesture in which familiar devices are simultaneously drawn upon and drawn into a foreground position in which they might be questioned.

A striking aspect of Araki's work is an aesthetic of excess based on garish, over-stylized images, the strongest example of which is the lurid use of colour in *The Doom Generation*. On exiting a QuickieMart, after the bloody and absurd decapitation of its proprietor, the three principals walk past a wall divided into successive fields of bright yellow, blue, orange and green, for which no realistic motivation is remotely available. In their car afterwards, they are enveloped in a red glow, with touches of blue, colours that also predominate in other sequences. They visit a bar done out in silver foil and a motel room where everything is chequered black and white: walls, floor, curtains, bedspread, lamp, phone, ashtray, towels, along with the white-skin/black-underwear favoured by Amy. The result is akin to the stylistic excess found in other examples of independent cinema. This can be an attraction in its own right, as suggested in Chapter 3, but it may have further, more specific appeal in queer cinema.

For Arroyo, the appeal of excess to the gay consumer of forms such as opera, melodrama and some women stars is related to the expressions of emotion they permit, an outlet for homosexual emotions traditionally repressed on screen:

> Just as our sexuality is often regarded as transgressing the bounds of the socially unacceptable, it has historically been forms that threaten to transgress the bounds of the aesthetically acceptable that seem to give us greater access to identification, that sometimes offer hints that 'we' [...] exist.[28]

Arroyo's analysis of excesses of prop and costume in Jarman's *Edward II* (1991) might also apply to *The Doom Generation*: that such excesses 'not only help communicate setting and character but signal a sensibility'.[29] An important ingredient of that sensibility is camp, a much-debated aspect of gay culture. Five dimensions of a distinctly

15. Excessive design as evidence of queer sensibility: *The Doom Generation* (1995).

queer form of camp – as opposed to the use of camp assimilated into the mainstream – are identified in Araki's work by Glyn Davis: a drawing to attention of performance (often through poor or bombastic acting, a style that resembles the earlier work of Paul Morrissey, or through excesses of costume); a delight in the use of trashy ephemera (the assorted detritus of pop culture found in Araki's films, often rubbing shoulders with high-art reference points such as the Godard poster in *The Living End*); the use of parody (of genres such as the road movie in *The Doom Generation*; the cartoon-like QuickieMart killing might be a parody of *Natural Born Killers*, released the previous year, in which case the colour-fields outside could be read as parody of a green-hued sequence at a drugstore in the original); a political ingredient, as already discussed; and references to earlier queer camp filmmakers (a Warhol poster in *The Living End*, a killing in *Nowhere* in which the victim is finished off with a can of Campbell's tomato soup).[30]

The effect of the strategies detailed above is to denaturalize the material, a move that has the potential to shift attention from form to content; from awareness of the constructed nature of film, and the world it represents, to consideration of the constructed nature of the social reality – including the gender frameworks – we all inhabit. Araki's films remind us that we are watching actors performing, as Davis suggests; the emphasis on performance 'exposes the supposed "naturalness" of everyday behaviour and identity as a sham'.[31] A similar effect is found in other examples of New Queer Cinema, including *Poison* and *Swoon*. The narrative structure of *Poison* remains in the foreground because of the problem it constantly poses of how to make sense of the relationship between the different strands, across which teasing but minimal connections are drawn. A conventional level of absorption into the material is blocked, encouraging a more critical-analytical level of response. *Swoon* also has a stylized surface – its black-and-white photography – that plays a substantial part in the maintenance of viewer distance. An impression of dissociation is created in a stylized sequence immediately after the murder, in which, in successive shots, the camera keeps sliding into and swinging away from the principals. The effect may partly be to figure the state of consciousness of the characters, especially Leopold, who plays a more passive role, but it also suggests a fracturing of the relationship between character and the perspective of the viewer. *Frisk* also employs a highly non-naturalistic aesthetic, closer in places to works of the avant-garde or underground, in a dense texture that includes the intrusion of rapidly cut sequences of 8mm found-footage, pixelvision, and a narrative frame that ultimately leaves open the question of whether or not the activities of Dennis remain in the realm of fantasy. Narrative disruptions and uncertainties of this kind in New Queer Cinema are seen by Monica Pearl as a response to the nature of the AIDS virus itself, in both its unconventional behaviour as an illness – one in which the body ends up attacking itself – and its depredations on the gay community.[32]

Qualities such as self-consciousness, parody, the use and abuse of existing genre formats and the mixing of elements ascribed to 'higher' and 'lower' cultural forms give New Queer Cinema much in common with prevailing definitions of the postmodern, as suggested in Rich's catchy original designation of the phenomenon as 'Homo Pomo'. New queer films and videos are not all the same and do not share a single aesthetic or concern, Rich argued in 1992, but they are united by a common style: 'There are traces in them of appropriation and pastiche, irony, as well as a reworking of history with social constructionism very much in mind.'[33] Denaturalization of both form and gender constructions is a strategy that mobilizes the wider resonances of the term 'queer'; not just as a reference to gay, lesbian or bisexual identity, but a more general making-strange or 'queering' of what usually passes for familiar or 'normal' in prevailing (bourgeois, heterosexist, patriarchal and often racist) terms. In some cases this entails a discovery of or shift towards non-heterosexuality, but it can also embrace a broader range of transgressive desires. Sexual orientation is not a matter of rigid binary opposites, or a strict separation between heterosexual and homosexual, but a potentially more fluid field of possibilities, a view of the world that often emerges in the films of Araki, in which characters can slide relatively easily and unfussily from one form of engagement to another.

A sense of queering that goes beyond material focused directly on issues of gay or lesbian sexuality is found in Todd Haynes' *Safe*, discussed in Chapter 3. *Safe*, along with the director's subversive short film, *Superstar: The Karen Carpenter Story* (1987), focuses on a disease that acts as a metaphorical equivalent of AIDS while not being restricted to its primary associations with the gay community.[34] *Superstar*, a 43-minute production tracing the events leading up to the title character's death from anorexia, offers an irresistible queering of the clean-cut Carpenters' image, confounding realistic conventions with its use of Barbie dolls and cardboard sets and juxtaposing the 'purity' of the song lyrics with contemporary footage including images from the war in Southeast Asia. *Safe* creates a more pervasive and subtle sense of dislocation in the form of an illness the precise source of which is not quite defined and that strikes not at the social margins but in the heart of upper-middle-class suburbia, qualities that make it an ideal vehicle for a more general queering or making strange of dominant and familiar social terrain.

It is at this point that a specific dynamic within New Queer Cinema crosses over into a wider segment of independent cinema, in its scope for creating unsettling impressions within otherwise more conventional forms. A subtle form of 'queering' is a useful term to describe the effect of some of the distinctly indie qualities outlined in earlier chapters, tending to work on and subvert rather than outrightly reject dominant norms. While *Happiness*, for example, does not celebrate the paedophile Bill Maplewood, it offers a perspective in which his activities are normalized, disturbingly – both in terms of his bland façade and the cinematic devices through which his desires are articulated – and in which a gulf is opened up in the construction of apparently 'normal' suburban family life. Something similar happens in David O. Russell's debut feature, *Spanking the Monkey* (1994), in which an incestuous relationship develops between a bright undergraduate, Ray (Jeremy Davies), and his mother (Alberta Watson), recovering from a broken leg and depression. What gives *Spanking the Monkey* a queer dimension is the fact that the relationship between mother and son is both eroticized and seems like an entirely 'natural' development, in context; but also that so highly charged an encounter does not become the sole or dominant centre of gravity of the film. Incest is just one ingredient in a blackly comic mix of dysfunctional family relationships. To include mother-son incest at all is likely to be a marker of independent status; to make it seem relatively natural, and to deny it a full melodramatic treatment, is to enter into the realm of queering the family context in which it occurs.

Its potential to overlap into qualities celebrated by some variants of indie cinema more generally might be one reason for the success queer cinema has enjoyed at the heart of the independent landscape in recent decades. A closer fit exists in some important respects between the core attributes of queer and indie cinemas than is found in the relationship between black independent film, for example, and the kind of filmmaking for which the term 'indie' has come to stand since the 1980s. The emphasis of queer cinema on transgression, specifically in the arena of sex and gender, gives it, almost by default, a commercial advantage in the independent sector. Sexual transgression can be sold as 'cool' and fashionable, to the particular niche audiences attracted by indie cinema. Sexual transgression, generally, is more subject to *commodification* than material that raises questions perceived as more socially intractable and 'political'. Issues of gender and gender transgression *are* essentially political in nature – entailing differential power relationships and embedded social constructions founded in inequality – but are less often experienced as such. The issues raised by queer cinema tend to be defined primarily as questions of culture and identity – rather than of politics and economy – that lend themselves more easily to niche-marketable quirky, individual-character-centred indie frameworks.[35] The separation of cultural dimensions from their political and economic contexts is a distinct characteristic of contemporary 'late' capitalism more generally, according to Rosemary Hennessy, a situation that enables the former to be commodified in the form of individual 'lifestyle' and consumption choices (including consumption of media) that appear divorced from their material ground. The material ground itself, including fundamental inequalities of class, race and gender, lends itself far less well to such treatment; attempts at its understanding tend (with the exception of the work of Spike Lee, up to a point) to encourage more dour and less niche-marketably entertaining approaches such as those found in the films of the LA School.

A substantial overlap exists between significant sectors of gay/lesbian or queer cultures and some of the specific target markets of indie cinema, reinforcing the mutual relationship between the two. A more prominent part of gay/lesbian culture falls into the regions of cultural-taste hierarchy occupied by independent cinema than is probably the case for society in general, and particularly for groups such as black Americans and others subjected to racially or ethnically defined inequality. The non-heterosexual population is divided, like the population in general, along lines such as race/ethnicity, gender and class. But organized gay and lesbian movements, and gay and lesbian culture, have been dominated by middle-class sectors of the population, a class bias that militates against more radical analysis of political and economic context and that encourages the consumption of particular kinds of cultural products.[36] The most influential components of gay and lesbian society are more likely than average to possess the cultural capital and/or aspiration associated with the consumption of products such as indie cinema, a culturally aware, educated, middle-class sector increasingly targeted in commodity culture since the 1990s.[37] A useful way of understanding this situation further is offered by Richard Dyer, in an analysis based on the earlier shaping of gay male culture in Britain. Gay culture, for Dyer, has a disproportionate tendency to lean towards art and expressive culture as alternative realms that have historically seemed hospitable to gay sensibilities. Working-class aspects of gay culture, he suggests, have generally been occluded from the formulations that have proved dominant and lasting, the tastes of a particular metropolitan gay milieu tending to be constructed as that of gay culture itself, to which others subsequently aspire, reinforcing 'the notion that this culture, very narrowly rooted in social terms, is what gays turn to spontaneously'.[38] In its wilful difference from the mainstream, New Queer Cinema, and indie cinema more generally, is a culturally elitist form, if not as much so as works of the avant-garde; as Dyer suggests, the same can be said of some of the defining characteristics of dominant constructions of queerness in gay subculture: distanced and 'superior' qualities such as irony, decadence, fashion and 'attitude'.[39]

Wider uses of the term 'queer' are valuable, both generally and in reference to independent cinema, in their ability to open up a range of aspects of non-normative or transgressive culture. There is a danger of a loss of specificity, however, that operates at more than one level. Using 'queer' or 'queering' to designate other forms of making-strange can have an appropriative effect, denying the specific conjunction of a range of non-heterosexual gender orientations. It can also have the same effect within the realm of non-heterosexuality. As an umbrella term, it suggests commonalities between gay, lesbian, bisexual and other orientations, and has been criticized for failing to attend to real differences among and between such communities. What goes under the name of queer culture, or queer cinema, has generally been dominated by the perspective of gay males, a replication within same-sex cultures of the gender inequalities of the wider society. It has also been overwhelmingly white, with a few notable exceptions. These include two documentary milestones in the first wave of 1990s queer cinema – Marlon Riggs' *Tongues Untied* (1990), an assertion of black gay male sexuality through a mixture including poetry recitation and personal testimony, and Jennie Livingston's *Paris is Burning* (1990), a portrait (albeit by a white filmmaker) of the complex gender, racial and class dynamics underlying the aspirations of participants in New York black and Latino drag balls – and Cheryl Dunye's *The Watermelon Woman* (1996), an example of an even more rare phenomenon, black lesbian cinema. *The Watermelon Woman* is a self-reflective work, in which Dunye herself plays a filmmaker tracing the history of a black woman performer from the racist Hollywood of the 1930s. New Queer Cinema includes a number of significant contributions by lesbian filmmakers such as Dunye, Rose Troche and Lisa Cholodenko, but these have generally been marginalized. The form of New Queer Cinema celebrated in the 1990s was dominated by figurations of male desire and, as Amy Taubin suggested at the time, films such as *Swoon* and *The Living End* have more in common with male-violence indie films such as *Reservoir Dogs* and *Laws of Gravity* than with a queer/feminist perspective.[40] A major exception to this tendency is the work of Todd Haynes, the themes of which, as Anat Pick says, 'are emphatically inclusive of, even exclusive to, women', especially in *Superstar, Safe* and *Far From Heaven* (2002).[41]

The lesbian component of New Queer Cinema was launched with the release of Troche's *Go Fish*, a hit at Sundance, in 1994. A number of other features followed, including Maria Maggenti's romantic comedy *The Incredibly True Adventures of Two Girls in Love* (1995) and Cholodenko's *High Art* (1999). The latter is a lesbian-oriented illustration of Dyer's point about the attraction of queer culture to 'decadent' arty milieux, in this case that of the photographer Lucy (Ally Sheedy) into whose heroin-fuelled downtown apartment-community is attracted the young, previously straight Syd (Radha Mitchell). *High Art* is another example that refuses a simple 'positive images' approach. It has a downbeat ending and gives a portrait of lesbian relationships that are more than one-dimensional, and in some cases painful, although it risks lapsing into stereotype in its association of lesbianism with an exotic and seductive *demi-monde*. Despite the attention gained by individual features such as *Go Fish* and *High Art*, lesbian filmmakers, like women more generally, usually find it hard to gain finance and/or distribution. More radical or outspoken lesbian- or feminist-oriented queer production has tended to be restricted to the commercial margins, often to production in video rather than higher-budgeted film, including the avant-garde work of Barbara Hammer and Sadie Benning.

The wider notion of 'queer' need not be surrendered, however, as Alexander Doty suggests, as long as recognition is given to each of the specific territories it contains: from 'straight' usages, for acts of making-strange that have no immediately non-heterosexual component, to broad conjunctions of non-heterosexuality and specific cultural and political locations such as 'gay', 'lesbian' and 'bisexual', in independent cinema and beyond.[42] More general and specific impressions of queerness can be merged, or one can modulate with the other, as is the case, for example, in *Chuck and Buck*. From the start, a suggestion is given of a homoerotic dimension to the attachment of the childlike adult Buck to his former best friend, Chuck. Buck's hand reaches down towards Chuck's groin, wandering off-limits during a hug between the two when they meet at the funeral of Buck's mother. It turns out later that the pair indulged in sexual activity as children ('Chuck and Buck, suck and fuck') but the impression of discomfort generated by the film is more pervasive than can be accounted for simply by the opening up of a queer/gay fissure in the successful/suburban/heterosexual life of Chuck. Chuck eventually agrees to one night of sex with Buck, in return for being left alone, a sequence that carries a hint of awakening his emotional investment in the relationship, and the respite it offers from the demands of his job as a record company executive. But the inappropriate nature of Buck's fixation is located more in its painful and embarrassingly non-adult qualities than in the specifically sexual dimension. The use of a naïve-but-honest childlike perspective to highlight the superficiality of particular constructions of adult normality is itself a familiar trope, but articulated here in a manner that is unusually unsettling.

The trajectory of New Queer Cinema has been very much that of the indie sector as a whole since the early 1990s: a period of initial innovation followed by consolidation, expansion, crossover success closer to the mainstream and, as a result, expressions of concern about a loss of radical edge. The volume of queer/gay/lesbian production increased throughout the decade, along with a rapid expansion in the number and scale of gay and lesbian film festivals. This was part of a more general expansion in the presence of gay and lesbian material in popular culture, including television shows ranging from *Will and Grace* to *Six Feet Under*, an increased visibility bought, as Hennessy suggests, at the price of increased commodification. The result, for Rich, among other commentators, was a dilution of quality, accompanied by a movement away from difficult, experimental or edgy work in

244 AMERICAN INDEPENDENT CINEMA

favour of material more likely to gain box-office success.[43] According to Rich, writing in 2000, New Queer Cinema:

> has become so successful as to have dispersed itself in any number of elsewheres. Lacking the concentrated creative presence and focused community responsiveness of the past, the New Queer Cinema has become just another niche market, another product line pitched at one particular type of discerning consumer.[44]

Queer cinema has, without doubt, become more firmly institutionalized, including a presence in the more mainstream parts of the indie sector and, on occasion, in Hollywood itself. A dialectic continues to exist, however, between more and less radical currents. If New Queer Cinema itself was, originally, an attempt to reclaim non-heterosexual difference and dissidence, in the face of the project of positive-image-based assimilation, its own commercialization has stimulated further anti-assimilationist forays, including fringe movements such as Queercore (of which *Frisk* might be taken to be an example) and queer punk.[45] Even within films that have enjoyed more prominent success, different degrees of 'queerness' can be detected, as can be seen in a comparison of two of the higher-profile examples of the late 1990s, *Gods and Monsters* (1998) and *Boys Don't Cry* (1999).

Neither has particularly queer antecedents, in terms of the filmmakers, although Christine Vachon, producer of transgressive indie features including *Poison* and *Happiness*, co-produced *Boys Don't Cry*, distributed by Fox Searchlight. The style of each is relatively slick and conventional on modest budgets ($3.5 million for *Gods and Monsters*, $2 million for *Boys Don't Cry*). Each offers a framework that operates effectively to contain the queer dimension, although this seems more strongly the case with *Gods and Monsters*, a portrait of the last days of the gay Hollywood director James Whale. The characterization of Whale is untroubling to familiar/dominant constructions of male homosexuality. In a mannered performance by Ian McKellen, a prominent gay rights activist himself, Whale offers a very 'safe' gay image: a mischievous theatrical old queer, playing on gay-coded qualities of 'distinction' and traits of upper-class 'Englishness', an example of the kind of class-aspirational, culture-oriented gay background described by Dyer. The wealthy ex-Hollywood milieu in which the film unfolds is one in which 'decadent' and 'excessive' behaviour might be expected, rather than appearing particularly transgressive, even if it is said to have been considered scandalous at the time.

The opposite is the case for *Boys Don't Cry*, the texture of which comes from a bored-youth, neon-lit, white 'trailer trash' Nebraska, in which the out-of-place gender ambiguity of the central character, Brandon Teena/Teena Brandon (Hilary Swank), proves a source of violent provocation. Brandon is presented as a young woman, physiologically, who passes as a man, is attracted to other women and seems to have plans for surgical gender realignment. 'I'm not a dyke,' Brandon insists. At times, particularly in the latter stages, the film plays with suggestions that Brandon's physiology may itself be ambiguous, although that proves not to be the case. Either way, the film queers conventional constructions of gender identity much more than *Gods and Monsters*. Brandon's lover Lana (Chloe Sevigny) maintains her attachment, physically and emotionally, despite indications that she is aware of his/her status before the forced revelation of the physiologically reductive 'truth'. The possibility of accepting so non-conventional a relationship is admitted; a relationship the ambiguity of which, the film suggests, is a greater threat to the prevailing gender economy than a simple and more easily accommodated case of lesbianism. Assertion of strictly physiologically defined conventional sex/gender boundaries is equated, literally, with violent assault, stripping and rape, followed by murder. The 'containing' narrative framework, in this case, is the format of 'doomed love', the potential of which to universalize in the name of commercialization is implied in Kimberly Peirce's invocation of *Romeo and Juliet* as one of the frames of reference for the film.[46] Doomed love, that is, with the particularly indie-marketable atmospherics of a going-nowhere, wasted-lives 'road' movie format, in which impressions of verisimilitude are mixed with estranging stylized time-lapse touches of the hyper-real.

Boys Don't Cry demonstrated the crossover potential of a film that retains a distinctly queer and unsettling dimension, including an angry attack on the violent policing of gender boundaries, even if this is blended with more familiar ingredients. It achieved the very high profile of a best actress Oscar award, among many others, for

Hilary Swank, if not any great box-office performance (a US gross of $11.5 million, respectable for the budget). The centrality of Swank's performance to the reception of the film is particularly important to its queer status, given its location at the heart of the issues of gender ambiguity confronted by the film. The spectacle of Swank's act of male drag is in many respects 'convincing', creating a plausible impression of 'maleness', but one in which a sufficient mix of signifiers is present to maintain the *frisson* provided by a destabilizing sense of androgyny. As far as the likely experience of the viewer is concerned, *Boys Don't Cry* is an example of the slippage that often occurs between distanced awareness of star/actor performing and absorption into the world of the fictional narrative. The two can work against each other, but in this case the 'quality' of Swank's performance, as validated by awards committees, seems to strengthen the impression created by the diegesis.

The dialectical relationship that exists between more or less radical/ alternative gay/lesbian/queer-oriented material can be explored further by looking briefly at some examples of uses made of one of the most familiar mainstream genre frameworks: romantic comedy. Gay- or lesbian-oriented romantic comedy is a good example of the use of existing formats within which to offer alternative perspectives, a strategy examined in detail in the previous chapter. In some cases, such as *Go Fish*, romantic comedy is given a distinctly indie/alternative quality, beyond the fact that the relationships on which it focuses are lesbian or gay. In others, the conventions of the form are played more or less 'straight', 'difference' being restricted to the shift from heterosexual to homosexual romance. The former is designed to appeal to both a gay/lesbian-specific and a broader indie niche audience. The latter is based on the assumption that alterity in one dimension – gender orientation – does not necessarily create a demand for products marked as particularly 'alternative' in others.

Go Fish clearly has the stamp of 'indie' movie, in its grainy, low-budget black-and-white photography, harsh sound quality, the use of a number of 'arty' expressive devices, and in the fact that it was the first lesbian-themed feature associated with the queer boom of the 1990s. Sequences of associative abstract imagery – spinning tops, hands, falling paper, a light going out; much of this shot against plain black backgrounds – recur throughout the film, along with other expressive effects that mark an injection of avant-garde experimentalism into the narrative texture. A group of four women's heads shot from above functions as a self-conscious running commentary on the status of the central plot thread, the developing relationship between Max (co-screenwriter Guinevere Turner) and Ely (V.S. Brodie). Much investment is put into the creation of an impression of the distinctive metropolitan lesbian milieu in which the action unfolds. While attending to such specifics, however, the basic structure of *Go Fish* remains rooted in mainstream romantic comedy convention: the romantic bringing together, eventually, after various delays, of two initially unlikely-seeming partners: the brash young Max and the older and more reserved Ely. The difference between more and less indie/ alternative treatments of such material can be seen in a comparison between *Go Fish* and *The Incredibly True Adventures of Two Girls in Love*. The familiar romantic comedy dynamic of differences-overcome-through-love is played up more strongly in the latter, a fact that increases the conventional nature of the production. The differences between 17-year-olds Randy (Laurel Holloman) and Evie (Nicole Ari Parker) are exaggerated (rebellious, butch, white, rock-oriented tomboy lesbian from poor background vs. rich, black, 'sophisticated', so-far-straight, classical music oriented Range Rover driver), to a point that makes their union a far more Hollywood-style magical fantasy than seems the case in *Go Fish*, an impression underlined by the absence of any other formal departures from the classical style.

A mix of milieu-specific and familiar-conventional features is also found in mainstream-style, gay-male-oriented romantic comedies such as *Jeffrey* (1995) and *Trick* (1999). In *Jeffrey*, a light, witty approach, including direct address to camera and other frame-breaking diversions, is given a darker, AIDS-era dimension in the revelation that Steve (Michael T. Weiss), the character romantically pursuing the reluctant title figure (Steven Webber), is HIV positive. The gay-specific spin of *Trick* lies in the fact that the will-it-happen/won't-it-happen relationship around which it revolves is reduced to the temporal dimensions of a one-night stand, following a wordless subway pickup of musical-comedy writer Gabriel (Christian Campbell) by go-go boy Mark (John Paul Pitoc). Both films obey basic romantic narrative conventions such as the presence of 'blocking' factors, or characters, that serve to frustrate the development of romance, as is also the case in *The Incredibly True Adventures*, but they are given specific resonance. In *Jeffrey*, the principal blockage is Steve's HIV status, and Jeffrey's attitude, only the latter of which can be overcome. In *Trick*, the problem is more pragmatic: the lack of a space in which to fuck, in a subculture based on gratification that cannot easily be delayed.

Anyone looking for an example from the domain of romantic comedy with which to argue the blunting of New Queer Cinema's edge might look no further than Gregg Araki's entry in the format, *Splendor* (1999), a much softer confection than his previous films. *Splendor*, a designer-stylish and snappily written homage to the screwball comedy of the 1930s and 1940s, celebrates an unconventional three-way relationship between early 20s Veronica (Kathleen Robertson) and the two men with whom she falls in love, Abel (Johnathan Schaech) and Zed (Matt Kesslar). In traditional romantic comedy style, Veronica leaves the two in favour of a more reliable suitor after becoming pregnant but follows her heart in the end, pursuing what the film marks as the emotionally appropriate course and settling down with Abel, Zed and what turn out to be twins. In some respects, the dynamic is akin to that of *The Doom Generation*, in which the two male leads are rivals for the girl. *Splendor* is uncharacteristically coy by Araki's standards, however, in its treatment of the relationship between Abel and Zed. In *The Doom Generation*, it is clear from the start that a strong homoerotic charge exists, and is to be developed, between Jordan and Xavier (also played by Johnathan Schaech). Similar *potential* exists in *Splendor* but is not realized in any explicit fashion. Abel and Zed share a kiss during one of their early meetings, but only in a 'dare' game played with Veronica. They embrace, Zed in tears, upset at the apparent loss of Veronica, towards the end. They live together in her apartment for the latter portion of the film, but no suggestion is given of any sexual relationship at this stage, or any clear impression that their three-way encounters with Veronica involved direct physical intercourse between the two. Potential exists to read this into the film, but the absence of anything more suggests a retreat by Araki from the more provocative nature of his earlier productions, in favour of a concoction more easily marketed to crossover audiences.

New Queer Cinema was certainly not 'new' by the late 1990s and early 2000s, but even if such a movement inevitably loses some of its freshness and impact over time, evidence exists for a continuing queer legacy, alongside less provocative lesbian- and gay-oriented production. The highly offbeat *Being John Malkovich* (1999), from the Indiewood zone (production and distribution involving then Universal affiliates Gramercy Pictures and USA Films), is nominated by Rich as a notable heir, its characters 'deeply implicated in the whole project of gender positioning'; specifically Lotte (Cameron Diaz), who immediately decides she is a transsexual, and then finds herself attracted to another woman, after being projected into the mind of the fictional version of Malkovich.[47] Features such as *Chuck and Buck* demonstrate the indie sector's continued potential for generating gay/lesbian and more diffuse impressions of queerness, and it would be a bold prediction to imagine that Araki had abandoned more provocative material with *Splendor*, his next project at the time of writing being an adaptation of Scott Heim's novel *Mysterious Skin*.

Left of Centre

In the case of New Queer Cinema, some kind of connection between indie cinema as an institution and an identifiable subject-specific culture/subculture has been important to the establishment of its sustained presence in the independent sector. The same might be said of elements of black independent filmmaking that have drawn on ghetto/youth/rap subculture, although the playing up of such components has, in this case, often led closer to the strategies of the mainstream. What about independent filmmaking of a left-oriented slant? Like the radical end of black cinema, it is harder to make a connection of this kind, between a definable cultural-political niche audience and the broader contours of the indie scene. If the dominant audience of much indie cinema is middle-class, educated and more than usually arts-oriented, as seems likely to be the case, this is less likely to be the core constituency of those concerned with issues such as socialism, class politics, socio-economic inequality and exploitation. This is far from an absolute distinction, of course, and the audience for indie cinema is likely to include plenty of left-leaning recruits from the middle classes, among others. But it might help to explain the paucity of films that can really be said to embody a leftist spirit in anything like the same way that many products of New Queer Cinema are distinctively and assertively queer. Questions of class politics and economy lend themselves far less well to dominant indie frameworks, as suggested above, especially at the level of exploring causal factors rather than symptoms – not that the causes of homophobia or other gender insecurities have been subject to much consideration in New Queer Cinema either.

Independent cinema remains primarily an individual-centred cinema (with some exceptions suggested above, especially work associated with the LA School), a quality it shares with the Hollywood mainstream and that limits its capacity to present radical alternatives to dominant American ideologies, in which conceptions of the freedom of the individual play such a central role in belying the impact of socio-economic determinations. This is apparent in the extent to which the formal innovations explored earlier in this book are so often motivated as expressions of individual consciousness. A central dynamic in much American indie cinema of recent decades revolves around notions of quirkiness, especially quirkiness of character, that run against the grain of a socialist or Marxist perspective. Critique of dominant ideologies tends to come in forms that are implicit more than explicit, in which the reassuring fantasies of Hollywood are undermined from within – the absence of neat reconciliations, the creation of moral ambiguity instead of clear-cut impressions of 'right' and 'wrong' – rather than being replaced by any politically radical alternative.

A more obviously socialist alternative has existed historically in independent cinema, especially in the 1920s and 1930s, a period in which socialism itself was a significant current in American politics. A number of low-budget features were produced by radical groups such as the Labor Film Service in the 1920s, screened primarily at union meetings.[48] The Depression of the 1930s saw the appearance of *Our Daily Bread* (1934), a hymn to the values of collective production in which unemployed workers group together to run a cooperative farm. Another landmark in socialist-oriented production is *Salt of the Earth* (1954), co-produced by the International Union of Mine, Mill and Smelter Workers, which revolves around a strike at a zinc mine in New Mexico. A striking characteristic of *Salt of the Earth* is the central role given to women, not just in supporting the strike but in making their own demands on the company in whose properties they live; a similar dimension is to the fore in Barbara Kopple's documentary *Harlan County, USA* (1976), a sympathetic portrait of a strike over the right to union recognition in the Kentucky coalfield.

The nearest to this kind of material visited in the independent feature movement of more recent decades is *Matewan* (1987), written and directed by John Sayles, the most consistently social-issues oriented of contemporary indie filmmakers. *Matewan* returns to the 1920s history of violent conflict between capital and labour, focusing on a strike in a coal-mining community in West Virginia. A number of points of similarity with predecessors such as *Our Daily Bread* and *Salt of the Earth* can be identified, in terms of both the left-oriented nature of the material and the way this is combined with the use of more dominant-conventional narrative devices. *Matewan* is clearly pro-worker, anti-company, although in a distanced, heightened and clear-cut historical context in which it is no great task to provoke sympathy for the forces of organized labour – a relatively 'easy' option, compared with the difficulties that might be experienced in achieving the same impression for most American viewers in a contemporary setting, especially given the use of brownish-yellow tints and gauzy effects that give the film a distinctly 'period' feel. *Matewan* presents a number of divisions between the workers, principally between 'native' local mine union members and black and recent-immigrant Italian recruits brought in by the company in an attempt to divide-and-rule, a dynamic based on real historical accounts of the period. A number of conventional fictional devices are imposed on the material, however, rendering it into a more familiar and melodramatic form. Much the same is the case in *Our Daily Bread* and *Salt of the Earth*, each of which builds its more political resonances around the often-troubled relationship between a central man-and-wife couple.

The catalyzing factor in bringing about unity in *Matewan* is the arrival of the union official Joe Kenehan (Chris Cooper), in some respects a typical American movie 'outsider' figure, who argues against the violent response the company seeks to provoke from the workers. Attention to the political dimension of the film, the specific nature of the conflict as one between labour and capital, is often displaced by generic resonances and the employment of melodrama. The 'bad guys', especially the lead hired thug, are irredeemably nasty, at a personal level. A highly melodramatic device involving allegations of sexual assault against a naïve widow is used at one point to put Kenehan under suspicion; melodramatic use is also made of another 'innocent' but more committed figure, a youth who manages to wrap an encoded message into a sermon to save Kenehan in the nick of time. *Matewan* owes a good deal to the Western tradition – the loner-with-a-past who comes into town, a climactic shoot-out in the main street, the generic resonances of which are played up in posters and video-cover artwork – although with some significant departures. These include the fact that Kenehan's disavowal of violence is maintained (unlike the classic Western protagonist, the former gunfighter who reluctantly picks up his weapon in defence of an embattled community) and that he dies unceremoniously off-screen in the end. In terms of narrative and formal strategies, departures from the mainstream are relatively minor: the bottom line of the film is to rely on very conventional patterns of emotional manipulation, probably considered a necessity in any attempt to put relatively radical material into any substantial form of commercial circulation.

A similar pattern is found in most of Sayles' work, including the ensemble pieces *City of Hope* (1991) and *Sunshine State* (2002) in which he deals most explicitly in areas of political controversy. In *City of Hope*, Sayles presents a much more complex and multi-layered set of competing interests, a function of turning from the relatively black-and-white issues of *Matewan* to the context of contemporary urban politics. The stance of the film is essentially liberal rather than radical, in its commitment to an emphasis on complexity and ambiguity, qualities more characteristic of commercial-indie cinema than indications of clear-cut commitment to a single cause. A black community group is shown to be prone to ritual oversimplification in its fight against injustice, too readily taking advantage of incidents that might promote its cause, without regard to the specific facts of the case (specifically, a malicious allegation of sexual molestation). The film revolves around the personal dilemmas faced by a small number of individuals at the centre of its web of tensions and allegiances, deploying a multi-strand narrative of the kind examined in Chapter 2 to depict a network of overlapping relationships, a dimension emphasized visually by Sayles' use of transitions in which the focus often moves from one thread to another within the same shot. The strength of the film is its refusal to admit the possibility of simplistic solutions to deeply ingrained problems. There is no unambiguously heroic individual action of the kind often deployed in Hollywood as an emotional displacement of irresolvable social issues. The end is distinctly downbeat, but without the abandonment of any prospect for meaningful action. One of the central characters is left bleeding, probably to death. Another, a black city councilman, decides to play to the crowd in relation to the alleged molestation, against his instincts, but quickly shifts the emphasis towards an intervention in the more substantial issue facing a inner-city black community threatened with displacement from its home. A similar issue is central to *Sunshine State*, in which an exclusive beach-resort development threatens a black community in Florida. A mixture of responses to the prospect is explored, mostly but not exclusively negative, along with an array of individual-character sub-plots, although in this case the *deus ex machina* device of the discovery of an important archaeological site creates an arbitrary resolution in which the development is abandoned.

The strategy adopted by John Sayles – a commercial necessity, to a large extent, even if also a personal preference – is to use typically indie variants on mainstream practice to make points that have specifically social-political resonances: multi-strand and/or low-key narrative structures, along with different attitudes towards genre (the use of genre resonances in *Matewan*; their deflation, primarily, in an example such as *The Brother From Another Planet* [1984], in which a mute black alien lands up in Harlem). Alternative material is conveyed through devices that remain largely, if not entirely, familiar-conventional, a position that would be located, in broader left-aesthetic theory, closer to that of Georg Lukács than Bertolt Brecht. In a series of debates among Marxist theorists, Lukács favoured the use of existing 'realist' fictional devices – principally those associated with the nineteenth-century novel – to produce a detailed picture of the surface texture of existence through which the 'underlying essence' could shine.[49] Brecht's theatre is associated with a formally more radical strategy, in which devices would be used to distance or 'alienate' the viewer from the fiction, to make clear its constructed nature and to create a more critical-analytical position for the spectator – an approach taken up most notably in film by Jean-Luc Godard and also manifested implicitly, to some extent, in some of the examples of New Queer Cinema cited above. In the work of Sayles, as in most American indie cinema, the viewer is encouraged into a position of close proximity with rather than distance from central characters, a distinctive feature of his ensemble works being the larger-than-usual number of characters who are presented either sympathetically or not entirely unsympathetically. Features that seek to keep the viewer at greater distance from central figures are notably thin on the ground, a striking exception being the mock-documentary *Bob Roberts* (1992), a political satire directed by and starring Tim Robbins as a blandly odious right-wing candidate for the US Senate.

It is the use of documentary-style convention that enables such distance to be kept from the central character of *Bob Roberts*. The title figure is seen only as viewed by the fictional filmmakers, which is, by definition, a more distanced perspective than that associated with the dominant fictional conventions – mainstream and indie, in many cases – through which we are presented with the illusion of a more intimate connection to character. An indication of the difficulty that can result from the more direct and positive presentation of political material is found in the impact on the film of a number of sequences in which we are presented with the opinions of Roberts' electoral opponent, Brickley Paiste (Gore Vidal). Paiste's interventions are entirely to the point, a critique of American foreign policy in the lead-up to the Gulf war of 1991. The material is precisely the kind of riposte to dominant perceptions that might be expected from a politically oriented independent production, but it sits a little awkwardly in the film, shifting its sharply satiric edge into a direction that seems overly sanctimonious, even for the viewer who agrees with the sentiment expressed. The reason for this may be that Paiste's comments are addressed more directly to the viewer than is usually the case, his arguments being put to the filmmaker in 'interview' segments in which he faces almost to camera. The effect is to upset the fictional balance and shift the mode of address, creating an impression of 'preaching' to the viewer rather than integrating the material more effectively into a diegetic universe, *from which* the viewer could draw the appropriate conclusions.

If *Bob Roberts* uses mock documentary to create an impression of satirical distance, documentary itself is a form in which it is generally possible to create a more analytical framework than is usually found in narrative fiction. As far as aspirations towards theatrical distribution/ exhibition are concerned, documentary filmmaking is more or less coterminous with the independent sector. Even in the indie scene, the number of documentaries that get far beyond the festival circuit is minimal, only rare examples achieving significant breakout status. Documentary in general is beyond the scope of this book, for reasons of space, except for its influence on fictional forms, as considered in earlier chapters. It is one of the major sources of more directly social-issues-oriented independent production, however, and will be considered briefly in that context. In addition to Kopple's *Harlan County, USA*, past examples include the blacklisted drama/documentary mix *Native Land* (1942), an angry outburst against state-sponsored oppression of American workers who fight for their rights, the films of Richard Leacock and Frederick Wiseman in the 1960s, and the work of Emile de Antonio. De Antonio was an influential figure in the creation of the infrastructure of the 'New American Cinema' of the late 1950s and early 1960s, performing roles including the distribution of the Beat cult film *Pull My Daisy* (1959) and the more general promotion and support of the movement.[50] De Antonio's own films – including *Point of Order* (1963), a compilation of footage from the televised Army-McCarthy hearings, *In the Year of the Pig* (1968), a pointed deconstruction of American policy in Vietnam, and the portrait of Nixon given by *Millhouse: A White Comedy* (1971) – were potent interventions in the politics of their time, combining a radical stance with formal innovations such as the abandonment of conventional narrative devices in *Point of Order* and the use of dissonant sound effects in *In the Year of the Pig*.

Documentary offers a number of modes of expression different from those used in both mainstream and independent narrative-oriented features, although points of overlap can also be identified. Documentary offers greater scope for investigation of causal factors involved in social phenomena. It is free, in principle, from the individual-character-centred nexus of most fiction-feature production, although many documentaries choose to orient themselves around central (real-life) characters and share some qualities with their fictional counterparts, a factor that helps to explain some of the more prominent successes. The unexpected box-office success of *Hoop Dreams* (1994), for example, a US gross of $7.8 million for a 170-minute non-fiction feature, was owed largely to the fact that its epic account of youthful aspiration to basketball stardom is focused closely around the compelling story of two individuals, the black Chicago-area teenagers Arthur Agee and William Gates. Although a work of non-fiction, shot over a period of several years, the film has many narrative qualities in common with those of fiction, principally a rollercoaster of dramatic ups-and-downs, successes and disappointments, in the lives of the two principals, at both the larger scale of ongoing life-events and in the close-up detail of numerous heightened key moments in which one player or the other holds the last-seconds fate of a basketball match in his hands. In the process, *Hoop Dreams* offers a vivid portrait of life in the black ghetto, including shortcomings in the welfare system and an implicit indictment of the way black basketball talent is exploited by white-dominated schools, colleges and universities. It is through an initial focus on individuals that this is achieved, however, and what emerge are symptoms rather than causes.

De Antonio's films offer a mixture of approaches. The basis of *Point of Order* and *Millhouse: A White Comedy* in the compilation of existing footage leaves the viewer to draw any wider conclusions from material focused on the players involved in individual-centred drama. Both are assembled to create specific impressions, but these are left implicit. *In the Year of the Pig* is more explicit and analytical in approach, using a mixture of stock footage (including the claims of administration spokesman) and its own interviews with commentators who provide a deeper context in which to understand the imperialist nature of American policy in Vietnam. In its more didactic approach, and in the use of strategies such as montage sequences in which the official line is juxtaposed with images supporting the case presented by the film, *In the Year of the Pig* has more in common than most of de Antonio's films with the work of Michael Moore, the most high-profile exponent of politically oriented non-fiction in contemporary indie cinema.

Moore's films depart from the norm for relatively high-profile independent features by focusing attention directly onto contentious socio-economic issues. The impact of the global corporate strategy of relocating jobs from America to low-wage economies overseas forms a central thread of Moore's first feature, *Roger & Me* (1989), and *The Big One* (1998), in which the focus is not just on effects but also on the strategy itself and its motivation: profit. In *The Big One*, Moore highlights the existence of 'welfare for corporations', the use of taxpayers' dollars to support private business operations, to counter more prevalent claims about the supposed burden of limited social welfare for working people. The post-war history of American foreign policy, from the installation of the Shah in Iran to the provision of aid and training to latterly demonized figures such as Saddam Hussein and Osama bin Laden, is sketched from a radical perspective during a montage sequence in *Bowling for Columbine* (2002), to the ironic accompaniment of Louis Armstrong's 'What a Wonderful World'. The theme of profit is also revisited in the film, which identifies a nexus between the cultivation of fear at home and the culture of consumerism. This is unusually radical material for anything other than marginal American media production, even if it does not dig very deeply into the underlying nature of the capitalist system of which these are manifestations. Any more general analysis tends to take second place to routines centred on exchanges with individuals. A good example is a sequence in *The Big One* in which Moore confronts the chairman of Nike, Philip Knight, and suggests that corporations such as his could settle for slightly less large profits in order to keep some jobs in the USA. The point seems well made as far as it goes: that there is not an absolute opposition between maximum exploitation and corporate failure; that some middle ground might be possible. To put the emphasis on individual moral choice and culpability, however, in a classically liberal-reformist manner, is to distract attention from overriding imperatives that result from the structural characteristics of US-centred global capitalism.

Moore is effectively tied into this level of engagement by a rhetorical strategy characteristic of all three films, the basis of which is the confrontation of individuals with the up-front Moore personality. The dynamic is Moore vs. Knight, the latter trying his best to play along as far as he can, to remain 'cool' under the pressure exerted by Moore rather than opting for the avoidance tactic used by the chairman of General Motors in *Roger & Me*. In this context, Moore can josh and probe and can pitch a number of options (he tries to persuade Knight to open a shoe factory in Flint, Michigan, the city hit by the closure of the GM plant documented in *Roger & Me*; he offers Knight free tickets to accompany him to inspect the factories used by Nike under an oppressive regime in Indonesia; he challenges Knight to a race; he eventually gets Knight to agree to match his own promise to donate $10,000 to the Flint school system). But this form of confrontation does not encourage any real examination of the factors that prevent Knight from suddenly agreeing to some individual-centred change of heart. Moore's is a style of documentary invested heavily in the presence of the filmmaker, both as active participant and commentator and as a figure whose individual history is often inserted into the narrative. The success of Moore's films in the commercially difficult arena of theatrically released non-fiction (most notably the $21 million US gross for *Bowling for Columbine*) can be explained largely by his personal style and presence, including a strong vein of ironic comedy and self-deprecation. The formula is one that permits the quirky character-centred style associated with many independent fiction features to be carried into the realm of social-issues-oriented non-fiction. It is notable, however, that the Moore personality plays a reduced role, even if it is still present, in his more overtly political and contentious – and, unusually, even more commercially successful – *Fahrenheit 911*, which out-grossed *Bowling for Columbine* several-fold in the months preceding the 2004 presidential election. Engagement with pressing social-political issues is also carried out at the less commercial, 'guerrilla' filmmaking end of the spectrum, by activists from groups such as anti-war and anti-globalization alliances, a form circulated outside mainstream-indie channels of distribution that has benefited from the advent of more easily accessible DV technology.

Independent cinema, in general, in its more institutionalized forms, is stronger at offering alternative visions through the creation of unsettling or ambiguous impressions than it is at conducting more explicit inquiries into social, economic or political territory.

The former lends itself to a particular niche-audience form of art/ entertainment production, just as much concerned with explorations of individual experience as the mainstream in most cases but oriented towards a more complex rendition of the qualities of contemporary life. *Happiness*, for example, confronts the viewer with paedophilia in a manner in which specifics are not ducked or elided, as might be expected to be the case in a studio production. When Bill Maplewood is questioned on the sofa by his young son, neither he nor the viewer is easily let off the hook. Maplewood is repeatedly asked to elaborate, to explain exactly what he did and why. Numerous opportunities to cut discreetly away, leaving the rest to the viewer's imagination, are spurned in a claustrophobic three-and-a-half minute sequence that could not remotely be contemplated in a conventional Hollywood production. An absence of simplistic, melodramatic moral condemnation is characteristic of many of the more challenging independent films examined in this book.

Independent films are far more likely than Hollywood productions to confront us with uncomfortable or prickly central characters and less likely to offer fantastical reconciliatory dynamics in which such characteristics are washed magically away. Alexander Payne's *Citizen Ruth* (1996), for example, offers both a gutsy treatment of the deeply contentious issue of abortion rights and an essentially selfish hard-drinking, glue-sniffing and drug-taking pregnant title character (Laura Dern), who is not softened or sentimentalized during the course of the narrative, even if the dynamic remains conventionally individualist (the film pitches Ruth against what are depicted as organized camps on either side of the issue, although the pro-choice lobby is presented in a relatively more positive light). A similarly shallow-seeming and self-serving character is presented in Payne's *About Schmidt* (2002), a portrait of the hollowness of the existence of the recently retired, widowed and penny-pinching Warren Schmidt (Jack Nicholson). *About Schmidt* does offer something of a more conventionally cathartic, reconciliatory ending, in the emotion that results when Schmidt receives a painting from an African child he has sponsored through a charity, an outlet for his own feelings – in letters to the child that provide a voice-over commentary throughout the film – that constitutes a genuinely unselfish commitment to the needs of another. The device has much in common with those typical of Hollywood films, in which an emphasis on local reconciliatory detail creates an emotionally rhetorical impression that tends to displace larger unresolved issues. In this case, however, the balance remains more ambiguous. An impression is left, as in a number of other indie films, of an existence that is somewhat desolate, despite the trippingly droll surface tone of much of the film, a denial of the myth/ideology of the American Dream that remains potent even if it offers no effective prescription for change.

Coda

Merging with the Mainstream, or Staying Indie?

The lines between the independent sector and Hollywood are in many places blurred, the difference between one and the other being sometimes radical, sometimes far less clear-cut. Hollywood has certainly learned some lessons from the independent sphere in the past decade. The indie sector has also been shaped by Hollywood, not always to its advantage, both in being embraced institutionally in some parts and in adopting – sometimes being forced to adopt – some of its strategies, such as the emphasis on breakout hits. For plenty of filmmakers, independence has been a one-way stepping stone to Hollywood. Some have remained resolutely independent over a period of decades, notable examples including John Sayles and Jim Jarmusch. Others have moved between the two, sometimes abruptly, sometimes more fluently. The best example of the latter is the recent career of Steven Soderbergh, which can be taken, briefly, as emblematic of the state of the relationship today between Hollywood and the independent sector.

After the breakthrough success of *sex, lies, and videotape*, which remains a milestone in the development of the indie sector as we know it today, Soderbergh's career underwent a series of rapid shifts and halts: the disappointing performance and reception of *Kafka* (1991) and the studio features *King of the Hill* (1993) and *The Underneath* (1995) and his return to low-budget basics with the zany *Schizopolis* and *Gray's Anatomy*, both produced on limited resources in 1996. From this point, Soderbergh has pursued a career based on more assured movement between Hollywood and the independent sector. To Hollywood, his films offer auteurist credentials and the ability to attract star performers: a stylized edge within familiar genre frameworks (*Out of Sight*, 1998, with its non-linear narrative structure, alongside the independently produced and distributed *The Limey*) or just a 'classy' mounting of more conventional material, with occasional showy touches (*Erin Brokovich*, 2000, *Ocean's Eleven*, 2001, *Solaris*, 2002). Where Hollywood has demurred, in the face of more unconventional material, Soderbergh has turned to the indie or Indiewood sectors, as in the case of *Traffic* (2000), a downbeat multi-strand epic of mixed visual styles tracing different threads in the drugs trade. He has also continued to work at the lower-budget end of the indie scale, examples including the mostly DV-shot *Full Frontal* (2002), which drew a number of stars to the prospect of working with Soderbergh on a very no-frills production.

Soderbergh's career demonstrates the richness of the seam that can be mined in the area between Hollywood and the indie sector, a zone also straddled by contemporaries such as David O. Russell, Spike Jonze, Wes Anderson, Paul Thomas Anderson and Alexander Payne. It is in this area that some of the most innovative, relatively mainstream filmmaking in America is currently to be found, a situation in which some independent-spirited filmmakers have found themselves courted by Hollywood while able to retain much of their own distinctive approach. Forms of independence continue to exist that remain separate from Hollywood, or Indiewood, however; that resist its pull either by choice or because Hollywood is willing to embrace only a limited quota of genuine novelty, and then often only when underwritten by the guarantee provided by a 'star' director's name, or by the stars attracted by the presence of such figures. The centre of gravity of American independent cinema has certainly shifted closer to Hollywood since the upsurge from the mid 1980s. Its outer reaches remain largely unaffected, however, as manifested by the inassimilable work to date of mavericks such as Harmony Korine and Todd Verow. Many shades of difference also continue to exist, as this book has argued throughout, between the extremes constituted by Hollywood and Indiewood, at one end, and the underground and avant-garde, at the other.

Notes

Introduction: How Independent?

1. The patents company preceded the independents on both counts, according to Janet Staiger, 'Combination and Litigation: Structures of US Film Distribution, 1896–1917', in Thomas Elsaesser (ed.), *Early Cinema: Space, Frame, Narrative*.
2. Ibid. 195.
3. Brian Taves, 'The B Film: Hollywood's Other Half', in Tino Balio (ed.), *Grand Design: Hollywood as a Modern Business Enterprise, 1930–1939*.
4. Tino Balio, 'Adjusting to the New Global Economy: Hollywood in the 1990s', in Albert Moran (ed.), *Film Policy: International, National and Regional Perspectives*, 30–1.
5. Greg Merritt, *Celluloid Mavericks: A History of American Independent Film*, 4.
6. Ibid. 60.
7. Geoff Andrew, *Stranger than Paradise: Maverick Film-Makers in Recent American Cinema*, 34.
8. Merritt, *Celluloid Mavericks*, xii.
9. Ibid.
10. For an example of a study of this kind, see Andrew, *Stranger Than Paradise*.

Chapter 1: Industry

1. Christine Vachon, *Shooting to Kill: How an Independent Producer Blasts through the Barriers to Make Movies that Matter*, 16.

2. Peter Broderick, 'Ultra-Low-Budget Moviemaking – The 2002 All-Digital Model', *Filmmaker*, Fall 2002, 46.

3. See especially 'The ABC's of No-Budget Filmmaking', *Filmmaker*, Winter 1993, archived at www.filmmakermagazine.com/winter1993/abc_no_budget.html; articles revisited by Broderick in 'Ultra-Low-Budget Moviemaking'.

4. See Rodriguez's own account in *Rebel Without a Crew; Or, How a 23-Year-Old Film-Maker with $7,000 Became a Hollywood Player*.

5. John Pierson, *Mike, Spike, Slackers & Dykes: A Guided Tour Across a Decade of American Independent Cinema*, 235.

6. Vachon, *Shooting to Kill*, 38.

7. James Schamus, 'To the Rear of the Back End: The Economics of Independent Cinema', in Steve Neale and Murray Smith (eds.), *Contemporary Hollywood Cinema*, 102.

8. In *Hollywood Reporter*, 'Summer Wrap 99; Artisan', 9 September 1999. This and other reports cited from *Hollywood Reporter* were accessed via www.hollywoodreporter.com, in archives available to paying subscribers only, unless otherwise stated. Page numbers cited are approximate, for pages as printed from the website.

9. This and the following detail on the avant-garde is from Juan Suárez, *Bike Boys, Drag Queens, and Superstars: Avant-Garde, Mass Culture and Gay Identities in the 1960s Underground Cinema*, 61–8.

10. Justin Wyatt, 'From Roadshowing to Saturation Release: Majors, Independents, and Marketing/Distribution Innovations', in Jon Lewis (ed.), *The New American Cinema*, 67.

11. Merritt, *Celluloid Mavericks*, 155.

12. Wyatt, 'From Roadshowing to Saturation Release'; on New Yorker and Bauer, see Pierson, *Mike, Spike, Slackers & Dykes*, 11–12.

13. Pierson, *Mike, Spike, Slackers & Dykes*, 10.

14. This and much of the following detail on New Line is from Justin Wyatt, 'The Formation of the "Major Independent": Miramax, New Line and the New Hollywood', in Neale and Smith (eds.), *Contemporary Hollywood Cinema*.

15. Lory Smith, *Party in a Box: The Story of the Sundance Film Festival*, 6, 24.

16. Ibid. 36

17. This and much of the following detail is from Merritt, *Celluloid Mavericks*, 261–3.

18. Merritt, *Celluloid Mavericks*, 262.

19. The following detail on this is from David Rosen, *Off-Hollywood*, 'Conclusion'.

20. Rosen, *Off-Hollywood*, 262.

21. Ibid. 263, figures cited from *Variety*.

22. Rosen, *Off-Hollywood*, 264.

23. Ibid.

24. Ibid. 264–5.

25. Ibid. 270.

26. Wyatt, 'The Formation of the "Major Independent"', 75.

27. A factor that may or may not dissipate as a result of the move of DVD to more mainstream status in the home entertainment market by the mid 2000s.

28. Rosen, *Off-Hollywood*, 270–1.

29. Pierson, *Mike, Spike, Slackers & Dykes*, 122.

30. Chuck Kleinhans, 'Independent Features: Hopes and Dreams', in Jon Lewis (ed.), *The New American Cinema*, 310–11.

31. Rosen, *Off-Hollywood*, 274.

32. Ibid. 272.

33. Ira Deutchman, 'Independent Distribution and Marketing', in Jason Squire (ed.), *The Movie Business Book*, second edition, 327.

34. This and subsequent detail about the release of *Welcome to the Dollhouse* is from the case study included in Tiiu Lukk, *Movie Marketing: Opening the Picture and Giving it Legs*, 115–124.

35. Mark Litwak, an entertainment lawyer and producer's representative for independent films, cited in Lukk, *Movie Marketing*, 120.

36. See Chris Gore, *The Ultimate Film Festival Survival Guide*, 106–33.

37. Lukk, *Movie Marketing*, 122.

38. Rosen, *Off-Hollywood*, 4–21.

39. Ibid. 14.

40. Ibid. 15.

41. Ibid. 139.

42. Tom Bernard, Co-President of Sony Pictures Classics, the distributor, quoted in Lukk, *Movie Marketing*, 123.

43. The following detail is from Rosen, *Off-Hollywood*, 244–58.

44. Ibid. 254.

45. Much of what follows is from Wyatt, 'The Formation of the "Major Independent"'.

46. Wyatt, 'From Roadshowing to Saturation Release', 70–1.

47. Wyatt, 'The Formation of the "Major Independent"', 80.

48. Ibid. 81.

49. Martin Dale, *The Movie Game*, 62–3; for more detail, see Peter Biskind, *Down and Dirty Pictures*, 145.

50. Wyatt, 'The Formation of the "Major Independent"', 81.

51. This and most of what follows on New Line is also from Wyatt, 'The Formation of the "Major Independent"'.

52. Ibid. 77.

53. Ibid.

54. Quoted in Dale, *The Movie Game*, 67.

55. Wyatt, 'The Formation of the "Major Independent"', 78.

56. Schamus, 'To the Rear of the Back End', 103.

57. Interviewed in Gore, *The Ultimate Film Festival Survival Guide*, 41.

58. Tom Bernard, Co-President, Sony Pictures Classics, interviewed in *IndieWIRE*, 20 December 1999, Part 1, 5, accessed via www.indiewire.com.

59. Joseph Steuer, '1996 Studio Wrap: The Indies: Too Much of a Good Thing', *Hollywood Reporter*, 9 January 1997.

60. Quoted in Steuer, '1996 Studio Wrap', 2.

61. Ibid. 2–3.

62. 'Indie Films: Life in the Cash Lane Down', *Hollywood Reporter*, 16 January 1998, 2.

63. Ibid.

64. Robert Marich, 'Indie Financing Fills in the Gap', *Hollywood Reporter*, 27 February 1997.

65. Charles Lyons, 'Darwinist dilemmas', *Variety*, posted at www.variety.com, 28 July 2002; Christopher Grove, 'Veteran players adapt to new rules of game', *Variety*, posted at www.variety.com, 25 July 2001.

66. Alan Baldachin, 'Financing Trends of the '90s', *Filmmaker*, Fall 2002, 45.

67. Geoffrey Gilmore, festival co-director, interviewed in *indieWIRE*, 21 December 1999, Part 1, 2, accessed via www.indiewire.com.

68. 'Year End Wrap 2001: The Indies. Newmarket Savors "Memento"', *Hollywood Reporter*, 4 January 2002.

69. Gary Susman, 'My Big Fat Greek Wallet', *The Guardian*, Review, 29 November 2002, 12.

70. See interview with Berney in *indieWIRE*, 28 August 2002.

71. This and the following detail is from Justin Lowe, 'Debut Peformance', *Filmmaker*, vol. 10, no. 4, 2002, 32–4.

72. Dan Cox, 'Sundance Tries Theatrical With New Series of Four Films', *indieWIRE*, 25 August 2003, accessed via www.indiewire.com.

73. Charles Lyons, 'Machine's Recharged by U Move', posted at www. variety.com, 5 May 2002.

74. Biskind, *Down and Dirty Pictures: Miramax, Sundance, and the Rise of Independent Film*, 156–7.

75. Dale, *The Movie Game*, 61, 63.

76. Wyatt, 'The Formation of the "Major Independent"', 84.

77. Ibid. and Dale, *The Movie Game*, 63.

78. Thom Geier, 'Mass Protest over "Dogma"', *Hollywood Reporter*, 4 November 1999.

79. Wyatt, 'The Formation of the "Major Independent"', 85–6.

80. 'Year End Wrap 98: October Now, Parental Guidance', *Hollywood Reporter*, 7 January 1999, 2; Biskind, *Down and Dirty Pictures*, 336.

81. Cathy Dunkley, 'Miramax Eyes Tentpole Vault', *Variety*, posted at www. variety.com, 18 May 2003.

82. David Rooney, 'Co-Prod a New Dimension', *Variety*, posted at www. variety.com, 3 March 2003.

83. Biskind, *Down and Dirty Pictures*, 363–6.

84. Ibid. 430.

85. Kleinhans, 'Independent Features', 323–4.

86. Ibid. 324.

87. Thom Geier, 'Indies Inside and Out', *Hollywood Reporter*, 6 January 2000, 1.

88. 'And the Success Goes to… Indies', *Hollywood Reporter*, 27 March 1995, 1–2.

89. Charles Lyons and Craig Offman, 'Madstone Plays Arty Library Card', *Variety*, posted at www.variety.com, 22 April 2002; Matthew Ross, 'Paul Speaker Exits Madstone Amidst Restructuring, New Yorker Team to Head Distribution', *indieWIRE*, 26 August 2002.

90. Charles Lyons and Matthew M. Ross, 'Stampede of Indie Players Coaxes Profit from Margins', *Variety*, posted at www.variety.com, 25 September 2001.

91.   Lyons, 'Cash-Strapped Micros Channel Alternative Rev Streams', *Variety*, posted at www.variety.com, 28 July 2002.

92.   Ibid.

93.   Eugene Hernandez, 'Cuban and Wagner's Deal for Magnolia Bolsters New "Vertically Integrated" Indie Company', *indieWIRE*, 5 January, 2004, accessed via www.indiewire.com.

94.   Matthew Ross, 'Still Dancing After 13 Years: A Conversation with Sundance Festival Director Geoff Gilmore', *indieWIRE*, 16 January 2003, accessed via www.indiewire.com.

95.   For details of some of the union requirements that might be imposed, see Vachon, *Shooting to Kill*, Chapter 3.

96.   Eugene Hernandez, 'Silicon Eyepiece/Digital Cameras Offer New Possibilities – and Lower Budgets – for Indie Filmmakers', *Hollywood Reporter*, 14 September 1999.

97.   Ibid. 2.

98.   Ibid. 3.

99.   Todd McCarthy, 'Ready for Heady at Sundance?', *Variety*, posted at www.variety.com, 2 December 2002.

100.   Merritt, *Celluloid Mavericks*, 356.

101.   Lauren Horwitch, 'Digital Auteurs Forge New Distrib'n Ground', *Variety*, posted at www.variety.com, 29 July 2002.

102.   Carl Diorio, 'Landmark Going Digital', *Variety*, posted at www. variety.com, 2 April 2003; Nicola Sperling, 'Landmark a D-Cinema Independent', *Hollywood Reporter*, 7 April 2003.

103.   See interview with Meistrich in Matthew Ross, 'Industry Spotlight: Film Movement's Meistrich Attempts to Reinvent Indie Distribution', *indieWIRE*, 19 December 2002, accessed via www.indiewire.com.

Chapter 2: Narrative

1.   Interviewed by Werner Herzog, *Interview*, November 1997, reproduced at www.angelfire.com/ab/harmonykorine/interviewmag.html, 2.

2.   David Bordwell, *Narration in the Fiction Film*, 158.

3.   Ibid. 159.

4.   Bordwell, 'The Classical Hollywood Style, 1917–60', in Bordwell, Janet Staiger and Kristin Thompson (eds.), *The Classical Hollywood Cinema: Film Style and Mode of Production to 1960*, 13.

5.   Ibid. 14.

6.   For a useful summary, see Bordwell, *Narration in the Fiction Film*, 49–51.

7.   Ibid. 57–61, 160.

8.   Bordwell, 'The Classical Hollywood Style', 12.

9.   See, for example, Elizabeth Cowie, 'Storytelling: Classical Hollywood Cinema and Classical Narrative', in Neale and Smith (eds.), *Contemporary Hollywood Cinema*.

10. Geoff King, *Spectacular Narratives: Hollywood in the Age of the Blockbuster* and *New Hollywood Cinema: An Introduction*, Chapter 6.

11. Suárez, *Bike Boys, Drag Queens, and Superstars*, 223.

12. Interviewed in Suranjan Ganguly, 'All That Is Light: Brakhage at Sixty', in Jim Hillier (ed.), *American Independent Cinema: A Sight and Sound Reader*, 17.

13. David James, *Allegories of Cinema: American Film in the Sixties*, 88.

14. Interview with Peter Keogh, 'Home and Away', in Jim Hillier (ed.), *American Independent Cinema: A Sight and Sound Reader*, 127.

15. Geoffrey Macnab, 'Moonshine Maverick', in Hillier (ed.), *American Independent Cinema*, 196.

16. Ellen Kim, 'Improvisation Drives *Julien Donkey-Boy*', Hollywood.com, 4 October 1999.

17. Keogh, 'Home and Away', 129.

18. Quoted in Chris Gore, 'Still Indie Indies', *Hollywood Reporter*, 22 March 2001, accessed via www.hollywoodreporter.com, 3.

19. Jonathan Romney, 'Robert Altman: In The Time of Earthquakes', in Hillier (ed.), *American Independent Cinema*, 169.

20. See Bordwell, 'The Classical Hollywood Style', 12.

21. Bordwell, *Narration in the Fiction Film*, 150.

22. Ibid. 206.

23. Ibid.

24. Ibid. 154.

Chapter 3: Form

1.   David James, *Allegories of Cinema: American Film in the Sixties*, 282.

2.   Gary Morris, 'Morris Engel and Ruth Orkin: Poets of Everyday Life', in *Bright Lights Film Journal*, 26, November 1999, accessed at www.brightlightsfilm.com/26.

3.   Ivone Margulies, 'John Cassavetes: Amateur Director', in Jon Lewis (ed.), *The New American Cinema*, 288.

4.   Ibid. 287.

5.   Shari Roman, *Digital Babylon: Hollywood, Indiewood & Dogme 95*, 104–12.

6.   Ray Carney (ed.), *Cassavetes on Cassavetes*, 151.

7.   Ibid. 97.

8.   Chuck Stephens, 'Aggressive Behaviour', interview with Clark, *Filmmaker*, Summer 2001, accessed at www.filmmakermagazine.com.

9.   Anthony Kaufman, 'Interview: Dazed and Enthused; Richard Linklater Proves He's No Slacker', *indieWIRE*, 18 October 2000, accessed at www.indiewire.com.

10. See Gavin Smith, 'Straight to Film', *Film Comment*, July–August 1997, reproduced in Shari Roman, *Digital Babylon: Hollywood, Indiewood & Dogme 95*, 215.

11. Margulies, 'John Cassavetes: Amateur Director', 299.

12. An interpretation with which Cassavetes concurred: see Margulies, 288.

13. For the essay that defined the form, see P. Adams Sitney, 'Structural Film', *Film Culture*, 47, 1969, reprinted in Sitney (ed.), *Film Culture Reader*.

14. Bordwell, *Narration in the Fiction Film*, 275.

15. Ibid.

16. For the classic reading of Hollywood in these terms, see Richard Dyer, *Only Entertainment*.

17. For the classic account of this perspective, associated with Russian Formalist literary criticism, see Victor Shklovksy, 'Art as Technique', in Lee T. Lemon and Marion J. Reis (eds.), *Russian Formalist Criticism: Four Essays*.

18. E.H. Gombrich, *The Sense of Order: A Study in the Psychology of Decorative Art*, 239, also cited in Bordwell, *Narration in the Fiction Film*, 281.

19. Gombrich, *The Sense of Order*, 18.

20. Rodriguez, *Rebel Without a Crew*, 204.

21. See interview in *The Onion*, 5 March 2003, accessed via www.theonionavclub.com.

22. Vachon, *Shooting to Kill*, 20.

23. Ibid. 21.

24. Rodriguez, *Rebel Without a Crew*, 62, 175.

25. Interviewed by Eugene Hernandez, *indieWIRE*, 20 December 1999, accessed via www.indiewire.com.

26. Bordwell, 'Intensified Continuity: Visual Style in Contemporary American Film', *Film Quarterly*, Spring 2002.

Chapter 4: Genre

1. Interview by Ray Pride, 'King of Infinite Space', *Filmmaker*, Winter 1999, accessed via www.filmmakermagazine.com.

2. For one of the best in-depth analyses of the complications of genre, see Rick Altman, *Film/Genre*.

3. This and the following point is from Fessenden's commentary in the 'Making of' segment accompanying the Fox Lorber DVD release.

4. Joan Hawkins, *Cutting Edge: Art Horror and the Horrific Avant Garde*.

5. Stephen Bissette, 'Curtis Harrington and the Underground Roots of the Modern Horror Film', in Xavier Mendik and Steven Jay Schneider (eds.), *Underground U.S.A.: Filmmaking Beyond the Hollywood Canon*, 49.

6. King, *Film Comedy*.

7. Rosen, *Off-Hollywood*, 131.

8. Tiiu Lukk, *Movie Marketing*, 25.

9. King, *Film Comedy*, 57–61.

Chapter 5: Alternative Visions

1. Ntongela Masilela, 'The Los Angeles School of Black Filmmakers', in Manthia Diawara (ed.), *Black American Cinema*.

2. Donald Bogle, *Toms, Coons, Mulattoes, Mammies, and Bucks: An Interpretive History of Blacks in American Films*.

3. See Ed Guerrero, *Framing Blackness: The African American Image in Film*, 88–90.

4. Toni Cade Bambara, 'Reading the Signs, Empowering the Eye: *Daughters of the Dust* and the Black Independent Cinema Movement', in Diawara (ed.), *Black American Cinema*, 119.

5. Teshome H. Gabriel, 'Toward a Critical Theory of Third World films', in Jim Pines & Paul Willemen (eds.), *Questions of Third Cinema*.

6. Quoted in sleeve notes, Connoisseur Video release.

7. Gabriel, 'Third Cinema as Guardian of Popular Memory: Towards a Third Aesthetics', in Pines and Willemen, *Questions of Third Cinema*, 57–8.

8. Fernando Solanas and Octavio Getino, 'Towards a Third Cinema: Notes and Experiences for the Development of a Cinema of Liberation in the Third World', reprinted in Michael Chanan (ed.), *Twenty-Five Years of the New Latin American Cinema*.

9.   Paul Willemen, 'The Third Cinema Question: Notes and Reflections', in Pines & Willemen (eds.), *Questions of Third Cinema*, 9.

10. Masilela, 'Women Directors of the Los Angeles School', in Jacqueline Bobo (ed.), *Black Women Film and Video Artists*, 38.

11. Guerrero, *Framing Blackness*, 172–3.

12. See S. Craig Watkins, *Representing: Hip Hop Culture and the Production of Black Cinema*, Chapter 4.

13. Mark Reid, *Redefining Black Film*, 95.

14. Ibid. 108.

15. Emanuel Levy, *Cinema of Outsiders*, 415.

16. Guerrero, *Framing Blackness*, 159.

17. Watkins, *Representing*.

18. Ibid., Part Three.

19. This and most of the following detail is from Lynne Johnson, 'The Distribution of Black Films', *Bright Lights Film Journal*, April 2002, accessed via www.brightlightsfilm.com.

20. This and the following detail is from Johnson, 'The Distribution of Black Films', and from documents on the Rainforest Films website, accessed at www.rainforestproductions.com.

21. Bobo, 'Black Women's Films: Genesis of a Tradition', in Bobo (ed.), *Black Women Film and Video Artists*, 9.

22. Patricia Thomson, 'Femme Helmers Strive for Level Playing Field', *Variety*, posted at www.variety.com, 28 July 2002.

23. For examples, see reviews of *Lovely and Amazing* by Stephen Holden, *New York Times*, 28 June 2002, accessed via www.nytimes.com, and Peter Bradshaw, *The Guardian*, 2 August 2002, accessed via http://film.guardian.co.uk.

24. 'Queer and Present Danger', *Sight and Sound*, March 2000, reprinted in Jim Hillier (ed.), *American Independent Cinema: A Sight and Sound Reader*, 114.

25. Suárez, *Bike Boys, Drag Queens, and Superstars*, 126–7.

26. Jackie Stacey, '"If You Don't Play, You Can't Win": *Desert Hearts* and the Lesbian Romance Film', in Tamsin Wilton (ed), *Immortal Invisible: Lesbians and the Moving Image*.

27. Arroyo, 'Death, Desire and Identity: The Political Unconscious of "New Queer Cinema"', in Joseph Bristow and Angela R. Wilson (eds.), *Activating Theory: Lesbian, Gay, Bisexual Politics*, 72.

28. Ibid. 81–2.

29. Ibid. 82.

30. Glyn Davis, 'Camp and Queer and the New Queer Director: Case Study – Gregg Araki', in Michele Aaron (ed.), *New Queer Cinema: A Critical Reader*.

31. Ibid. 59.

32. Monica Pearl, 'Aids and New Queer Cinema', in Aaron (ed.), *New Queer Cinema*.

33. Rich, 'Homo Pomo: The New Queer Cinema', *Sight and Sound*, Vol. 2, No. 5, September 1992; reprinted in Pam Cook and Philip Dodd (eds.), *Women and Film: A Sight and Sound Reader* and in Aaron (ed.), *New Queer Cinema*. Many different accounts of postmodernism have been offered. For a useful example of a version centred on notions of the simultaneous use and subversion of existing cultural formats, see Linda Hutcheon, *A Poetics of Postmodernism*.

34. See interview with Haynes in Amy Taubin, 'Nowhere to Hide', *Sight and Sound*, May 1996, reprinted in Jim Hillier (ed.), *American Independent Cinema: A Sight and Sound Reader*, 102.

35. See Rosemary Hennessy, *Profit and Pleasure: Sexual Identities in Late Capitalism*.

36. Urvashi Vaid, *Virtual Equality: The Mainstreaming of Gay and Lesbian Liberation*, 256–9.

37. See Hennessy, *Profit and Pleasure*, Chapter 4.

38. Richard Dyer, 'The Politics of Gay Culture', in Dyer (ed.), *The Culture of Queers*, 18.

39. Dyer, Introduction to *The Culture of Queers*, 6.

40. Amy Taubin, 'Queer Male Cinema and Feminism', *Sight and Sound*, September 1992, reprinted in Cook and Dodd (eds.), *Women and Film*, 179.

41. Anat Pick, 'New Queer Cinema and Lesbian Films', in Aaron (ed.), *New Queer Cinema*, 106.

42. Doty, *Making Things Perfectly Queer*, Introduction and 'There's Something Queer Here', in Corey Creekmur and Doty (eds.), *Out in Culture: Queer Essays on Popular Culture*.

43. Rich, 'Queer and Present Danger'; see also Marcus Hu, of the gay-oriented distributor Strand Releasing, 'New Queer Cinema', *Filmmaker*, Vol. 11, No. 1, Fall 2002.

44. Rich, 'Queer and Present Danger', 116–17.

45. See, for example, Dennis Cooper, 'Queercore', in Donald Morton

(ed.), *The Material Queer*, and Matias Viegener, '"The Only Haircut that Makes Sense Anymore": Queer Subculture and Gay Resistance', in Gever, Greyson and Parmar (eds.), *Queer Looks*.

46. Interview in Danny Leigh, 'Boy Wonder', *Sight and Sound*, March 2000, reprinted in Hillier (ed.), *American Independent Cinema*, 112.

47. Rich, 'Queer and Present Danger', 118.

48. Merritt, *Celluloid Mavericks*, 36–7.

49. Georg Lukács, 'Realism in the Balance', in Ernst Bloch et al., *Aesthetics and Politics*, 39.

50. See Douglas Kellner and Dan Streible, 'Introduction. Emile de Antonio: Documenting the Life of a Radical Filmmaker', in Kellner and Streible (eds.), *Emile de Antonio: A Reader*.

Select Bibliography

Aaron, Michele (ed.), *New Queer Cinema: A Critical Reader*, Edinburgh: Edinburgh University Press, 2004

Altman, Rick, *Film/Genre*, London: BFI, 1999

Andrew, Geoff, *Stranger than Paradise: Maverick Film-Makers in Recent American Cinema*, London: Prion Books, 1998

Arroyo, José, 'Death, Desire and Identity: The Political Unconscious of "New Queer Cinema"', in Joseph Bristow and Angela R. Wilson (eds.), *Activating Theory: Lesbian, Gay, Bisexual Politics*, London: Lawrence and Wishart, 1993

Balio, Tino, 'Adjusting to the New Global Economy: Hollywood in the 1990s', in Albert Moran (ed.), *Film Policy: International, National and Regional Perspectives*, London: Routledge, 1996

Bambara, Toni Cade, 'Reading the Signs, Empowering the Eye: *Daughters of the Dust* and the Black Independent Cinema Movement', in Manthia Diawara (ed.), *Black American Cinema*, New York: Routledge, 1993

Biskind, Peter, *Down and Dirty Pictures: Miramax, Sundance, and the Rise of Independent Film*, New York: Simon and Schuster, 2004

Bissette, Stephen, 'Curtis Harrington and the Underground Roots of the Modern Horror Film', in Xavier Mendik and Steven Jay Schneider (eds.), *Underground U.S.A.: Filmmaking Beyond the Hollywood Canon*, London: Wallflower, 2002

Bogle, Donald, *Toms, Coons, Mulattoes, Mammies, and Bucks: An Interpretive History of Blacks in American Films*, New York: Continuum, 1993

Bordwell, David, 'The Classical Hollywood Style, 1917–60', in David Bordwell, Janet Staiger and Kristin Thompson, *The Classical Hollywood Cinema: Film Style and Mode of Production to 1960*, London: Routledge, 1985

Bordwell, David, *Narration in the Fiction Film*, London: Routledge, 1986

Bordwell, David, 'Intensified Continuity: Visual Style in Contemporary American Film', *Film Quarterly*, Spring 2002

Broderick, Peter, 'The ABC's of No-Budget Filmmaking', *Filmmaker*, Winter 1993

Broderick, Peter, 'Ultra-Low-Budget Moviemaking – The 2002 All-Digital Model', *Filmmaker*, Fall 2002

Carney, Ray (ed.), *Cassavetes on Cassavetes*, London: Faber, 2001

Cooper, Dennis, 'Queercore', in Donald Morton (ed.), *The Material Queer*, Boulder: Westview Press, 1996

Cowie, Elizabeth, 'Storytelling: Classical Hollywood Cinema and Classical Narrative', in Steve Neale and Murray Smith (eds.), *Contemporary Hollywood Cinema*, London: Routledge, 1998

Dale, Martin, *The Movie Game: The Film Business in Britain, Europe and America*, London: Cassell, 1997

Davis, Glyn, 'Camp and Queer and the New Queer Director: Case Study – Gregg Araki', in Michele Aaron (ed.), *New Queer Cinema: A Critical Reader*, Edinburgh: Edinburgh University Press, 2004

Deutchman, Ira, 'Independent Distribution and Marketing', in Jason Squire (ed.), *The Movie Business Book*, second edition, New York: Fireside, 1992

Doty, Alexander, *Making Things Perfectly Queer*, Minneapolis: University of Minnesota Press, 1993

Doty, Alexander, 'There's Something Queer Here', in Corey Creekmur and Alexander Doty (eds.), *Out in Culture: Queer Essays on Popular Culture*, London: Cassell, 1995

Dyer, Richard, *Only Entertainment*, London: BFI, 1992

Dyer, Richard, 'The Politics of Gay Culture', in Richard Dyer (ed.), *The Culture of Queers*, London: Routledge, 2002

Gabriel, Teshome H., 'Toward a Critical Theory of Third World Films', in Jim Pines and Paul Willemen (eds.), *Questions of Third Cinema*, London: BFI, 1989

Gabriel, Teshome H., 'Third Cinema as Guardian of Popular Memory: Towards a Third Aesthetics', in Jim Pines and Paul Willemen (eds.), *Questions of Third Cinema*, London: BFI, 1989

Gombrich, E.H., *The Sense of Order: A Study in the Psychology of Decorative Art*, Oxford: Phaidon, 1979

Gore, Chris, *The Ultimate Film Festival Survival Guide*, Hollywood: Lone Eagle, 2001

Guerrero, Ed, *Framing Blackness: The African American Image in Film*, Philadelphia: Temple University Press, 1993

Hawkins, Joan, *Cutting Edge: Art Horror and the Horrific Avant Garde*, Minneapolis: University of Minnesota Press, 2000

Hennessy, Rosemary, *Profit and Pleasure: Sexual Identities in Late Capitalism*, New York: Routledge, 2000

Hillier, Jim (ed.), *American Independent Cinema: A Sight and Sound Reader*, London: BFI, 2001

Hutcheon, Linda, *A Poetics of Postmodernism*, New York: Routledge, 1998

James, David E., *Allegories of Cinema: American Film in the Sixties*, Princeton: Princeton University Press, 1989

Kaufman, Anthony (ed.), *Stephen Soderbergh: Interviews*, Jackson: University Press of Mississippi, 2002

Kellner, Douglas, and Dan Streible, 'Introduction. Emile de Antonio: Documenting the Life of a Radical Filmmaker', in Kellner and Streible (eds.), *Emile de Antonio: A Reader*, Minneapolis: University of Minnesota Press, 2000

King, Geoff, *Spectacular Narratives: Hollywood in the Age of the Blockbuster*, London: I.B. Tauris, 2000

King, Geoff, *New Hollywood Cinema: An Introduction*, London: I.B. Tauris, 2002

King, Geoff, *Film Comedy*, London: Wallflower, 2002

Kleinhans, Chuck, 'Independent Features: Hopes and Dreams', in Jon Lewis (ed.), *The New American Cinema*, Durham: Duke University Press, 1998

Levy, Emanuel, *Cinema of Outsiders: The Rise of American Independent Film*, New York: New York University Press, 1999

Lukács, Georg, 'Realism in the Balance', in Ernst Bloch, et al., *Aesthetics and Politics*, London: Verso, 1980

Lukk, Tiiu, *Movie Marketing: Opening the Picture and Giving it Legs*, Los Angeles: Silman-James Press, 1997

Lyons, Donald, *Independent Visions: A Critical Introduction to Recent American Film*, New York: Ballantine Books, 1994

Margulies, Ivone, 'John Cassavetes: Amateur Director', in Jon Lewis (ed.), *The New American Cinema*, Durham: Duke University Press, 1998

Masilela, Ntongela, 'The Los Angeles School of Black Filmmakers', in Manthia Diawara (ed.), *Black American Cinema*, New York: Routledge, 1993

Masilela, Ntongela, 'Women Directors of the Los Angeles School', in Jacqueline Bobo (ed.), *Black Women and Video Artists*, New York: Routlege, 1998

Merritt, Gregg, *Celluloid Mavericks: A History of American Independent Film*, New York: Thunder's Mouth Press, 2000

Pearl, Monica, 'AIDS and New Queer Cinema', in Michele Aaron (ed.), *New Queer Cinema: A Critical Reader*, Edinburgh: Edinburgh University Press, 2004

Pick, Anat, 'New Queer Cinema and Lesbian Films', in Michele Aaron (ed.), *New Queer Cinema: A Critical Reader*, Edinburgh: Edinburgh University Press, 2004

Pierson, John, *Mike, Spike, Slackers & Dykes: A Guided Tour Across a Decade of Independent American Cinema*, London: Faber, 1996

Rich, B. Ruby, 'Homo Pomo: The New Queer Cinema', *Sight and Sound*, Vol. 2, No. 5, September 1992; reprinted in Michele Aaron (ed.), *New Queer Cinema: A Critical Reader*, Edinburgh: Edinburgh University Press, 2004

Rich, B. Ruby, 'Queer and Present Danger', *Sight and Sound*, March 2000; reprinted in Jim Hillier (ed.), *American Independent Cinema: A Sight and Sound Reader*, London: BFI, 2001

Rodriguez, Robert, *Rebel Without a Crew; Or, How a 23–year-old Film-maker with $7,000 Became a Hollywood Player*, London: Faber, 1996

Roman, Shari, *Digital Babylon: Hollywood, Indiewood & Dogma 95*, Hollywood: Lone Eagle, 2001

Rosen, David, with Peter Hamilton, *Off-Hollywood: The Making and Marketing of Independent Films*, New York: Grove Weidenfeld, 1990

Schamus, James, 'To the Rear of the Back End: The Economics of Independent Cinema', in Steve Neale and Murray Smith (eds.), *Contemporary Hollywood Cinema*, London: Routledge, 1998

Shklovksy, Victor, 'Art as Technique', in Lee T. Lemon and Marion J. Reis (eds.), *Russian Formalist Criticism: Four Essays*, Lincoln and London: University of Nebraska Press, 1965

Sitney, P. Adams, 'Structural Film', *Film Culture*, 47, 1969; reprinted in Sitney (ed.), *Film Culture Reader*, New York: Cooper Square Press, 2000

Smith, Lory, *Party in a Box: The Story of the Sundance Film Festival*, Salt Lake City: Gibbs-Smith, 1999

Stacey, Jackie, '"If You Don't Play, You Can't Win": *Desert Hearts* and the Lesbian Romance Film', in Tamsin Wilton (ed.), *Immortal Invisible: Lesbians and the Moving Image*, London: Routledge, 1995

Staiger, Janet, 'Combination and Litigation: Structures of US Film Distribution, 1896–1917', in Thomas Elsaesser (ed.), *Early Cinema: Space, Frame, Narrative*, London: BFI, 1990

Suárez, Juan, *Bike Boys, Drag Queens, and Superstars: Avant-Garde, Mass Culture and Gay Identities in the 1960s Underground Cinema*, Bloomington: Indiana University Press, 1996

Taves, Brian, 'The B Film: Hollywood's Other Half', in Tino Balio (ed.), *Grand Design: Hollywood as a Modern Business Enterprise, 1930–1939*, Berkeley: University of California Press, 1995

Thompson, Kristen, *Storytelling in the New Hollywood*, Cambridge, Mass.: Harvard University Press, 1999

Vachon, Christine, *Shooting to Kill: How an Independent Producer Blasts through the Barriers to Make Movies that Matter*, London: Bloomsbury, 1998

Vaid, Urvashi, *Virtual Equality: The Mainstreaming of Gay and Lesbian Liberation*, New York: Anchor, 1995

Viegener, Matias, '"The Only Haircut that Makes Sense Anymore": Queer Subculture and Gay Resistance', in Gever, Greyson and Parmar (eds.), *Queer Looks*, New York: Routledge, 1993

Watkins, S. Craig, *Representing: Hip Hop Culture and the Production of Black Cinema*, Chicago: University of Chicago Press, 1998

Willemen, Paul, 'The Third Cinema Question: Notes and Reflections', in Jim Pines and Paul Willemen (eds.), *Questions of Third Cinema*, London: BFI, 1989

Wyatt, Justin, 'From Roadshowing to Saturation Release: Majors, Independents, and Marketing/Distribution Innovations', in Jon Lewis (ed.), *The New American Cinema*, Durham: Duke University Press, 1998

Wyatt, Justin, 'The Formation of the "Major Independent": Miramax, New Line and the New Hollywood', in Steve Neale and Murray Smith (eds.), *Contemporary Hollywood Cinema*, London: Routlege, 1998

Index